A HISTORY OF MILITARY ENCOUNTERS with UFOs

This book is dedicated to my loving wife, Kim Van, and our loyal sons, Austin and Jordan, for all of your love and support through all the years, through good times and not so good ones as well.

A HISTORY OF MILITARY ENCOUNTERS with UFOs

EXPLANATIONS and COMBAT STRATEGIES

ROBERT ALLRED

A HISTORY OF MILITARY ENCOUNTERS WITH UFOs
Explanations and Combat Strategies

First published in Great Britain in 2024 by
Air World
An imprint of
Pen & Sword Books Ltd
Yorkshire – Philadelphia

ISBN 978 1 39906 376 0

A CIP catalogue record for this book is available from the British Library.

Typeset by SJmagic DESIGN SERVICES, India.

Printed and bound in the UK by CPI Group (UK) Ltd.

Pen & Sword Books Limited incorporates the imprints of Atlas, Archaeology, Aviation, Discovery, Family History, Fiction, History, Maritime, After the Battle, Military, Military Classics, Politics, Select, Transport, True Crime, Air World, Frontline Publishing, Leo Cooper, Remember When, Seaforth Publishing, The Praetorian Press, Wharncliffe Local History, Wharncliffe Transport, Wharncliffe True Crime and White Owl.

For a complete list of Pen & Sword titles please contact

PEN & SWORD BOOKS LIMITED
George House, Units 12 & 13, Beevor Street, Off Pontefract Road,
Barnsley, South Yorkshire, S71 1HN, England
E-mail: enquiries@pen-and-sword.co.uk
Website: www.pen-and-sword.co.uk

or

PEN AND SWORD BOOKS
1950 Lawrence Rd, Havertown, PA 19083, USA
E-mail: uspen-and-sword@casematepublishers.com
Website: www.penandswordbooks.com

Contents

Acknowledgements

I thank all of the dedicated professionals who have gone before me who investigated and reported on the history of military encounters with UFOs, and more than that, to the many more who worked tirelessly, some to within hours of the ends of their lives, to inform us about all things UFO, and related phenomena.

Among those to whom I owe a lot are John Grehan, at Pen and Sword Books for his patience and sage advice in helping me make this a publishable book. Also to be thanked at Pen and Sword is editor Karyn Burnham for her invaluable editorial input. In the production department at Pen and Sword, I am indebted to Amy Jordan for her prompt and on-target ironing-out of the many wrinkles I had left behind. Thanks to Olivia Camozzi at Pen and Sword Books, Yorkshire, UK, Marketing Department; Matthew Potts Author Liaison & Marketing Coordinator Pen & Sword Books Ltd; and to Daniel Yesilonis, at Casemate Publishers, Philadelphia, PA, USA for their great help in making this book known to the world.

I must, of course, thank my loving wife, Kim Van, and our loyal sons, Austin and Jordan for all of their assistance – spiritual and tangible.

My gratitude extends to the persons and forces unknown that caused the first draft of this manuscript to be sent back in a condition that forced me to conduct extensive rewriting and updating, making the book more timely and better crafted, and generally improved overall.

Introduction

In this book I will be asking readers to "suspend disbelief" on the subject of UFOs/UAP (*) just long enough to keep an open mind until all of the evidence is presented, then make an informed decision regarding the existence of UFOs/UAP. We will also investigate the curious, intriguing, even sometimes disturbing encounters between Earth's people and militaries and as yet poorly understood extraterrestrial biological entities – EBEs (also known as extraterrestrials – ETs), or alien beings from beyond our world. (Should we find that they exist.) I know that I am asking a great deal from people, especially those whose minds are made-up either in favor of or against accepting UFOs/UAP and EBEs/ETs as realities. Many people hold strong convictions of skepticism about the reality of UFOs/UAP as anything other than mere light effects in the sky that always have mundane explanations. This is so even though we are presently unable to completely identify all of the possible unknown causes of what are sometimes seen. The situation also applies even to this writer, who, despite having observed what was to me unexplainable – or, more accurately, for me to quickly explain away – in an occurrence that was witnessed by two others.

There are many people who have investigated UFOs/UAP and concluded that these apparitions in our world are probably not alien spacecraft. Rather, they posit that UFOs/UAP are likely psychological – including extrasensory, or psychic – in nature. Or, more bizarrely, these phenomena may indicate the presence of interdimensional craft and beings, or time travelers. I disagree with these theories, as will be shown in this book. Briefly: it is true that over a very long period of time people in different eras in our past perceived and interpreted UFOs/UAP and possible ETs in ways that were shaped by the prevailing world view at the time, and

* "Unexplained aerial phenomena," as the British and American governments, among others, now prefer to call what most of us refer to as UFOs – unidentified flying objects. The British government was the pioneer in this practice, starting in the early 1950s.

within their own belief systems. What they described were "cloud ships," "chariots in the sky," "dragons," and other Earthbound or imaginary visions translated into celestial phenomena. When it comes to the supposed EBEs/ ETs, they were perceived as angels, demons, fairies, monsters, spirits, ghosts, and a host of other entities – real and invented. I now interpret these observations as possible sightings of alien beings of a physical nature with an extraterrestrial – other planetary – origin. I do now – after reviewing the evidence – believe that there probably are EBEs/ETs coming to our planet, with the apparent if not proven ability to affect our perceptions, memories, even consciousness; (**) and that these psychic/psychological effects have caused many people, now as in the past, to sometimes or even often misinterpret these alien visitations.

While investigating the subject of UFOs/UAP, I was confronted with the fact that many of the eyewitnesses who reported observing and otherwise interacting with UFOs/UAP and EBEs/ETs were experienced, trusted, dependable people such as commercial airline pilots, and those in law enforcement, and in the world's militaries. This made me into less of a skeptic, but still not (yet) a total, out-and-out believer. Moreover, a few years ago when reading about, then watching on television, the testimony of UFO observers who were military personnel, including pilots and others who had been assigned to very sensitive duties that included working with nuclear weapons, it seemed odd to me that they would possibly be mistaken, were making their sightings up, or were suffering from delusions. This fact alone told me that something tangible probably was there, that the testimonies if not the actual events were accurate as described.

Further confirmation for me was the fact that, for example, radar returns, photographs, films and videos also underlined the genuine basis of certain UFO/UAP sightings. I then read the reactions of well-known psychologist Carl Gustav Jung, PhD, who wrote in the 1950s that illusions, hallucinations, fantasies and fabrications do not leave impressions on radar screens, or film, or other sensors such as the then current technology of video-tube cameras. I subsequently fell more into the category of one who accepts the reality of UFOs/UAP as more than just strange light effects in the skies.

The subject of UFOs/UAP is rife with mistakes, misinformation, and disinformation. However, many or even most people who may have found reports of UFOs and ETs to be lacking in credibility in times past are reassessing their attitudes since the release of the "Tic-Tac," "Gimbal," and

** We shall see later that recent scientific discoveries indicate how this may be possible.

"Go-Fast" videos, and other visual recordings made by people aboard United States Navy jet fighters and ships of "unexplained aerial phenomena" that could or could not be alien spacecraft. The United States Navy has verified the validity of these videos.[1] This development has placed the entire matter of UFOs/UAP in a different perspective.

Despite my ambition to remain an "open-minded skeptic," I also have too often dismissed out-of-hand reports that seemed at first to be too fantastic to believe. This applies to the initial accounts of the UFOs/UAP being encountered by the very same aircraft whose recordings were later released, and which proved that "there is something there," even if we cannot as yet fully understand or explain it, and which no one – in or out of government – can in honesty, logically try to explain away. These early reports, unsubstantiated by videos as of then, were published in the online magazine *The Aviationist*,[2] and again I, for one, did not at first accept them, and wondered what had happened to the editor and originators of the story to prompt them to either make something up, or to so radically misinterpret phenomena that would almost certainly not prove to be from "out of this world." Then, when I saw the "Tic-Tac," "Gimbal," and "Go-Fast" videos recorded by U.S. Navy pilots off both coasts of the United States, it was almost impossible for me to reserve judgment any longer. Those images – again, later acknowledged by the Navy as being genuine – tipped me and many others off of our perches on the fence and placed us firmly in the camp of UFO/UAP believers, even though we as yet do not have anywhere near a complete understanding of what is plainly, factually in existence.

However, the real clincher came to me in the form of the United States government's confirmation, on 25 June 2021, that UFOs/UAP are evident physical realities and not something without material substance, (or, again, are not merely lights in the sky).[3]

I understood from the reactions of others when I presented my thesis at the University of California at Berkeley for one of my majors – American Studies, about UFOs and their impact on American society and culture, that the subject was, as of 2015, still regarded as marginally taboo – more than a bit of a joke. I further realized that getting a book published that had anything at all to do with UFOs/UAP could be more of a handicap than a hand-up when attempting to continue writing with a maximum of

1. https://www.cnn.com/2019/09/18/politics/navy-confirms-ufo-videos-trnd/index.html
2. https://theaviationist.com/
3. https://www.dni.gov/files/ODNI/documents/assessments/Prelimary-Assessment-UAP-20210625.pdf

credibility. Then, fortunately for me – but even more so for the many other writers who were the true pioneers and giants in giving us later arrivals such as I am a boost to acceptability in writing about UFOs/UAP – the release of the aforementioned Navy videos and the U.S. government's report of 25 June 2021 assured our credibility with all but the most cynical of observers. These developments also guaranteed that what we have to write will be accepted by a much larger readership across the spectrum that ranges from the truly open-minded to the most obdurate of doubters, nay-sayers, and habitual debunkers.

Readers will notice that many of the most prominent, or famous, or their favorite UFO incidents will not be found in this book. There are many reasons for this, including: there was little to no military connection. Although a very few events without direct military involvement are included, they were covered because they illustrate a problem or aspect of UFO/UAP phenomena that has implications or complications requiring military consideration. Some events have insufficient evidence to be included; others were found to be grossly exaggerated and/or misinterpreted, such as the overly dramatized and overstated disappearance of an American pilot off the east coast of England. In that case there was no UFO connection, despite attempts by some to inject one into the incident. The "UFO" in question was a mock UFO, in the form of an RAF Shackleton bomber playing the role of an unauthorized intruder. The mission was for training purposes and, while the pilot was never found, it was plainly a training accident, not some sort of bizarre alien-abduction of the pilot from inside his aircraft. Moreover, members of the unfortunate man's family have asked that he be allowed to rest in peace without the further disrespectful sensationalism or undue attention being drawn to the case through writings that can only be described as melodramatic. Then there are limitations of space as there are far too many (known and/or acknowledged) encounters with UFOs by the world's military organizations to be listed, and much less so to be adequately explored, despite the fact that it is very likely that the vast majority of the incidents remain hidden from public awareness.

So, please feel completely free to accept, wonder at or deny what is presented herein as I launch into delivering a history of military encounters with UFOs.

From Northern California, 28 May 2024.

Maps

UFO Encounters and strange events in the United States and Canada.

MAPS

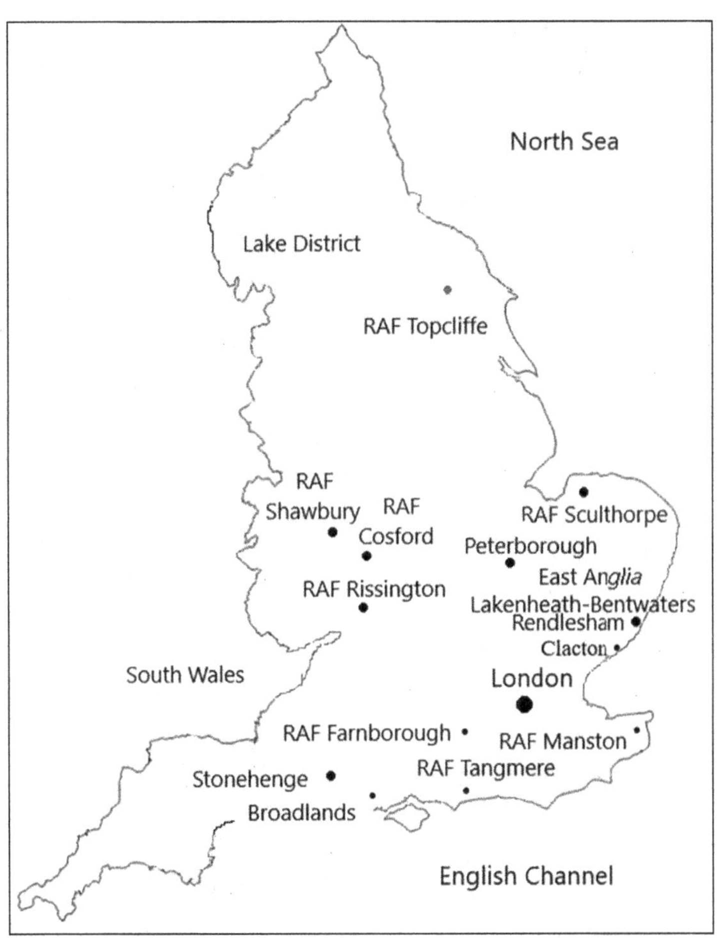

UFO Incidents in and around England.

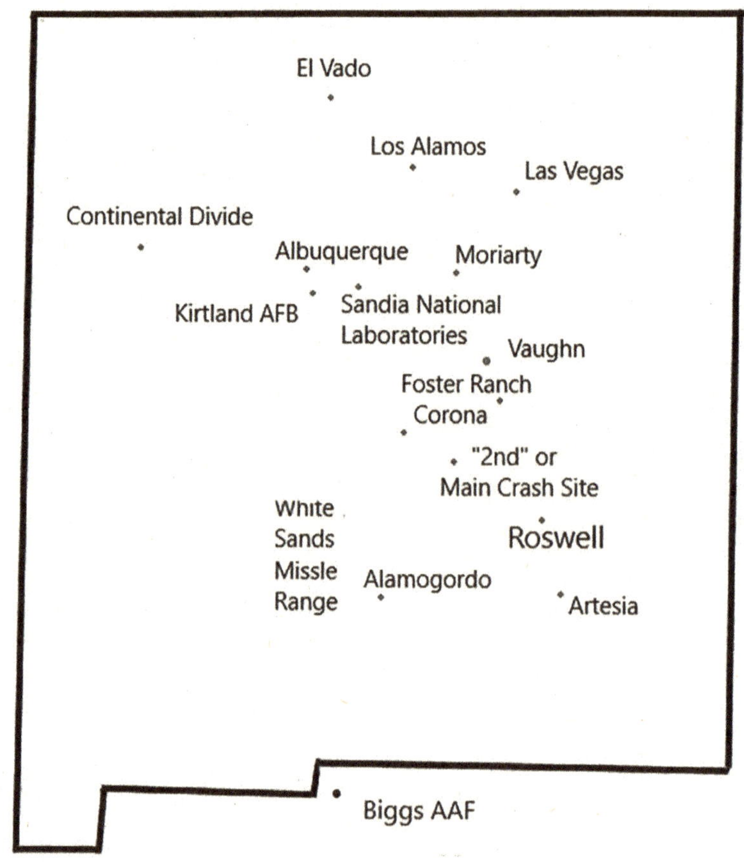

Military and Defense, and UFO Crash Sites in New Mexico as of 1947.

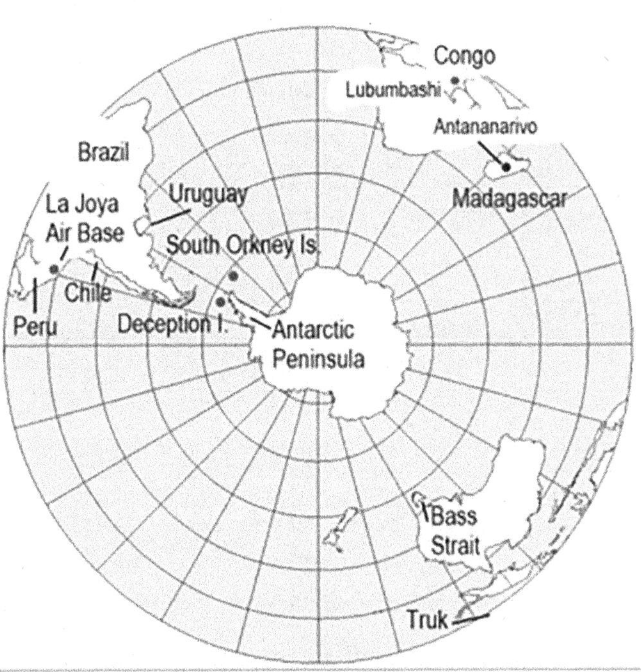

UFO Sightings and Incidents in the Southern Hemisphere.
Map Courtesy of the Central Intelligence Agency

UFO Encounters in Europe

UFO Encounters in Asia

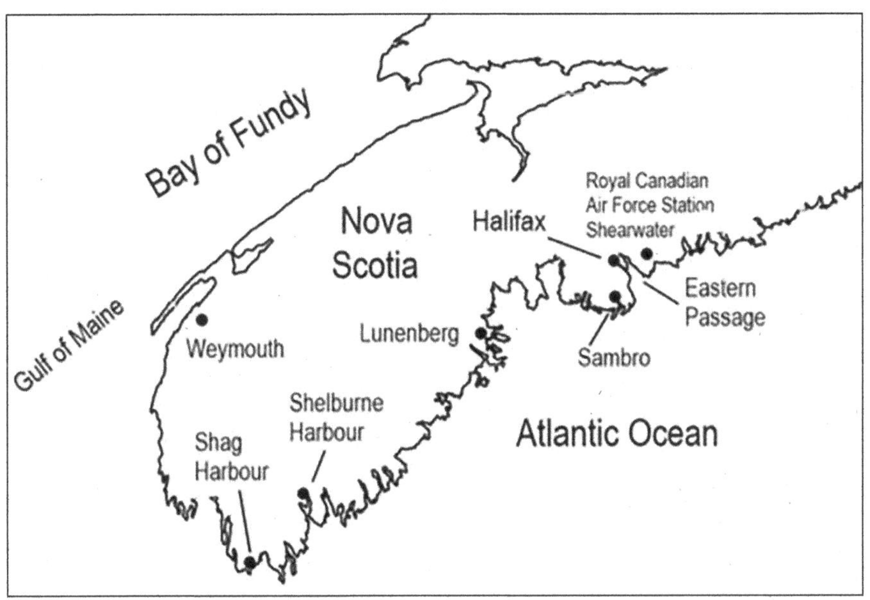

UFO sightings and events above and around Nova Scotia, 4 October 1967.

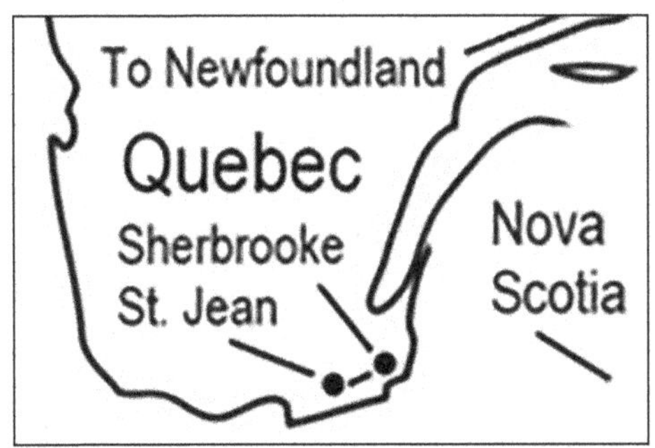

Route of airliner whose crew saw complex UFO events, 4 October 1967.

Chapter 1

Military Action and Recently Recorded Events

Preliminary Briefing

Before embarking on our journey into the unknown in our investigation of UFOs/UAP, due to the controversial and even emotionally explosive nature of the issue, I feel compelled to note that there are volumes of solid information and thousands of pages of validating documentation on the subject. Those who do not accept this fact are invited not only to read this book all the way to the end but also to consult the bibliography and obtain other printed and electronic works that, if read with care and an open mind, confirm this statement. Of course, some books were written in earlier times without the benefit of more up-to-date techniques to investigate, interrogate, appraise and research records, witnesses, physical evidence, and the reliability of sources. These newer information resources include recently released records, new witnesses stepping forward with reliable and confirming testimony, blogs and other internet assets that have further vetted and either authenticated or disproved earlier claims. There is also the unfortunate reality that some who have written on this subject have done so with the aim of building a reputation and career and to maximize profits, rather than to seek to uncover the truth. Some of the "research" performed on the topic of UFOs/UAP consists of merely consulting lists of reported incidents, paraphrasing existing accounts – some of which have already been shown to be inaccurate, if not outright fabrications – and merely resorting to their own creative writing skills instead of performing deeper research to either confirm or invalidate prior coverage of UFOs/UAP. In some cases I was able to perform such research, in others the additional information was not (and still is not) available – sometimes due to government secrecy. Some events required no further validation or dismissal. Still other incidents called for no more coverage because the point was made, with qualifications, and it was time to move on, otherwise this book would run to many hundreds of pages.

Even though there are reports of UFO/UAP incidents going back to medieval and ancient times, they are necessarily mostly fragmentary, tenuous, and extraneous to our investigation of encounters by military organizations on our planet with these phenomena. This study will begin with the turn from the nineteenth to the twentieth century, when such incidents led to consequential developments, advances and considerations of not only a socio-political but also a military nature.

For about three-quarters of a century there have also been intensive propaganda campaigns by many of the world's governments to discredit even hard evidence regarding UFOs/UAP through outright attacks on the information itself or on those who have witnessed and/or conveyed it.

Valid reports by numerous eyewitnesses of UFO/UAP sightings and related incidents have been ignored by those in positions of authority and responsibility. Hard evidence such as photographs, physical traces left behind, and corroborative testimony by very reliable eyewitnesses has been seized, filed away and "forgotten" by government agencies and media outlets. Compelling evidence has been suppressed, hidden or even stolen by people in several government agencies and in many countries. For all of these reasons and more, investigators reporting on UFO/UAP sightings and related incidents are sometimes forced to rely on sources of information for confirmation who have been hindered in their effectiveness by government and institutional attempts to keep the entire UFO/UAP subject out of public awareness. Due to these and other considerations, the following investigation will necessarily be heavily dependent on eyewitness testimony as reported by researchers, ufologists, journalists, and writers at large.

Eyewitness testimony makes up the bulk of evidence presented in courts of law around the world, and carries a great deal of legal, social, cultural, intellectual and emotional weight. (Except – some people in governments and a few societal institutions have hoped – for UFOs/UAP.) Eyewitness testimony becomes almost irrefutable when corroborated by other eyewitnesses reporting nearly identical versions. Habitual doubters may object that eyewitness testimony in this book and elsewhere is often conflicting in many details and also sometimes in the more substantial aspects in news reports, or even of a legal case. However, slight or more major differences in eyewitness accounts are almost always present in all areas of life. Ironically, such divergence tends to buttress the validity of eyewitness testimony overall because people's memories vary, and when several eyewitnesses do on occasion relay identical reports, that fact itself is an indication that they conspired or were coached to recite from the same prearranged script.

To me, as with most people, eyewitness testimony becomes even more convincing when reported by individuals in positions of great responsibility (not necessarily of high rank but instead engaged in serious duties), including law-enforcement officers, commercial airline pilots, and military personnel such as pilots and the crews of ships and missile squadrons who are charged with the ominous obligation to possibly deliver nuclear weapons to foreign targets.

Probably most significant of all is the fact that while a majority of military enlisted personnel reporting UFO incidents to higher commands were told to keep quiet, intimidated, threatened, or even transferred (and this also happened to more than a few officers), some enlisted people and most officers recounting UFO incidents were not mistreated or transferred to "less sensitive" duties. Obviously, senior commanders in these lattermost instances did not suspect that their subordinates who had reported UFOs, or even spacecraft or alien beings on the ground, were insane, perpetrating hoaxes, or mistaken. This brings us back to our main point: in that so much in the way of other evidence has been stolen, destroyed, lost, hidden, lied about, ignored, we are forced to rely herein on eyewitness accounts in general and in the majority of cases. However, again, many of these reports were made by several people observing the same incident, while a few were not.

With regard to the former Soviet Union and in other countries subject to authoritarian rule, often only a single and anonymous eyewitness has been brave enough to tell what happened. Under those regimes, making personally acknowledged reports or giving attributed testimony contrary to the official stance of the government (that UFOs are part of a foreign plot against the regime) could be detrimental for one's prosperity, liberty, or even life. Therefore, while as many cases as possible cited in this book have been substantiated to a greater degree by multiple eyewitnesses, in some instances we are forced to rely on a single observer who may or may not be in one of the categories listed above as being assumed to be more reliable. However, just because a person is not in law enforcement, commercial aviation, or in a responsible position in the military, that does not mean we should necessarily and arbitrarily dismiss what she or he has to say, for, to quote many of them who had an identical reaction when his or her word was challenged: "I know what I saw." (I am included in this statement.)

In this investigation of the UFO/UAP phenomenon, I have found that eyewitnesses have only one request: that we not instantly leap to a dismissive misjudgment that they are stupidly mistaken, hallucinating, perpetrating a hoax, or simply lying. They just want to be taken at their word. This is what I intend to do in this report. I will accept what eyewitnesses have to say based on what they personally observed, and I will even consider with as open a mind as possible some hearsay testimony. What I will not do is unquestioningly believe what these eyewitnesses were allegedly told by media people, and/or government officials or agents – such as mysterious people who sometimes show up and attempt to intimidate, threaten, or just pose as friends, fellow eyewitnesses, or experts, whose intent is to silence or discredit genuine experiencer testimony. Moreover, I certainly will not just accept what eyewitnesses relay from their alleged direct encounters with supposed EBEs/ETs. Any messages the aliens are said to have communicated to them are suspect, for, as will be shown, and is presented in much more detail in other works to be found in the bibliography, the extraterrestrials, should we decide they exist – and numerous accounts strongly suggest that they are real – then, again according to experiencers, the alien beings are operating from a hidden agenda and seek to attain their own secret goals without being honest and direct with humans. To me, the actions of the EBEs/ETs, should they exist, speak louder than the reported – but, to be honest about it, unsubstantiated, except by others who were involved in unrelated incidents – communications to humans, almost all of whom have said they were captives and not invited guests. In these regards, I will draw my own conclusions and share them with you, our increasingly aware members of the general public, throughout this work.

Now: we begin.

Why Would a Military Engage With Alien Spacecraft?

Our planet remains separated into diverse cultures and distinct nations. There are differing views on whether this is a good circumstance or not. However, it is today's reality. There could possibly one day be a world government – perhaps brought on by the presence of EBEs/ETs. A world government would no doubt likewise seek to defend or at least regulate its airspace and eventually a defensive sphere in space around our planet of autonomy from outside penetration or interference with Earth's air and space traffic; open space lanes free of dangerous debris; and for the safety of our facilities such as satellites, orbiting space stations, and our own spacecraft.

All nations, without exception, maintain military, border and internal police forces to protect their physical, philosophical and theoretical boundaries. These include coastal defense and resource zones offshore and, of course, the air space above each nation. When unidentified intruding aircraft encroach upon a nation's air space, they are challenged by radio when they enter an "air defense identification zone" (ADIZ), or even after they fly above a given country's land territories, including islands. (Note that English is the official language as far as international air communications are concerned, so every licensed, commercial pilot is expected to have at least a basic understanding of spoken English.)

If an aircraft fails to reply, and does not possess a "friend-or-foe" tracking and navigation device – a transponder – then it becomes an "unidentified flying object," not necessarily an alien spacecraft, just an unknown aerial vehicle that may or may not be hostile or engaged in illegal activities such as drug smuggling. At that point, air-defense controllers will usually call the military planes on standby alert, and the interceptor aircraft will scramble and approach the infringing "UFO." Most often, the pilots of the air-defense interceptors will observe a standard aircraft such as an airplane, blimp, or helicopter. Radio contact might be made, and the pilot of the UFO will be required to identify the flight and purpose, including destination. If the pilot of the UFO does not respond, then the air-defense plane or planes may, after giving a final warning – including hand signals if the mystery aircraft's pilot is within visual contact but, for example, does not understand English – that unless the UFO follows the interceptor and lands at a friendly airfield, the military aircraft will shoot down the UFO.

However, some UFOs are not identifiable as conventional aircraft. As we will see in eyewitness accounts, some of these objects may look like spheres – either metallic in appearance or seeming to be glowing balls of fire. Or they may be "cigar-shaped objects" (CSOs), discs (flying saucers), crescent-shaped, pear-shaped, looking like a teardrop, a cylinder, a diamond shape, a cone, or may even seem to be a "glowing cloud." Naturally, some of these UFOs are more like the usual identification by governments as UAP (such as glowing clouds, fireballs, streaks of light, or even strange apparitions that seem to change shape while being observed) or, again, "unexplained aerial phenomena."

However, even exotic and strange-looking UFOs or UAP could conceivably be the aforementioned possible drug smugglers or, more concerning, disguised aircraft from a hostile nation attempting to penetrate friendly airspace for sinister purposes. Therefore it is, as noted, standard practice to contact the UFO/UAP and, failing that, to promptly engage – forcefully.

It is claimed that when military air-defense planes – and sometimes missiles – have attempted to (or possibly did) shoot at or bring down the occasional UFO that turned out to be an alien spacecraft they were able to close with and fire upon, that action has sometimes resulted in the UFO allegedly "firing back," or, worse, making the intercepting aircraft disappear entirely. (This lattermost event was almost always reported from the former Soviet Union.) We will investigate a few of these supposed occurrences of hostile action on the part of a UFO as we report on military encounters – and a very few civilian ones – over many decades. However, to properly set the stage it is best to start off with the "confirming evidence" of the existence of UFOs/UAP as physical realities, as proven by the US Navy videos cited earlier, and also by pilot and other witness testimony.

Seeing is Believing

From 10 to 16 November 2004, the nuclear-powered aircraft carrier USS *Nimitz* and accompanying ships in the *Nimitz* Strike Group (NSG) were on maneuvers off the west coasts of Mexico and the United States to prepare for deployment to the Arabian Sea. On at least three separate occasions, the NSG's guided missile cruiser USS *Princeton* detected several "anomalous aerial vehicles" (AAVs) in flight near the ships. The AAVs would drop from an altitude of 60,000ft to just 50ft above the surface of the sea within a few seconds, hover there briefly, then zoom away at tremendous speeds while turning rapidly.[1] "[T]hese craft exhibit technology far more advanced than any known craft on Earth."[2]

Kevin Day was the senior radar operator aboard the *Princeton*. He said his team's radar screens indicated well above 100 UFOs/AAVs for several days. Reporting that the objects generally remained above 80,000ft, higher than most aircraft, military or civilian, operate; Day said that at times the radar blips were so numerous they looked like snow falling from the sky. He added that radar crews initially thought their equipment was malfunctioning, but after investigations proved their instruments were performing as they should, the operators became alarmed when the UFOs/AAVs dropped to lower altitudes where they could collide with other, positively identified

1. Duncan Phenix. Mystery Wire. From the USS *Nimitz* Tic-Tac Executive Report. Posted 19 August 2020. Updated 19 May 2021. https://www.mysterywire.com/ufo/former-navy-pilot-and-current-us-rep-says-he-listened-in-real-time-to-tic-tac-ufo-encounter/ Also: https://s3.documentcloud.org/documents/20743466/nimitz-unredacted.pdf
2. Entropy (Basel). 21 October 2019. Published online 25 September 2019. "Estimating Flight Characteristics of Anomalous Unidentified Aerial Vehicles." By Kevin H. Knuth, Robert M. Powell, and Peter A. Reali. https://www.ncbi.nlm.nih.gov/pmc/articles/PMC7514271/

aircraft. At that point, Day asked the *Princeton*'s commander if he could take action. "I just really wanted to intercept these things," he said.[3]

On 14 November 2004, the *Princeton*'s radar detected a UFO/AAV while two U.S. Navy F/A18F aircraft were on a routine training mission close to the NSG. [4] The planes were contacted and directed to investigate. When the Navy jets approached to within about a mile of the AAV they reported to the controllers aboard the Princeton that it looked like "an elongated egg," or had a shape "like a Tic-Tac"; and with an observable "midline horizontal axis." (Referring to a raised "seam" around the object, lengthwise, from end to end as the UFO/AAV hovered horizontally – in a configuration level with the surface of the sea.) It was further described as being uniform in color, and "solid white."

> This was not the only time and place where such an object was recently observed: "Infamous 'Tic-Tac' UFO seen by Navy pilot now spotted over England." By Paula Froelich. 19 June 2021.[5] "… The UFO resembling a 'white Tic-Tac' spotted in 2004 by Former U.S. Navy pilot Cmdr. David Fravor while on duty at the USS *Nimitz* is back – but this time it's floating over England.
>
> "Pictures of the notorious UFO were snapped by Lucy Jane Castle, from Hinckley in south-west Leicestershire, who managed to grab a snap of the unexplained object and posted it on a UFO hunter's Facebook page, which was found by the *Daily Star*.
>
> "'It was hovering for a while and within a blink of an eye it had gone,' Castle said.
>
> "'Never seen anything like this before in that shape… Quickly took a picture while it was very still and within a blink of an eye it disappeared.'
>
> "Dan Watson, a fellow of the private UK UFO Sightings group, then posted a pic of two similar objects he claims to have seen over Swindon last year … " The AAV had no observable wings, pylons or engine nacelles. Its estimated length was

3. The History Channel. https://www.history.com/news/uss-nimitz-2004-tic-tac-ufo-encounter
4. Duncan Phenix. Mystery Wire. https://www.mysterywire.com/ufo/former-navy-pilot-and-current-us-rep-says-he-listened-in-real-time-to-tic-tac-ufo-encounter/
5. https://nypost.com/2021/06/19/tic-tac-ufo-seen-by-navy-pilot-now-spotted-over-england/

> approximately 40ft.[6] To maneuver an aircraft at even close to the performance shown by the AAVs in the videos, which is not possible for our current Earth-based technologies, would demand great propulsive power.

When the UFO/AAV was at high velocity the fighter planes' radar could not lock on to the object. However, when it was at lower speeds and hovering, the Navy jets could track the UFO/AAV with "forward-looking infrared radar" (FLIR). While the object took evasive action after interception by the Navy jets, exhibiting advanced acceleration, propulsion and aerodynamic capabilities, it did not engage in offensive actions against the planes, or the ships in the CSG. However, the UFO's demonstrated advanced capabilities clearly showed that it had the potential to approach the CSG and to possibly engage in "undetected reconnaissance," leaving the CSG with only a limited capacity "to detect, track, and/or engage the AAV."[7]

A U.S. Marine Corps Lieutenant Colonel flying another F18 was directed to the area and made a single pass over the site of the reported position of the UFO/AAV. He was at a higher altitude to remain clear of the two Navy planes that were heading toward the object. From his vantage point at an altitude of some 15,000ft, he could see that the ocean surface, presumably beneath the hovering UFO, was frothing as if stirred by a sinking ship or surfacing submarine. The disturbance was about 150 to 300ft in diameter. Otherwise, he said the sea was calm. He said he did not see the UFO/AAV itself or the other two fighter planes. In the words of the quote from the report: "It is possible that the disturbance was being caused by an AAV but that the AAV was 'cloaked' or invisible to the human eye." Impossible? Guess again. See: "Weird quantum effect that can turn matter invisible finally demonstrated."[8] On the *Coast-to-Coast AM* radio program of 25–26 March 2022, UFO researcher Rich Hoffman told fill-in host George Knapp that a United States Marine Corps pilot involved in a chase of a UFO observed that it had a "mirage-like, fuzzy appearance." Hoffman, who is prominent in the Scientific Coalition for UAP Studies – https://www.explorescu.org/ – said that this account, as with many others citing the same effect, indicates some sort of electromagnetic or microwave field enveloping UFOs. He detailed that this is probably why

6. Ibid.
7. https://www.mysterywire.com/ufo/former-navy-pilot-and-current-us-rep-says-he-listened-in-real-time-to-tic-tac-ufo-encounter/
8. By Ben Turner published 19 November, 2021. https://www.livescience.com/gas-made-so-cold-invisible

plant life at locations where UFOs are reported to have landed or hovered just above the surface were partially "cooked," as if in a microwave oven.[9] This possibility suggests to me that one and all are advised to keep a safe distance from any such objects hovering or on the ground nearby. This suspicion was later partially confirmed in an official report by the U.S. Defense Intelligence Agency.[10] As we shall see toward the end of our coverage, not being cautious in this regard possibly led to the death of a woman in Texas.

Upon arriving at the scene, the first intercepting aircraft's pilot, Commander David Fravor, flight leader of the Black Aces squadron, who was a Top Gun program graduate with more than sixteen years flying experience, also saw the frothing ocean surface, then spotted the UFO/AAV. When asked about the disturbed water, he reported that it remained under the object, and did not appear as a wake or trail, and looked as if the ocean there were boiling.[11]

Commander Fravor ordered the second intercepting jet pilot to remain at higher altitude (20,000ft) while he swept down toward the surface for a closer look.

The second pilot, Lieutenant Commander Alex Dietrich was among some pilots in this and other incidents to reveal their identities only later, she explained, because they feared "being labelled kooky."[12]

Diving to between 12,000 and 16,000ft, the lead plane was unable to obtain any sensor locks on the UFO/AAV. Fravor added, according to the official USS *Nimitz* report, that he forgot to activate his helmet recording system, which is seldom used by most pilots anyway. He and the second officer on board, who has wished to remain anonymous, depicted the object as described earlier, with the only difference being that Commander Fravor perceived it to be hovering while the second officer thought it was flying straight and level at about 500 to 1,000ft, and traveling at some 500 nautical mph.[13]

The official report states that the UFO/AAV was in a horizontal position, darting forward and back and from side to side for short distances as Fravor

---

9. https://www.coasttocoastam.com/
10. Defense Intelligence Reference Document: Anomalous Acute and Subacute Field Effects on Human Biological Tissues. 11 March, 2010. https://www.dia.mil/FOIA/FOIA-Electronic-Reading-Room/FileId/170026/
11. https://www.mysterywire.com/ufo/former-navy-pilot-and-current-us-rep-says-he-listened-in-real-time-to-tic-tac-ufo-encounter/
12. https://www.the-sun.com/news/4038088/fighter-pilots-intercepted-ufos-radiation-warped-time/
13. https://www.mysterywire.com/ufo/former-navy-pilot-and-current-us-rep-says-he-listened-in-real-time-to-tic-tac-ufo-encounter/

took the F-18 even lower for a better look. He rolled his plane in from about 10,000ft and approached at approximately 350kt toward what was estimated to be aft of the object. As he did so, he said the UFO/AAV seemed "to recognize us," and turned on its axis so that it was end-on to the closing aircraft. Fravor said that at that point the frothing of the otherwise calm sea ceased.

As Fravor completed his aerial maneuver, the UFO/AAV quickly gained altitude, then shot toward and past his aircraft at supersonic speed. He set the radar to short range and asked the *Princeton*'s controllers for their own radar update. At first, the ship's radar had no target blip, then the controller radioed to Fravor, "You're not going to believe this; it's at your CAP," adding that it was now at 24,000ft altitude. (CAP: Combat Air Patrol location, where the two F-18s had been performing their training assignment prior to being ordered to investigate the UFO/AAV. This development indicates to me that perhaps whoever was controlling the AAV was sending a not-so-subtle hint that the Navy planes should return to where they were before intercepting the UFO.)

After landing on the USS *Nimitz*, the F-18 crew was asked about any problems with the aircraft or its instruments, and both men said everything was in good order, adding that it was a brand-new plane with fewer than 100 hours flying time. They said that nothing had been electronically interfered with or "jammed." Also when asked, they reported no physiological effects from the encounter.

A second flight was scheduled that day, and the crews of those planes were asked by members of the first flight to see what they could find and to record it on their FLIRs. That flight included Lieutenant Chad Underwood. The planes took off and their crews were alerted to an AAV, via their aircraft radar, to be at a distance of about 30 to 40 nautical miles to the south. The Navy planes were at about 20,000ft, and the object was at approximately -5° ahead and below – between 15,000 and 20,000ft in altitude – when they flew toward it. As Underwood's plane drew closer, the object slewed to the left, and out of the FLIR's view. He said that then he made no attempt to pursue the UFO; and the planes continued on to their point of operations and initiated their planned training activities.[14] (Later, "Lieutenant Commander Chad Underwood revealed how his weapons system was disabled during the eerie encounter.")[15]

---

14. https://www.history.com/news/uss-nimitz-2004-tic-tac-ufo-encounter
15. https://www.the-sun.com/news/4038088/fighter-pilots-intercepted-ufos-radiation-warped-time/

So, in accordance with the release of the Defense Intelligence Agency documents to be introduced much later, already air crews were being asked if they suffered any untoward physiological side-effects after their close encounters with UFOs/UAP.

When Commander Fravor delivered his report to the *Nimitz* air wing intelligence officer, initially he was not taken seriously, and the man said he didn't know what to do about it. However, cognizant of the fact that Fravor was an experienced and well-respected commander, the intelligence officer changed his attitude, noting that had the report come from a less experienced pilot of a lower rank, the account would have received little attention. Consequently, the statement and the FLIR tape from the second plane were sent to higher echelons of command.[16]

Unbelievably, in my opinion, a more senior intelligence officer offered his theory that the "Tic-Tac" incident reflected the activities of an anti-drug operation. In view of the ridicule to which many witnesses – even those in the military (including Commander Fravor and his fellow flyers), commercial airline crews, and law-enforcement professionals – have been subjected after reporting UFOs, I laughed out loud at this notion, thinking, "*Now* who is hallucinating, lying, or hoaxing us?" As we shall see, such an extraordinary assertion requires extraordinary – or at least some – evidence, not just an utterly unfounded verbal shrug-off.

I am not going to vet the *Nimitz* reports further at this stage, but there will be additional confirming information presented later. This is because the evidence and testimony of credible witnesses has already buttressed the factual basis of the events as established so far. Moreover, as mentioned previously, the U.S. Navy has announced that the video from the second flight – and others to be introduced later – is genuine.

It is not the intent of this investigation to examine every incident to the last detail, stopping only when a statement can be made to "explain" – or, to put it more accurately, to *try* to explain away – UFO/UAP incidents. Readers should keep this in mind when I believe it necessary to try to explain away some reported occurrences that should – in my opinion and/or that of others – be put to rest. They need to be set aside as they detract from the credibility of numerous reports by reliable witnesses that are supported by material evidence such as films, videos, photographs, traces of radiation, radar returns, and physical changes to soils, plants and people involved in what are very likely actual events of lasting impact on human beings and our planet.

16. https://www.mysterywire.com/ufo/former-navy-pilot-and-current-us-rep-says-he-listened-in-real-time-to-tic-tac-ufo-encounter/

The *Nimitz* incident remained largely unknown except among Navy people and UFO enthusiasts until 2017 when the *New York Times* covered the story and released the aircraft FLIR video.[17] In a related article the *Times* also reported on the existence of a largely unknown Defense Department bureau called the Advanced Aerospace Threat Identification Program (AATIP). It was created largely due to the efforts of the then Senate Majority Leader, the late Senator Harry Reid of Nevada, who had a longtime interest in UFOs.[18] The Defense Department informed the *New York Times* that the AATIP had been shut down in 2012.[19] However, its director, Luis Elizondo, said it was still in business, but that he had resigned in October 2017 because it was not being taken seriously enough within the Department of Defense.[20] Moreover, as we will see later, the entire UFO/UAP phenomenon is being taken very seriously by at least one other branch of our military.[21] [22] We will also take a look at some corroborating testimony regarding the "Tic-Tac" incident, as if that were necessary; but, for now, let us return more than a few steps back in time to find out what we can learn from a history of military encounters with UFOs in earlier days.

---

17. https://www.nytimes.com/2017/12/16/us/politics/unidentified-flying-object-navy.html
18. https://www.nytimes.com/2017/12/16/us/politics/pentagon-program-ufo-harry-reid.html
19. https://www.reuters.com/article/us-usa-pentagon-ufos/does-pentagon-still-have-a-ufo-program-the-answer-is-a-bit-mysterious-idUSKBN1EA0QP
20. https://www.nytimes.com/2017/12/16/us/politics/pentagon-program-ufo-harry-reid.html
21. https://www.cnn.com/2019/09/18/politics/navy-confirms-ufo-videos-trnd/index.html
22. In this regard, Donald R. Schmitt – who, along with Lieutenant Colonel (Retired) Kevin D. Randle, uncovered the facts of the 1947 Roswell, New Mexico UFO crash, asked the pertinent question when he observed that we know about the US Air Force studies of UFOs, but where are the data collections by the Army, Navy, Coast Guard, Marine Corps? This was during his appearance on the *Coast-to-Coast AM* radio program hosted by George Noory, 1–2 June 2022. As we shall see, other government agencies such as Customs and Border Protection have compiled video footage and documentation of UFO/UAP incidents. https://www.coasttocoastam.com/

Chapter 2

From the Nineteenth Century to the First World War

Mystery Aircraft: Made by Domestic Inventors, or Sinister Foreigners, or … ?

During the mid- and late 1800s, almost as soon as the news was relayed that human beings had become airborne – first in balloons, then in rigid "airships," and just after the nineteenth century turned into the twentieth, in airplanes – reports of mystery aircraft in the skies proliferated around the world – and, of course, the world's militaries took heed. At first, the only viable use for balloons in military applications was for observation, and the Union Army did utilize them as surveillance platforms to direct the fire of field guns and siege artillery during the American Civil War.

The influence of the sight of people in balloons inspired German former military man Count Ferdinand von Zeppelin to design and launch in 1900 the first of his many later airships, which originally bore his name. (Afterward to become known as "dirigibles" or "blimps.") Starting off as experimental and exploratory, then commercial and later as military aircraft, rigid-framed Zeppelins took to the air – initially for reconnaissance, then during the First World War, as bombing platforms.

Through those early years, all around the world there were increasing reports of "airships" or "cigar-shaped objects" (CSOs) and later "mystery aeroplanes." In the United States, observations of these unidentified flying objects were treated with wonder, awe and a hopeful anticipation for the future of air travel; but in Great Britain – with the close proximity of adversarial Germany – home of the Zeppelin, and with the then current "dreadnought race" to see which of those two countries could build the most battleships – the growing numbers of mystery airship and airplane sightings were cause for alarm and dread in the British Isles. Thus was born the era of "scareships."

The wave of airship reports peaked in the United States in 1896 and 1897, with only indirect and incidental references to the potential military use of these craft in warfare – occasionally thought to be by Cuban revolutionaries arming against Spain. But in Great Britain the perceived threat of "enemy" airships flying above had a more immediate military connection.

The wave kicked off in 1909 with a few, then a flurry of reports. This mini-wave began on 23 March when a police constable with the surname of "Kettle" said he saw a CSO fly over Peterborough at about 5 a.m.[1] His story was welcomed with skepticism until two other sighting reports came in on the 25th. By 17 May there were nineteen accounts of mystery objects in the skies above sixteen communities, concentrated in East Anglia and South Wales, as reported in *The Standard*.[2] One factor they had in common was that these "torpedo-shaped" unidentified flying objects only came out at night, and were equipped with two powerful searchlights.[3] This description fits airships, so they were branded as such, being referred to as "mystery airships," "phantom airships," "scareships," etc.

However, there was a problem: the first edition of *Jane's All The World's Airships* came out that year and listed only two such craft in all of the British Isles. One small airship belonged to the army and was named "Baby"; the other was on exhibition in London at the time. In reality, neither craft was large, dependable or robust enough to account for these sightings. This left theorizers with only one alternative – Germany.

By 1909 Count Zeppelin's creations were few in number, did not have a great range, and were not yet accepted by the German military. The world's first airline, "DELAG" (Deutsche Luftschiffahrts-Aktiengesellschaft, or German Airship Transportation Corporation, Ltd.) was not even established until months after the above-cited observations – on 16 November 1909.[4] So, while the speculation about German airships invading British airspace was a valid fear, the technology was not quite there yet. Many of these early Zeppelins were destroyed by fire or crashed, but fortunately with almost no loss of life. (That would change as the First World War developed, with British air defense inflicting heavy losses on Germany's airship fleet.)

However, the reports of airships seen aloft, or their motors heard above the clouds persisted in the pre-war years. This wave of anxiety, fear and

1. https://airminded.org/2006/12/22/the-scareship-age/ This blog says, in its "About" section: "'Airminded' is the research blog of Dr Brett Holman, a historian from Melbourne, Australia." He conducted extensive searches of news stories from each era covered.
2. Ibid. Here Holman cites: *The Standard* (London), 17 May 1909, p.9.
3. Ibid. Holman again cites *The Standard*, same date and page.
4. https://www.airships.net/delag-passenger-zeppelins/

alarm did have one beneficial result: advocates for a stronger military and the creation of an air arm were able to pressure the then Liberal government to move faster in these areas, which aided Great Britain in wars to come.[5] This was especially true of the even larger wave of airship sightings in 1913.[6]

With regard to the earliest reports, Dr Brett Holman wrote in his blog that there could be little doubt that something had been observed because the eyewitnesses resided many miles apart, but all agreed on specifics such as that the craft moved rapidly and were under control – piloted.[7] To my mind, these sightings rule out natural phenomena or the random movements of balloons or Zeppelins that had broken loose from their moorings and were being driven about by the wind – as did happen on occasion in that time period.

Foreshadowing what would be the reactions of governments and militaries to observations of UFOs/UAP in the air, the War Office and the Aeronautical Society both stated that they had made "extensive inquiries," but were unable to explain the sightings. With regard to the competing theories about the mystery flying craft, *The Standard* mentioned a theory that the airship had been launched from a German warship, but added that it would be the "wiser" course to decide that it was the product of an English inventor who was yet attempting to keep his innovation secret.

Dr Holman goes on to inform us that this later theory was countered in a report by a Mr Egerton Free, who described a mystery airship over Clacton. Quoting *The Globe* but found on page 7 of the *Daily Mail* the following day, the story by Free is that he went to the spot below where the airship had passed and discovered a "curious object" said to be about 5ft long, forged from steel and India rubber, and weighing 35lb. The artefact was also described as an ovoid of dark grey rubber, between 2 and 3ft long, which was encased in "a network of mesh," and with a steel rod passing through its center and projecting on each side by about a foot, with one end capped by a steel disc, like a miniature railway-wagon buffer. In a further foretelling of actions by authorities in subsequent decades, it was reported that the War Office had confiscated it.[8]

5. https://cupdf.com/document/scareships-over-britain.html
6. "Conservative newspapers such as the *Daily Mail* did not hesitate to use the 'fact' of the supposed German aerial espionage of Britain as a cudgel with which to beat the Liberal government for its slow progress in forming a military wing." https://airminded.org/2009/06/11/post-blogging-the-1909-scareships-thoughts-and-conclusions/
7. https://airminded.org/2009/05/17/monday-17-may-1909/
8. https://airminded.org/2006/12/22/the-scareship-age/

At first seeming to be the damning evidence, the rubber bag, or "piston" as it was variably described, was stamped with the label "Müller Fabrik Bremen."[9] However, investigations in that German port city led nowhere.

This is the first example of what would become a pattern: a sighting of a mystery craft in the sky. The alleged discovery of an artefact of unknown origin. The War Office is claimed to have confiscated the only evidence. I think we can accept the fact that reports of unidentified aircraft can be believed, if we choose to do so. As for the strange object allegedly found that seemed to tie Germany to the mystery airships, and its subsequent supposed seizure by the War Office, it is too convenient and could easily be the work of one or more hoaxers, perhaps working in league with those who hoped to sell materiél to the government for a future air arm.

With the start of the First World War, mystery airship sightings increased, obliging the War Office to dispatch one of its precious few airplanes in a futile air search for a rumored airship base in the Lake District during August 1914.

While the interaction of UFOs in the form of mystery airships with the British military was not all that direct, its indirect effects would be long-lasting with regard to subsequent preparations in the UK for aerial warfare. However, the question remains: if these phantom airships – and the many more of them reported from Russia, the United States, Canada, South Africa, France, Denmark, New Zealand, Australia, Sweden, Belgium, the Netherlands, Germany, Romania, Austria-Hungary, and Norway[10] until 1918 – were not German or another nation's airships, or the work of unknown inventors, what were these UFOs being seen by many people all around our world?

First Attack on an Unidentified Flying Object by a Military Aircraft

Just before 9 p.m. on 31 January 1916, Royal Naval Air Services Flight Sub-Lieutenant J.E. Morgan piloted his BE2c fighter plane up to 5,000ft in search of German Zeppelins intent on bombing his British homeland.[11] Within moments he spotted, straight ahead and slightly above, an object

9. https://airminded.org/2009/05/17/monday-17-may-1909/
10. https://airminded.org/2006/12/22/the-scareship-age/
11. https://airminded.org/2010/03/13/something-like-a-railway-carriage/ Brett Holman citing: *Out of the Shadows: UFOs, the Establishment and the Official Cover-Up*. David Clarke and Andy Roberts. Piatkus. London. 2002.

he said looked "something like a railway carriage" with its row of lighted windows muted by having the blinds drawn. Believing the object was some sort of German aircraft assigned to bomb London, Morgan made use of his only option; he drew his service revolver and fired several shots at the mystery craft. This was his "only option" because, when redesigned as a night fighter, the BE2 in its "c" model carried a pilot, with no observer-gunner. The plane was equipped instead with incendiary bomblets and a grapnel hook with an explosive charge attached to blow a hole in, ignite the contained hydrogen gas, and tear apart a Zeppelin's airbags. Both weapons systems were to be dropped from the plane as it flew above an enemy airship; there was no forward-firing or ring-mounted gun. The only gun aboard would have been the pilot's sidearm.[12] He reported that the "row of lights" immediately rose rapidly and disappeared into the dark night above.[13] Thinking that instead his plane was losing altitude, Morgan attempted to keep it aloft, lost control, and crash-landed into the Thames Haven Marshes.

Dr Holman in his blog adds some perceptive observations, commenting that they are omitted from reports by most ufologists.[14] He cites another source[15] to propose that the "phantom airship" was the German Zeppelin L16, whose gondola could, conceivably, "look something like a railway carriage," but adds that it would not have been well lit (in a combat situation – RA).[16] Holman states that the L16 had been intent on bombing well to the north of London; but he also explains that neither airship captains nor British interceptor pilots often knew where they were, and that observation

12. https://en.wikipedia.org/wiki/Royal_Aircraft_Factory_B.E.2#cite_note-Bruce68-15-18-47 Citing: Bruce, J.M. *British Aeroplanes 1914–18*. Putnam. London. 1957. pp.15-18.
13. https://airminded.org/2010/03/13/something-like-a-railway-carriage/ Brett Holman citing: *Out of the Shadows: UFOs, the Establishment and the Official Cover-Up*. David Clarke and Andy Roberts. Piatkus. London. 2002.
14. https://airminded.org/2010/03/13/something-like-a-railway-carriage/
15. Christopher Cole and E.F. Cheesman, *The Air Defence of Britain 1914-1918*. Putnam. (London. 1984). pp.83-9.
16. And: Holman also cites David Clarke, who in an article for "The UFO Project" in turn cites: H.A. Jones, *The War in the Air, Volume 3*, The Clarendon Press, Oxford, 1931. C. Cole and E.F. Cheeseman, *The Air Defence of Britain 1914-1918*, Bodley Head, London, 1984. PRO Air 1/611 16/15/286. Report from Officer in Command, Royal Flying Corps, Hainault Farm, 2 February 1916. PRO Air 1/438 15/300/1. Rochford Station (Naval): report on night landing ground, 1916. PRO Air 1/720 36/1/6 GHQ Home Forces Intelligence Circular No. 6 May 1916. See: http://www.uk-ufo.org/condign/hist19162.htm) https://airminded.org/2010/03/13/something-like-a-railway-carriage/

and anti-aircraft ground crews usually saw nothing at all (presumably due the frequent cloudiness of Great Britain's maritime climate). He goes on to explain that the L16 had been forced to turn back toward the continent by engine trouble, which could explain why Morgan encountered it, and possibly why another British defense pilot spotted it briefly.

Further, Holman reminds us that with the airship's engine noise it is likely a Zeppelin captain would not have heard Morgan's pistol shots. Also, he speculates that the L16 could have quickly dropped ballast bags to gain altitude rapidly and escape, adding that it could have "disappeared" by entering a cloud layer above. Holman's conclusion is identical to my own thought: "But otherwise, if it wasn't an airship, what might Morgan have seen?"

While I strive to whenever possible rely on reports from at least two sources, we can only take this pilot's word in this case, which I am prepared to do as he had no reason to lie because he was not claiming a kill, only that he saw a mysterious aircraft and fired at it. The report of Sub-Lieutenant Morgan's encounter with the UFO is absent from the official record released by the War Office after the war. However, another British pilot told of briefly seeing a Zeppelin caught in the beams of London's anti-airship searchlights just a few minutes after Morgan said he encountered the mystery object.[17]

I sincerely doubt the notion that what Sub-Lieutenant Morgan saw that night had been thought of by him as an alien spacecraft or other exotic device such as an interdimensional or time-travel vehicle. I do not believe such thoughts ever entered his or anyone else's mind at the time. Moreover, there were few to no widespread reports in that era of strange craft with what appeared to be rows of lights, and of unidentified flying objects fleeing from Earthly aircraft, vehicles or people by shooting straight up and away. The similarities in his account to other, later reports do add credence to Morgan's story, giving it added believability. So, I accept this as being the first attack by a powered aircraft from Earth on a UFO – which to my mind, in this case, (possibly but not conclusively) represents an extraterrestrial spacecraft.

A Fantastic Story – Too Easily Dismissed?

I now ask readers to bear with me while I cover a story that, in the words of Conrad Bauer in his book, *Military UFO Encounters*, "is a fantastic tale

---

17. Ibid. Brett Holman, citing: *Out of the Shadows: UFOs, the Establishment and the Official Cover-Up*. David Clarke and Andy Roberts. Piatkus. London. 2002. And: https://en.wikipedia.org/wiki/Royal_Aircraft_Factory_B.E.2#cite_note-Bruce68-15-18-47 Citing: J.M. Bruce *British Aeroplanes 1914–18*. Putnam. London. 1957. pp.15–18.

to be sure, bordering on the utterly absurd."[18] I agree, but let us take a brief look at it, then add another remark or two.

A man named Peter Waitzrik, who identified himself as one of the wingmen of Baron Manfred von Richtofen – popularly known as the German First World War fighter ace the "Red Baron" – stepped forward near the end of his life to report that after he and von Richtofen took off on 13 March 1917 from an airfield in Belgium they encountered a strange aircraft.

At the age of 105, Waitzrik told the tabloid *Weekly World News*, "We were terrified because we'd never seen anything like it before. The U.S. had just entered the war, so we assumed it was something they'd sent up."[19] There is no publication date for the story given at the *Weekly World News* archive's website, but Bauer states that Waitzrik told his tale shortly before his death in 1999.[20] Waitzrik continued with his fantastic account by stating that von Richtofen promptly fired at the craft, and that it dropped from the sky "like a rock, shearing off tree limbs as it crashed in the woods." Waitzrik then said that "two little baldheaded guys climbed out and ran away."[21] I know … but please stay with me momentarily while I complete this tale, and add some commentary.

Waitzrik explained that he and the Red Baron made a complete report of the incident to headquarters, but were ordered to not mention it again. Waitzrik detailed that he had never told anyone except his wife and grandchildren. He added the comment, "But it's been over eighty years, so what difference could it possibly make now?" Good point. And, whether his tale is tall or not, other military witnesses have also spoken out with the same thought in mind, more or less: "It's now or never." Back to the Waitzrik account: Waitzrik described the UFO as being about 40m (136ft) in diameter, and said it "looked just like those saucer-shaped spaceships that everybody's been seeing for the last fifty years." He added that he was certain the craft he saw the Red Baron shoot down was not an American reconnaissance plane; that it had been "(a) spacecraft from another planet – and those little guys who ran off into the woods weren't Americans, they were space aliens." He concluded with a final remark that, "You know, sometimes I wonder whatever became of those guys, anyway."

---

18. *Military UFO Encounters*. Conrad Bauer. Maplewood Publishing. No city listed. 2019. p.5.
19. http://astro.wsu.edu/worthey/astro/html/im-ufo/im-aliens/aliens19.html
20. *Military UFO Encounters*. Conrad Bauer. Maplewood Publishing. No city listed. 2019. p.3.
21. http://astro.wsu.edu/worthey/astro/html/im-ufo/im-aliens/aliens19.html

While I declared my intention to give UFO eyewitnesses the benefit of a doubt, and I still intend to, I must admit that when I first encountered this story while researching this study I laughed out loud, and almost threw the book containing the item across the room (it was not Bauer's book), but Bauer, among others, did make a couple of additional points worth considering. First of all, it *is* utterly absurd to think that a few 7.92mm[22] bullets fired from a rickety biplane[23] could bring down a very sophisticated alien spacecraft – assuming that is what happened. However, if there are extraterrestrial spacecraft penetrating our airspace, as so much evidence to be presented later indicates, then they would very likely be protected by a force-field shield of some kind to guard them from interstellar and interplanetary debris; but, the presumed aliens may have, for some reason, switched off their defensive screen upon entering the relative safety of Earth's atmosphere, leaving them vulnerable to the German pilot's primitive firearm.

Counting heavily against the reliability of this story is the fact that it was released through the tabloid *Weekly World News*, which covered the tale in its usual sensationalistic, lurid style. But author Frank Joseph further informs us that Waitzrik and his family tried to interest standard press outlets until, despairing of his story not coming to light prior to his death, they were driven to take the tabloid route. However, yet again, just a little bit of deeper digging throws more light on the Waitzrik account.

Enter the Aerodrome Forum, with participant "Volker_Nemsch, Forum Ace of Aces." He posted that Waitzrik "seemed to be a ghost himself." Nemsch explained that he had performed "a short research" but found no records of 'Peter Waitzrik,' or any other details regarding his supposed "rank, service record, address, other documents" on the internet. Nemsch posted that the only time "Waitzrik" appears is in connection with this very strange tale.[24]

---

22. *Early Aircraft Armament.* Harry Woodman. Smithsonian Institute Press. Washington, D.C. 1989. http://www.worldhistory.biz/download567/EarlyAircraftArmament.TheAeroplaneandtheGunupto1918_worldhistory.biz.pdf
23. It's been pointed out that von Richtofen's squadron was not yet equipped with the Fokker triple-winged aircraft the *Weekly World News* reporter said was flown that day. Elsewhere, it is affirmed that another aircraft type was then being used. But, as far as the story quoted goes, Waitzrik did not claim they were in Fokker triplanes. In his book, *Military Encounters With Extraterrestrials*, Frank Joseph reports that in that particular month von Richtofen's squadron flew bi-winged Hablerstadt pursuit planes. *Military Encounters With Extraterrestrials*. Frank Joseph. Bear & Co. Rochester, VT. 2018. p.16.
24. The Aerodrome Forum. http://www.theaerodrome.com/forum/showthread.php?t=68877

So, while a true believer or two may protest that Waitzrik is telling the truth, and that Nemsch is not. Nemsch's report is, to me, far more believable. So I now risk the wrath of those who want others to believe this tale – at this point, without hesitation, I state that the Waitzrik story is too far out of the bounds of sound reasoning for me to accept as being genuine. If anyone can produce solid proof to the contrary, I will change my opinion. To quote economist John Maynard Keynes: "When my information changes, I change my mind."[25]

However, overall, while I do not accept the validity of the Waitzrik story, please allow me to quote an observation from another First World War hero: "'UFOs are real. Too many good men that don't experience hallucinations have seen them.' (Captain Eddie Rickenbacker, leading U.S. fighter ace of the First World War.)"[26]

The War Office Took Airship Reports Seriously, For a While…

In response to the "scareship" waves, the War Office evidently called forth a team of intelligence officers to investigate sightings in British skies during the First World War. Thus, the world's first official group investigating unidentified flying objects – anticipated as being airships and airplanes, not alien spacecraft – was born in the second decade of the twentieth century, preceding the United Kingdom's post-Second World War "Flying Saucer Working Party" by thirty-seven years.[27]

As we have seen as revealed to us by Dr Brett Holman, whose research found that the early twentieth century "scareship" wave was regularly featured in British and other nations' newspapers, there were plenty of opportunities for misidentified, hoaxed or imagined sightings to interfere with governmental and military efforts to detect actual German air-assaults on Great Britain during the First World War. Therefore, a regular, scientific, more analytic approach to the problem was required. Organized and under the control of a Lieutenant Colonel Kell, the group was reportedly called the "Military Observation Department Five" (MO5).

25. https://quoteinvestigator.com/2011/07/22/keynes-change-mind/
26. *Military Encounters With Extraterrestrials*. Frank Joseph. Bear & Co. Rochester, VT. 2018. p.14.
27. https://www.yahoo.com/news/the-first-x-files-how-britain-investigated-ufos-100349038.html

Since he was not fully identified, I performed an internet search and found that Lieutenant Colonel (later General) Vernon Kell had served in military intelligence at that time, and had been assigned to the domestic branch, later to become the Security Service, then to be known as MI5. However, there was no mention of his working at MO5 and being occupied with identifying unknown aerial intruders into British airspace. Nevertheless, despite the absence of direct confirmation, in view of the overall trajectory of his military career, I am willing to accept his assignment as fact.

The wartime reports of mysterious lights and objects in the skies were also analyzed by Lieutenant Colonel W.S. Brancker, then Assistant Director of Military Aeronautics, in the Department of Military Training. Brancker and Kell coordinated the British military's efforts to identify, track, intercept and destroy German airships assaulting Great Britain from the sky. Of course, British curiosity was directed not at the mysterious aspects – or phantom airships – but rather in focusing on real-world threats to the health and safety of Britons in the here and now.

Britain's air defenses quickly evolved to include an ingenious system that incorporated a network of sound detection and ranging devices, rings of human ground observers, searchlights, and belts of anti-aircraft guns around London. Improved anti-aircraft guns, night-fighting pursuit planes equipped with illuminated instrument panels, night-fighting training for pilots, and new types of explosive and incendiary ammunition to ignite the hydrogen gas that held Zeppelins aloft all contributed to the defeat of Germany's terror-bombing campaign that was waged against Great Britain throughout the war.[28] So, indirectly, and one step removed, the "scareship" wave led to innovations in aerial defense that were unimagined prior to the First World War.

The 1920s and 1930s were much more quiescent as far as military encounters with UFOs were concerned, probably due in part to the massive demobilization of their armed forces by the combatant nations; and, with the onset of the Great Depression, people – military people included – had more pressing problems in mind than scanning the skies or paying attention to evidently harmless unidentified flying objects and/or unexplained aerial phenomena; but the outbreak of the Second World War would soon change all of that.

---

28. "1914-1918-online. International Encyclopedia of the First World War." By Charles Dusch https://encyclopedia.1914-1918-online.net/article/zeppelin_airship

Chapter 3

Second World War

The 1941 "Crash of a UFO" Near Cape Girardeau, Missouri

It has been alleged that a saucer-shaped aerial vehicle crashed in southeastern Missouri, near Cape Girardeau, in April 1941 – eight months before the United States was brought into the Second World War. The supposed crash is further reported to have drawn the prompt attention of the United States Army.[1] The accounts of this incident are sparing and tenuous, so we will take a quick look at as much of the information as practical.

After consulting *MO41 The Bombshell Before Roswell*, I found myself less convinced that any such incident really happened than before I had forced myself to finish reading the account. Unfortunately, for the sake of the telling of the tale, the text suffers from being imprecise in language, circular in its lack of organization, repetitive in content, burdened with huge doses of unfounded speculation, a general lack of proper structure, and it is without the benefit of good editing.

Putting aside the problems with this flawed item of reportage, there is the fact that the tale originated not with a direct witness, or even a second-hand witness, but with the testimony of a granddaughter of the participant, and not from the man himself but from his widow. Mitigating this circumstance is the fact that the widow in question relayed the story on her deathbed. So, let me declare at the outset that the witness and those relaying the story – living and dead – seem to be sincere in their belief about what happened.

Supposedly, the primary witness was a Baptist minister who had been called to what at first seemed to be a conventional aircraft crash to perform last rites, and console survivors and witnesses. However, when he arrived he observed a damaged saucer-shaped craft, two dead aliens, and one in the

1. *MO41, The Bombshell Before Roswell* Paul Blake Smith. W & B Publishers. Kernersville, NC. Revised, 2020 edition.

process of dying as it, too, lay on the ground. What followed is what will become the usual story of arriving military people, witnesses being warned to keep quiet about the whole thing, a quick removal of the victims and crashed vehicle, and a complete cleanup of the site.

Consulting Ryan S. Wood's account at the "Mutual UFO Network Symposium, Evidence for a Crash" web page,[2] one finds supporting "evidence," much of it newer, but some of which was available prior to the publication of *MO41 The Bombshell Before Roswell.* I did find some supposedly corroborative materials. However, the origins of the documents alleged to have been penned by President Franklin D. Roosevelt and senior government officials have not been authenticated beyond a reasonable doubt. While many individuals are listed as likely but not definitely confirmed to have been there, certain facts such as the presence of a local airfield with military connections and a new FBI office are, I believe, irrelevant and inconsequential.

I am not faulting the efforts of Mr Wood and his co-investigators; but to me the corroborating circumstantial indications, testimony and documents just are not sufficient to prove that the incident really occurred. Again, my opinion could change if the facts change. So, for now, I must conclude that the Cape Girardeau crash is a myth founded on family and community legends, not provable, material facts.

The "Battle of Los Angeles," 25 February 1942

Just a few weeks after the Japanese air strikes on the United States Pacific Fleet at Pearl Harbor, Hawaii, and but one day following a submarine-launched deck-gun attack on an oil field 100 miles up the California coast, an air-raid alert sounded at 2:25 a.m., Wednesday morning, 25 February 1942, in the Los Angeles Basin.[3]

A *Los Angeles Times* overview, in a retro-look published in 2011, citing a 1992 article, updated in 2012, 2017 and 2021, tells us further that widespread fears were supposedly realized with the Great Los Angeles Air Raid – an apparent Japanese air attack on mainland America.

2. https://pdf4pro.com/fullscreen/evidence-for-a-crash-retrieval-in-cape-girardeau-missouri-53b595.html
3. https://www.latimes.com/visuals/framework/la-me-fw-archives-1942-battle-la-20170221-story.html

The *L.A. Times* reported that the U.S. Army announced the approach of potentially hostile aircraft. Air-raid sirens wailed, air-raid wardens scrambled from their beds, interceptor pilots raced to their aircraft and started their engines, searchlight and anti-aircraft gun crews scanned the skies.

Just after 3 a.m., air-defense troops who had been stationed in Santa Monica let loose with their anti-aircraft and 50-caliber machine guns.[4] Within moments other batteries joined the battle. To quote from History.com, which in turn refers to *Los Angeles Times* reports: "Powerful searchlights … stabbed the sky with brilliant, probing fingers … anti-aircraft batteries dotted the heavens with beautiful, if sinister, orange bursts of shrapnel."[5]

Let us look at the photographic evidence: the copies of the photo displayed in most books and at almost all websites supporting the idea that Los Angeles had been overflown 25 February 1942 by a UFO – in the meaning that it was an alien spacecraft or other paranormal phenomenon – show an overly contrasted image with a blob – an excessively unfocused blob – of light at the point where the air-defense searchlight beams converge. This gives the impression that a single, large, saucer-shaped or cigar-shaped object is being lit up. However, a better – more realistic – version of this same photo appeared in the *Los Angeles Times* on 26 February 1942, and another version is also displayed at the aforementioned History.com website.[6]

I have performed some photo-journalism work, including dark-room, film-processing chores in developing and printing photographs. This was in the days when camera settings had to be adjusted manually and judged by eye without the benefit of computerized advice. I am far from being an expert in photographic analysis and interpretation as a professional. However, I do have a certain level of skill in these regards as an "informed amateur."

I believe the photograph posted on the front page of the *Los Angeles Times*, and the other photo accompanying the History.com story regarding the Los Angeles incident are much better, because: in the second photo the haze, clouds and smoke are plainly visible. In both photos, the searchlight beams and, especially, the all-important point where they converge, are much more easily discerned. In both photographs, the relatively small

4. https://www.history.com/news/world-war-iis-bizarre-battle-of-los-angeles
5. Ibid. Citing: *The Los Angeles Times*.
6. https://www.history.com/news/world-war-iis-bizarre-battle-of-los-angeles Also: The *Los Angeles Times*, 26 February 1942.

explosions from the anti-aircraft shells are more distinct; especially the ones just above where the searchlight beams meet. In the second photo the light shafts – three from the left, two from the right, three from the center and pointing slightly toward the camera that took the photo – are clearly shown to have been dispersed and distorted by the smoke, haze and/or thin clouds aloft over the city that very early morning. (The three centermost beams are smaller, probably due to being farther away, and the leftmost of the trio is actually a double beam, likely created by two searchlights being placed close together, perhaps in a single "bank.")

In the *Los Angeles Times* photo displayed at the History.com website, also plainly evident is the dispersal of the searchlight beams, especially in the topmost portions. This is likely caused by a thin stratum of clouds, haze or smoke that is also scattering into this atmospheric layer. Crucially, there is no 'bent' light beam, as is asserted at more than one website; it is a combination of what are apparently the nearest beams, at the far left and far right, being directed away, and having the top portions dispersed and absorbed by moisture and smoke in the air, and some light being refracted and reflected that makes these shafts of light seem to sag or curve in the distance. Most important, the blob or mass where the searchlight beacons converge is much smaller than in the blurred images that attempt to show some sort of cigar-shaped or saucer-shaped object in their depictions.

When I lived in the Los Angeles Basin, on many occasions, particularly in cool-weather months, the sea air and coastal haze would cause bright lights (including the searchlight beams from Hollywood premieres or the opening of a new automobile dealership) to cast blurred and fuzzy auras, blobs and hazy or "bent" shafts of light skyward.

In the images, the "sphere" of light at the upper part of the convergence of the searchlight beams can be clearly seen, especially in the second *Los Angeles Times* photo (at History.com) to be the effects of an anti-aircraft shell bursting a bit closer to the camera. There is another one, being smaller – probably due to its distance from the camera – slightly above and just behind.

Individuals who are either sloppy, uncaring or unscrupulous insist on reproducing images taken from this photo that are less clear and that tend to reinforce the mistaken notion that the blob or mass at the center of the converging searchlight beams has a sort of dome, or crest on top.

Taken altogether, I believe the photographic evidence, such as we have always had, does not prove the existence of an unidentified flying object (as in an alien spacecraft), or any aircraft or objects at all. What the best images demonstrate is that the sky above Los Angeles, at least at the instant these photographs were taken, is devoid of any sort of UFO – alien, paranormal, unexplainable, or just plain conventional enemy.

I anticipate that the preceding paragraphs will come under attack from UFO true believers, and photographic "experts," and even genuine authorities in photo analysis and interpretation, especially those who are also true believers themselves. Without going into what are irrelevant, extraneous, even misleading further details, I stand firmly with my interpretation being the correct one.

History.com seems to support my contention, with the observation: "It appeared that Los Angeles was under attack, yet many of those who looked skyward saw nothing but smoke and the glare of ack-ack (anti-aircraft) fire." Moreover, History.com further reports: "'Imagination could have easily disclosed many shapes in the sky in the midst of that weird symphony of noise and color,' Coastal Artillery Corps Colonel John G. Murphy later wrote. 'But cold detachment disclosed no planes of any type in the sky—friendly or enemy.'"

In response to anxious questions about why the interceptor aircraft warming their engines on area airfields were not sent aloft are easily answered by observing that the last thing an air commander wants to do is order his interceptors into the air amid a flak-storm hurled up by co-defending gunners aiming at perceived enemy aircraft – real or imagined, mistaken or off course. Except in the most desperate of circumstances, such as those faced by Axis air forces toward the end of the Second World War, intercepting aircraft were only to be deployed relatively safely well outside the ring of anti-aircraft artillery sites defending the target to prevent the loss of the planes to "friendly fire."

After more than an hour, over 1,400 shells had been fired into the air, but with the arrival of daylight there was an amazing discovery: it seemed there had been no enemy air attack. No wrecked planes were found. No bombs had fallen. There was damage on the ground, all caused by metal shrapnel raining down, and anti-aircraft ammunition that had not exploded until falling from the sky. There were no serious injuries; the five deaths were caused by three traffic accidents and two heart attacks.

In the aftermath, inter-service discord continued, as it had since the Pearl Harbor air raid. The Navy Secretary declared that it had been a false alarm, while the Secretary of War sided with the Army in claiming that at least fifteen planes had taken part in the "raid." As always, eyewitness accounts varied from some who thought they saw a single, large, balloon-shaped object, to those who claimed to have observed from one to up to dozens of planes. History.com cites the *New York Times* in printing: "The more the whole incident … is examined, the more incredible it becomes."[7]

History.com further observed, "In 1983, the Office of Air Force History … noted that meteorological balloons had been released prior to the barrage to help determine wind conditions."[8] The "lights" seen flying overhead were evidently anti-aircraft search beams bouncing off panels of thin, reflective tinfoil affixed to the balloons so they could be more easily detected by radar, and the balloons' silver color could have been what first triggered the alerts. Once the shooting began, the disorienting combination of searchlights, smoke and anti-aircraft flak might have led gunners to continue to "believe they were firing on enemy planes even though none were actually present." I completely agree.

History.com concluded with: "Even at the time, many journalists noted that it was fitting that the incident had taken place in the home of the film industry." In an article from March 1942, the *New York Times* wrote that as the 'world's preeminent fabricator of make-believe, Hollywood appeared to have played host to a battle that was 'just another illusion.'"[9]

I lived in the Los Angeles Basin in 1960 and in 1970–74. Discussions with older Angelenos about the "Battle of Los Angeles" would prompt the remark: "Japanese destroyers shelled Santa Barbara." Someone else replied with, "It was a submarine, and it shot-up the oil fields." Another comment would be, "They bombed Culver City with a blimp." Then someone would dispute that with, "It was Santa Monica, and they used planes." Other contentions included, "We shot down some Zeroes." Another older Los Angeles resident said, "They [the Japanese] tried a landing down around Long Beach, but when they saw what we had in store for them when we shot-up their planes all night, they turned around and went back to Japan." Also alleged was, "They were going to land up by San Francisco, but we turned 'em back." Yet that was "corrected" by, "It was Oregon. They tried to set fire to the oil refineries all up and down the coast," etc. However, no one – ever – said anything about spaceships, interdimensional vehicles, time machines, or even mystery objects – it was all either a Japanese blimp, balloon, ships or planes, not aliens from outer space, which were not on anyone's mental radar at the time. What we now see in some coverage of the events of 25 February 1942 is UFO enthusiasts reading their own

7. Ibid. And: *The New York Times*.
8. https://www.history.com/news/world-war-iis-bizarre-battle-of-los-angeles Also: The *Los Angeles Times*, 26 February 1942.
9. https://www.history.com/news/world-war-iis-bizarre-battle-of-los-angeles

preferences into the testimony and evidence of what was purely an Earthly Second World War phenomenon, not an otherworldly, paranormal incident.

I must agree that the "Battle of Los Angeles" was a case of mistaken identity aggravated by "war nerves." There was a military encounter with an unidentified flying object, or perhaps just a misperception of one; but it had nothing to do with extraterrestrial spacecraft. As we shall see, other incidents will produce contrary conclusions.

Fireballs: Strange Craft, Or…? The "Foo-Fighters" of the Second World War

While popularly known as "Foo-Fighters" among American air crews, their British counterparts called the mysterious manifestations "the light," or "the thing."[10] On 14 December 1943, Beaufighter pilot Squadron Leader P. Wells wrote in the log-book entry, "Screaming dogfight with the light."

In the first part of October 1944, British, Canadian and American night fighter pilots and bomber crews reported peculiar "balls of light" that seemed to be intelligently controlled as they flew in various formations and engaged in spectacular aerial maneuvers above Belgium, Holland and western Germany.[11] These odd apparitions were seen to be following Allied aircraft – tailing them, or dogging their planes from alongside or even slightly ahead, as if flying with them in echelon formation.[12]

In February 1945, American and British night fighter crews also began to report encounters with "balls of light" and "jets" over the Po Valley of northern Italy.[13]

One sighting, this time over the Rhine Valley area of western Germany, is documented in military records as follows:[14] From the official report of the

---

10. *Out of the Shadows: UFOs, the Establishment & the Official Cover-up*. By Dr David Clarke and Andy Roberts. Piatkus. London. 2002. p.7.
11. jeff.lindell@comcast.net [Jeffery A. Lindell, B.A. Indiana University Folklore Institute. Electronic Warfare Systems Analyst USAF (Retired)]
12. Chamberlin, Jo. "The Foo Fighter Mystery." *American Legion Magazine*. December 1945. By Jo Chamberlin. pp. 9, 43, 44, 47. https://archive.legion.org/handle/20.500.12203/3811
13. jeff.lindell@comcast.net
14. This writer, other researchers, the general reading public are in debt to the Computer UFO Network (CUFON) for these records. (https://www.cufon.org) The records were located after painstaking research by Barry Greenwood, co-author of the breakthrough book on the subjects of UFOs and government attempts to keep information about them secret – *Clear Intent*.

415th Night Fighter Squadron, for the night of 13–14 February 1945, at about 7:10 p.m., while flying between Rastatt and Bischwiller an aircraft encountered two sets of lights at 3,000ft. The pilot turned his plane toward them, and one winked out as the other shot up 2,000 to 3,000ft before it, too, went out.[15]

There are many accounts written some decades later that attribute this phenomenon to "Saint Elmo's fire," which is an electromagnetic glow seen atop church steeples, at the tips of the masts and yardarms of ships, utility poles, and even treetops. Other attempts to explain away this anomaly include pilots experiencing hallucinations due to exhaustion, combat fatigue – more recently called Post-Traumatic Stress Disorder (PTSD), pilot inexperience or other observational errors, etc. Other theories at the time attributed the mystery phenomena to Axis secret weapons; and, of course, some people in recent decades connect them to UFOs – meaning extraterrestrial spacecraft, inter-dimensional vehicles or effects, or time machines. We shall address those theories later.

I thought it preferable to get as close as possible to the source of these stories. Other than a brief column in *Time* magazine published in January 1945, the best report is located in the *American Legion Magazine*, from December of that year. The article can be found at the magazine's archives website.[16] The observations therein come directly from quoting the Second World War flyers who witnessed the incidents themselves.

Correspondent Jo Chamberlin reported that American B-29 bombers – the type responsible for delivering high-explosive and incendiary bombs to targets in Japan, as well as later dropping the atomic bombs that would end the war in the Pacific – encountered these mystery objects or effects that tagged along with the planes, changing colors from a "phosphorescent orange glow" to red, then white, and back to orange again. Chamberlin added that the balls of light "never closed in to attack or crash into Allied aircraft, suicide-style."

Chamberlin also described how the pilot of one particular B-29 bomber attempted to "shake" the light off the plane's tail by cruising into a cloud, performing evasive maneuvers there, then flying back into clear air, only to have the apparent fireball emerge from the cloud behind the aircraft and in the same relative position, indicating that it had a way of tracking the B-29 through the overcast. The crew estimated that it was 500 yards away, and about 3ft in diameter. After a few minutes it disappeared as mysteriously as it had arrived, just as dawn broke and the plane was above Mount Fujiyama.

15. https://www.cufon.org
16. "The Foo Fighter Mystery." *American Legion Magazine*. December 1945. By Jo Chamberlin. pp. 9, 43, 44, 47. https://archive.legion.org/handle/20.500.12203/3811

On another occasion in the Pacific, a B-24 Liberator was flying at 11,000ft above the Japanese South Pacific stronghold of Truk when two red lights quickly rose from a lower altitude, then followed the plane for an hour before one light turned back. The other kept on – sometimes following, then alongside, at other times ahead about 1,000 yards – until daybreak, when it climbed to 15,000ft and hovered in the disc of the sun, "hiding" there, as would an attacking fighter plane. During the encounter, the crew observed the sphere change colors – from red to orange, then white, and back to red again. They reported that it appeared to be about the size of a basketball, with no fuselage or wings visible. When the crew radioed to friendly bases to ask if any other aircraft were in the area, they replied that all radar screens were clear.

What follows below is extracted from an official report. This document is available through the CUFON website.

The official report was later forwarded on 22 January 1953 to then U.S. Air Force Director of Intelligence, Lieutenant General John A. Samford – six months after the mass UFO sightings above Washington, D.C. in July 1952. It originated with the USAF Air University Research Studies Institute's Chief of the Historical Division, Albert F. Simpson. The summary cited the mission report from 2 May 1945 by the B-24 bomber crew as they flew near Truk atoll cited above, in part as follows:

> ... observed 2 airborne objects at their 11,000-foot altitude changing from cherry red to an orange, and to a white light which would die out and then become cherry red again. These objects were out on either wing and not within range of .50 [caliber] machine guns ... followed the B-24 through all types of evasive action ... one of the pursuers dropped off ... after accompanying ... for an hour. The other continued to follow ... speeding up when the B-24 went thru [*sic*] the clouds to emerge on the other side ... In daylight ... seen to be bright silver in color, one of which burst.

There were other incidents cited in this same Army Air Forces account.[17]

As we can see in this formerly secret communication subsequently sent to the United States Air Force Director of Intelligence, not only was the testimony of the crew of the B-24 as published in the *American Legion*

17. https://www.cufon.org

Magazine in 1945 corroborated, the official document provided additional information and further confirmation as it had been transmitted internally and secretly within the Air Force in 1953.

From April until late May 1945, American bomber crews in the 20th Air Force experienced hundreds of sightings of "Foo-Fighters" in the night skies over Japan.[18] Army Air Forces intelligence services remained puzzled by the flood of "Foo-Fighter" sightings.

Meanwhile, in the European Theater of Operations, in November 1944, Lieutenant Ed Schlueter guided his Bristol Beaufighter Mark VIF into the air near Dijon, France. The plane was the night fighter variant of the versatile, British-manufactured aircraft. Also aboard was his observer/radar operator, Lieutenant Donald J. Meiers. Tagging along for further observation and information-gathering was Lieutenant Fred Ringwald, intelligence officer of their 415th Night Fighter Squadron.

Scanning the skies as best they could while Schlueter flew the plane above the Rhine Valley, he and the others awaited a possible radio call from controllers directing them toward a radar indication of enemy aircraft within their patrol zone. Instead, Lieutenant Ringwald said, "I wonder what those lights are, over there in the hills."

Schlueter answered, "Probably stars," knowing from long-time experience that the size and character of lights are hard to estimate at night, especially from the air, with no nearby points of reference.

"No, I don't think so," Ringwald told him.

"Are you sure it's not a reflection from us?" Schlueter asked, meaning reflected lights from the illuminated instrument panel bouncing off the inside of the windows of their darkened aircraft cabin.

"I'm positive," Ringwald said as the lights, now eight or ten glowing orange balls of fire, traveled in a row at high speed.

Then pilot Schlueter saw them, too, off his left wing. Concerned the lights could be the glowing engine exhausts of enemy fighter planes, he turned toward them, ready to engage, and radioed ground radar stations to see if they had any returns on their screens. The replies came back negative. Neither did Lieutenant Meiers see any blips illuminating his on-board radar scope.

The lights disappeared, and reappeared, but far off and, about five minutes later went into a flat glide, then vanished.

When they returned to base, the men did what "any other prudent soldiers would do – keep quiet for the moment." This because they knew, "If you

18. "The Foo Fighter Mystery." *American Legion Magazine*. December 1945. By Jo Chamberlin. pp. 9, 43, 44, 47. https://archive.legion.org/handle/20.500.12203/3811

tried to explain everything strange that happened in a war, you'd do nothing else." Also, Lieutenants Schlueter and Meiers had almost completed their required number of missions and "didn't want to chance being grounded by some skeptical flight surgeon for 'combat fatigue.'"

However, they had not been "seeing things," because a few nights later pilot Lieutenant Henry Giblin and radar operator-observer Lieutenant Walter Geary crewed another night fighter and, as they patrolled at 1,000ft they observed a huge red light another 1,000ft above them, moving at an estimated 200mph. They, too, did not hurry to report the incident.

Early on the morning 23 December 1944, another 415th pilot and radar operator-observer were on patrol, flying at 10,000ft when they saw two lights climbing toward their plane from the ground. At altitude, the lights leveled, and tailed the night fighter. They were said to be "large orange glows" that stayed with the plane two minutes before "they peeled off and turned away, (seemingly) flying under perfect control, and then went out."

The following night the same airmen, again patrolling at 10,000ft, spotted a single red flame.

Another crew – pilot Lieutenant David L. McFalls and observer-radar man Lieutenant Ned Baker – also saw "A glowing red object shooting straight up." But, unlike all of the other unidentified flying objects, it suddenly changed in appearance to that of "an aircraft performing a wing-over, and going into a dive, then disappearing." This was the first and only report suggesting what had previously been observed to be just glowing balls of light now included "a controlled flying device."

Correspondent Chamberlin further informed his *American Legion Magazine* readers that by then all 415th Night Fighter Squadron crewmen who had seen something reported it, adding that when the information was received at higher levels of command it was acknowledged with smiles, and the question, "Have you been getting enough sleep?"

Despite the skepticism, the reports continued, with bomber crews observing what looked like silver-colored spheres – resembling huge Christmas-tree ornaments. Could they be weather balloons? No. Experienced air crews knew they traveled generally straight up, then burst at height in the decreased air pressure. Were our flyers seeing experimental enemy aircraft? That was highly unlikely as neither wings nor a fuselage had been seen, with the one possible exception in the McFalls-Baker sighting. Could the glows have been exhaust plumes from the German Me-262 jet fighters? No – because the German jets had no observable exhaust flames. Could our air crews be seeing the after-effects of nearby explosions of anti-aircraft shells? No – because the "Foo-Fighters" were often seen when there had been no anti-aircraft fire. Could they be seeing Saint Elmo's fire? No – because the glows of Saint Elmo's fire stay near to the protrusion where they flare, are not hundreds of yards away, and do not travel at high speeds. Besides, Saint Elmo's fire was only known to occur in stormy conditions, not in clear skies.

Elsewhere, a P-47 pilot saw a metallic "gold-colored ball" that seemed to be cruising slowly along, but, because the sun was low, it was impossible to tell if its surface reflected the golden hue of the setting sun or if the light came from within; and yet another P-47 pilot reported seeing "a phosphorescent golden sphere, 3 to 5ft in diameter, flying at 2,000ft."

The official reaction at group headquarters was that the accounts of the "Foo-Fighters" had been "noted," which – as correspondent Chamberlin informed his readers – in the Army meant the reports were neither approved nor rejected; and not that anything would be done about the situation. Being "noted" covered everything, including, presumably, the hindquarters at headquarters. (This lattermost remark is the author's, and not to be blamed on the war correspondent.)

Eventually, the men of the 415th began referring to the balls of light as "Foo-Fighters." The attribution's conjectured genesis varies as to who came up with the term first, and even its origin, but these phenomena quickly became widely known as such. There was a popular comic strip at the time named "Smokey Stover," and its firefighter characters were shown in a dilapidated, cartoonish fire truck with "Foo-Fighters" emblazoned on the side. This evident play on words was making reference to the French word "feu," which means "fire." Other explanations merely leave in the "feu," without including the cartoon characters. The comic book explanation works well for me because so many Allied aircraft had cartoon art painted onto the sides and noses of their planes – in addition to cartoon-like illustrations of scantily clad young women. I speculate this was because the color illustrations in the Sunday newspapers at the time were the only colorful and entertaining media in that era – along with a few magazines. – because monochromatic and then color television, personal computers and the internet were years or decades in the future.

These were not the only incidents, by far. What follows is a summary. These encapsulated excerpts are a few more from official reports reproduced at The National Archives: On the night of 23–24 April 1945, near the Rhine River, an aircraft of the 415th Night Fighter Squadron spotted four lights traveling in a square pattern, which went out as the plane approached. On the night of 17–18 December 1944, again the crew of a plane from the 415th saw "5 or 6" lights – red and green – flying in a T-formation, which followed their aircraft about 20 miles north of Breisach. In January 1945, once more a plane from the 415th reported that "Foo-Fighters were at it again last night." The Operational Report stated that about halfway between Wissembourg and Landau, amber lights (evidently a pair) were spotted at 2,000ft altitude, one proceeding above the other by about 20 to 50ft. They were seen for around thirty seconds; were approximately 1ft in diameter, and 1,000ft behind, following the Beaufighter, but disappeared when the aircraft was turned toward them.

In a Special Flak Report from the 42nd Bomb Wing for September–October 1944: On 18 October "a shower of silver objects about the size of silver dollars" was observed near Alfonsine (15km northeast of Ravenna, Italy). They were seen to be floating "at 10,500ft and descending very slowly."

As noted, these strange apparitions would sometimes play tag with Allied aircraft, and there is one photo that purports to show the phenomenon in relation to Japanese planes.[19] It is also written, however, that German pilots observed the phenomenon of UFOs – but not necessarily glowing balls of light, or "Foo-Fighters" – on 3 February 1942 and 14 March 1942.[20] Likewise, Japanese flyers are alleged to have encountered UFOs at least once, on 24 April 1945.[21] Of course, Allied flyers thought the mysterious lights were German or Japanese secret weapons whose purpose was either reconnaissance or to act as a distraction to enemy (meaning "Allied") air crews.

The same incident previously cited concerning aircraft from the 415th Night Fighter Squadron encountering balls of light on 13–14 February 1945 was found again in this batch of records but was omitted herein as being overly repetitive. While we are on the subject of repetition: Night Fighter squadrons had numerous encounters with glowing balls of light, as opposed to other air units, because most Allied (especially American) aircraft operated during the day in the Second World War, partly due to the strategy of "round-the-clock bombing," wherein British bombers would hit Germany at night, and American bomb groups would attack in daylight, which contributed to the heavy losses experienced by the United States' airmen – one quarter of the total American combat deaths for the entire war.

---

19. https://sped2work.tripod.com/foo_fighters.html
20. *Military UFO Encounters*. Conrad Bauer. Maplewood Publishing. No city listed. 2019. pp.62-64.
21. Ibid. pp.67-68.

No matter what their origin or ultimate fate, as they seemed to have almost completely disappeared for a time after the war, the "Foo-Fighters" presented another enigma for investigators in militaries and governments – and UFO organizations – to ponder. The most important fact about "Foo-Fighters" is that there was no known instance at the time of them attacking or colliding with Allied aircraft, in any theater of the war.

The mystery of the "Foo-Fighters" continues to this day, but I am prepared to offer a theory. However, first we must lay the ground (or aerial or celestial) work to get there from here.

Chapter 4

Post-Second World War and Early Cold War

The Ghost Rockets of 1946

While the wave of sightings of "ghost rockets" over Scandinavia and elsewhere, mostly in 1946, has a tenuous and tangential – but possibly significant – military involvement, it is part of a progression of events that potentially hold major implications for further military developments in all things UFO from shortly thereafter until now.

On 26 February 1946, several people in Finland spotted what they described as a rocket-like craft zooming past overhead.[1] A mere fifteen days previous, Russian Soviet Communist Party boss and dictator of the Soviet Union, Josef Stalin had stopped just short of declaring that a state of war existed between his communist system and capitalism. In his inflammatory speech, Stalin further stated that the Soviet Union would embark on a five-year plan to prepare for war. So, the sighting of what could have been a V-1 or V-2 war rocket the Soviets had captured from the Germans was cause for alarm among Western leaders – civilian and military. The Western Allies knew they had not launched the rocket, so that left only one alternative – the Soviet Union.

The press in Sweden and other countries referred to the UFOs as "ghost rockets," and the Swedish government quickly ordered that all information about the ghost rockets' flight paths, and times and places of additional sightings be excluded from news stories about them. This was because it was generally believed among the political and military leadership of Sweden, Britain and the United States that the ghost rocket incursions were the results of secret tests by the Russians, and allowing the publication of information about the rockets' times of sighting and trajectories would merely aid Soviet scientists and engineers.

1. http://fly.historicwings.com/2013/02/ghost-rockets/

A more detailed analysis of the phenomenon was published in the U.S. War Department General Staff Circular, "Intelligence Review," from January 1947.[2] In that report, the ghost rockets were most often described as either balls of fire, but with a tail, or as "shiny, cigar-shaped objects." The UFOs were seen traveling in all directions, with a slight preference for a south-to-north course. The "missiles," as the report called them, moved mostly at high speeds, but could cruise as slowly as about 65mph. They were said to fly at all altitudes, and many were perceived to either explode in the air or crash into the ground or a lake. The wave of sightings increased and expanded to include Norway, and extended to as far away as Greece and Portugal.

While the Second World War still raged, a V-2 missile launched from the German rocket base at Peenemünde had crashed in Sweden. At that time, Swedish authorities had collected the crashed rocket's debris and sent it to England for analysis. Thus began increased cooperation between the Western Allied powers and "neutral" (but frequently German-leaning) Sweden. Small steps closer to one another were being taken between Sweden and Allied Britain and America in 1943, including the placing of a British radar installation and listening post on Öland Island to track German aircraft and intercept Axis communications.[3] Further political and diplomatic developments would affect the ghost rocket phenomenon.

After the war ended, Swedish society and political leaders became increasingly uneasy regarding the Soviet intimidation and partial subjugation of neighboring Finland – the buffer between Russia and Sweden; so, while officially maintaining its "neutrality" Sweden sought closer relations with Great Britain and the United States.

It was time for Sweden to try to make amends for its slanted "neutrality" toward the now defeated and extinct Nazi Germany. Negotiations were being held with the United States government and Great Britain regarding Sweden's partly pro-Axis involvement during the war.

Sweden's entanglements had included supplying Nazi Germany with high-grade Swedish iron ore; and providing the Nazi regime (through a Swedish-owned factory in Schweinfurt, in Germany) with ball bearings, which were essential to the production of the Luftwaffe's aircraft, among other war materiél. The Swedes had allowed armed German troops in uniform to cross Swedish territory; permitted German soldiers on leave to

2. https://passingstrangeness.wordpress.com/2011/01/14/the-ghost-rockets/
3. Leifland, Leif (1995). *...Secret Matters Not So Far Disclosed.* Vårstormar 1944. Stockholm: PROBUS Förlag. ISBN 91-87184-37-0. Also: https://www.konditori100.se/SiWW2/sww2sbc.htm

visit and then cross Sweden to new assignments; had also looked the other way as the Germans shipped weapons across their country; had transported oil and other essentials in "neutral" Swedish ships to Germany; had provided Swedish Navy escort ships for German transports in the Baltic Sea. Moreover, Swedish individuals and financial institutions had participated in buying and marketing diamonds and gold from Nazi Germany, which had later been identified as having been looted from – among others – Belgium and the Netherlands. Swedish banks had been involved in the money-laundering of Nazi funds as well.[4]

Sweden had a lot to atone for, despite having provided shelter for thousands of Jewish refugees, and clandestinely training and supplying young men from Norway and Denmark for the post-war re-establishment of democratic regimes in their then Nazi-occupied homelands. There were negotiations, conducted mostly during the first half of 1946 with the United States and Great Britain, which eventually resolved all of these issues, while Sweden also paid reparations. On the other side, the United States government unfroze Swedish assets and removed individuals and companies from blacklists for being too pro-Nazi Germany. The accord was attained even as the ghost rocket wave reached a crescendo, on 18 July 1946. This, "coincidentally," – if one believes in coincidences, which I do not – occurred just as Washington and London were eager for more cooperation with Sweden in resisting the then increasing power of the Soviet Union.

It seems the sudden ghost-rocket near-hysteria, with up to 2,000 sightings overall, came at a time that was, perhaps "coincidentally," convenient for both Swedish authorities and Allied leaders. Investigative teams from America, including Second World War hero General James Doolittle – who had launched the first air raid on Tokyo, in April 1942, where elsewhere all across the Pacific, American military might had been laid low by sudden Japanese attacks – arrived in Sweden. Observers and intelligence officers from the American, British and Swedish militaries all remained convinced that the ghost rockets originated from secret Soviet tests. Sweden henceforth continued to be very cooperative and eager to forge closer ties with Great Britain and the United States.

In my view the ghost-rocket wave proved to be very opportune for all parties involved, which leads me to walk out onto a limb and speculate that perhaps – just maybe – much of the ghost rocket wave was partly the product of a media-inspired mass inclination to keep eyes on the skies, and,

4. https://1997-2001.state.gov/regions/eur/rpt_9806_ng_sweden.pdf

as soon as anything unusual – such as, for example, a meteor – was seen, to promptly report the "sighting" to news outlets and authorities. Also maybe – just possibly – some of the sightings could have been "helped along" in a few subtle or not-so-subtle ways, by, for example, having jet planes[5] zip by at high speeds, defying proper explanation in an overwhelmingly pre-jet era. Some of these planes, whatever their true origin, could have fired unarmed air-to-ground rockets into remote lakes, or not. I know – some skeptics on both sides of the UFO/UAP issue are now screaming (silently or not) "Conspiracy theory!" But, please allow me to remind one and all that there is a precedent, albeit one that antedated and did not predate the ghost rocket wave: In August 1964, United States Navy destroyers patrolling in the Gulf of Tonkin were allegedly attacked by North Vietnamese patrol boats – twice. As a result, the United States Congress authorized President Lyndon B. Johnson to take all necessary action to protect American and Allied military forces in the region. Thus was the Vietnam War approved, obliquely and indirectly, and under false pretenses, because, according to the U.S. Naval Institute:

> The Truth About Tonkin: Questions about the Gulf of Tonkin incidents have persisted for more than 40 years. But once-classified documents and tapes released in the past several years, combined with previously uncovered facts, make clear that high government officials distorted facts and deceived the American public about events that led to full U.S. involvement in the Vietnam War.[6]

As a result of the ghost rocket wave, Western intelligence agencies held the Soviets to be responsible, with a minority view that the UFOs could be alien spacecraft.[7] Moreover, the near-hysteria provoked renewed interest in Congress for increasing the budget of the Department of Defense to combat this new Soviet threat. It was all very well-timed, indeed.

---

5. These could have included captured German ME-262, or British Gloster Meteor, or even American XP-59 and/or YP-59 Airacobra jet planes – more than a dozen of the latter having been produced, even though they were not officially in operational service with military units.
6. The U.S. Naval Institute. https://www.usni.org/magazines/naval-history-magazine/2008/february/truth-about-tonkin
7. http://fly.historicwings.com/2013/02/ghost-rockets/

I must add that I am fully supportive of (nearly) any and (almost) all efforts to improve national (and planetary) defense, because doing so increases both national and international (and interplanetary) security, and the prospects for peace. This is so because, since ancient times, average citizens and national rulers have been advised: "To prevent war, prepare for it." Sage advice, because weakness invites aggression, which was a major cause for many of the nations of the Earth falling into the Second World War and other armed conflicts to begin with.

However, the message of peace through strength can be forgotten, misplaced, or lost. In totalitarian societies, if the political bosses decide to increase spending for war, they increase spending for war. But in more democratic societies the taxpaying and voting public must be convinced that war-spending is advantageous, which is not always possible. At that point, all too often political leaders and their friends in the military and defense industries may decide to resort to deceit, as was done in the Gulf of Tonkin in the 1964 example cited above. In open societies such extreme dishonesty is a bad habit to fall into when an individual, a group or a faction feels driven to trickery and manipulation to convince the voting and taxpaying public that increased military spending is the proper course. Such attitudes and actions are habit-forming and ultimately detrimental to the freedom and well-being of all and, if continued, eventually endanger the democratic republic itself.

Based on the evidence, and lack of the same (due to government secrecy), I conclude at this point in our investigation that the post-Second World War ghost rockets were more about a fear-driven frenzy of anxious sky watching, and opportunistic military professionals and political and economic influencers manipulating public perceptions. This is true no matter if what people were seeing, or thought they saw, were actual, material objects of mysterious and possibly extraterrestrial origin; the products of adrenalin-powered over-enthusiasm; and/or actual, conventional aircraft deployed in a cynical campaign to fool taxpayers and voters.

In some ways the ghost rockets exhibited similar behaviors and displayed perceived shapes that align with later sightings of UFOs – in the interpretation of being alien spacecraft. According to the official analysis of the ghost rockets, their individual descriptions consisted primarily of looking like "'a ball of fire with a tail' and a 'shiny cigar-shaped object.'"[8] Later UFO sightings would also include these shapes, with added odd effects

8. https://passingstrangeness.wordpress.com/2011/01/14/the-ghost-rockets/

to their form, possibly caused by the manipulation of electromagnetic and/or gravity/anti-gravity fields, and/or the ability to partially or fully "cloak," or visually distort and conceal themselves from view.

I believe these distortions in the visible spectrum also confused earlier observers of "Foo-Fighters," and their behavior would continue to do so in future years as numerous eyewitnesses could see strange optical oscillations of UFOs, saw them shift in shape, would perceive them undergo color changes – many of which tended toward the orange and red end of the spectrum, while other colors such as yellow, blue, purple and green also alternated within and around them. Further, based on size, behavior – such as evident signs of intelligent control, I postulate that smaller UFOs, of whatever nature and description, may be extraterrestrial versions of our recently developed "remotely piloted vehicles – RPVs, or "drones" – some of which may be fully or partially autonomous probes – only coming under remote control if a situation arises that is beyond the pre-programmed operational parameters of a particular "mission" or assignment.

Altogether, the preceding step of the ghost-rocket wave in the sequence of events concerning a history of military encounters with UFOs/UAP was another link in a chain of occurrences that could, if we accept the existence of UFOs as alien spacecraft, have further consequences.

I do not necessarily believe that the ghost rockets were all illusions; or perhaps, hoaxes (government-perpetrated in this case); exclusively sightings of meteors; or were in their entirety probable alien spacecraft. Rather, I do believe the ghost rocket reports were likely a result of a combination of some or all of these phenomena that were exploited by governments and interest groups who stood to gain from it all.

1947: The Pivotal Year

The year 1947 kicked off with a Royal Air Force interceptor pursuing an unidentified radar target over the North Sea, 50 miles from the Netherlands and heading toward Norfolk, Great Britain.[9] It was reported to be at 22,000ft and traveling at a speed equal to or greater than that of the pursuit plane. (Estimated to be about 400 to 425mph.)[10] This was on 16 January at 10:30

9. Comprehensive Catalog of 1,500 Project BLUE BOOK UFO [*sic*] https://studylib.net/doc/8048891/comprehensive-catalog-of-1500-project-blue-book-ufo
10. *Out of the Shadows: UFOs, the Establishment & the Official Cover-up* Dr David Clarke and Andy Roberts. Piatkus. London. 2002. p.41.

p.m., which means the British Mosquito aircraft was probably a post-Second World War Mark 36 Night Fighter model with a crew of two.[11] The object appeared on the radar screen but the Mosquito was unable to catch up to the UFO.[12] It became known within the Royal Air Force as a "ghost plane."

The pilot who attempted the intercept reported that ground control told him the radar plot would stop and hover at great heights, then dart in different directions at high speed, only to stop and hover yet again. It was estimated that the object at times traveled at 1,000mph.[13] (This is more than 300mph faster than any airplane in the world could fly at that time. The Bell X-1 flew at 700mph in October of that year.)[14] The Mosquito pilot added that "This was not an aircraft; it was something very odd."[15] The Air Ministry asked the pilot to write "a confidential report," which as of 2002 still remained a secret document hidden from the public.[16] I have no information about its possible subsequent release.

There were other unsettling "ghost airplane" incidents, prompting the RAF to investigate further, causing the commanding officer of 12 Group to theorize that the radar return was the product of a partially deflated meteorological balloon. Years later, the United States Air Force's UFO consultant, Dr J. Allen Hynek, would look over the "ghost airplane" reports and conclude that the radar echoes were caused by "Weather effects on radar."[17] In the meantime, the Air Ministry also determined, as of the end of January 1947, that the "unidentified tracks" on radar screens were caused by meteorological balloons.[18] My comment: weather balloons do not travel at 1,000mph, or even 400 to 425mph. As we shall learn later, radar operators with even a minimum of experience can discriminate between aircraft and "weather effects" on their displays. Moreover, the pilot verified

11. https://aviation-safety.net/wikibase/145342
12. https://studylib.net/doc/8048891/comprehensive-catalog-of-1500-project-blue-book-ufo
13. *Out of the Shadows: UFOs, the Establishment & the Official Cover-up* Dr David Clarke and Andy Roberts. Piatkus. London. 2002. p.42.
14. https://www.smithsonianmag.com/smart-news/remembering-chuck-yeager-exploring-plane-broke-sound-barrier-180976479/#:~:text=Over%20the%20course%20of%20several,an%20altitude%20of%2043%2C000%20feet.
15. *Out of the Shadows: UFOs, the Establishment & the Official Cover-up* Dr David Clarke and Andy Roberts. Piatkus. London. 2002. p.46.
16. Ibid. p.44.
17. Ibid. p.46. Citing Mike Hall in a personal communication with information derived from Captain Edward J. Ruppelt's personal papers. (Note 19.)
18. Ibid. p.46.

the physical existence of an unidentified flying *object* in the 16 January 1947 observation.

A next big link in the chain of events that featured heavily during and after 1947 is encapsulated in a report at the History.com website, which states, in part:

> On June 24, 1947, the civilian pilot [looking for a crashed military plane] Kenneth Arnold reported seeing nine objects, glowing bright blue-white, flying in a 'V' formation over Washington's Mount Rainier. He estimated the objects' flight speed at 1,700 mph and compared their motion to 'a saucer if you skip it across water.'[19]

In newspaper reports of Arnold's sighting, this description was mistakenly understood to mean that these objects were shaped like saucers, leading to the popularization of the term "flying saucers" as a synonym for UFOs.

The Kenneth Arnold experience was a sighting heard about round the world, although it was hardly the original, or even the first, in 1947, or before. On 1 August 1946, Captain Jack E. Puckett, Second World War combat veteran, and later Assistant Chief of Flying Safety, Tactical Air Command, Langley Field, Virginia, piloted a C-47 transport plane from Langley to Southeast Air Base, Tampa – later known as MacDill Air Force Base, Florida. His co-pilot was Lieutenant Henry F. Glass; there was also a flight engineer who remains anonymous. When they were 30 miles from SAB Tampa, the crew observed a large UFO speeding toward their plane on an evident collision course. Captain Puckett reported that the UFO veered to "cross our path" when about 1,000 yards away. He said, "We observed it to be a long, cylindrical shape approximately the size of a B-29 bomber." The craft evidently streamed an exhaust trail. Startling "to Air Force analysts" [*sic* – the U.S. Air Force did not exist yet; it was still the U.S. Army Air Forces] was the observation that the UFO had a row of windows – a first, according to the same source.[20] (That is, if we exempt Sub-Lieutenant Morgan's little-known First World War description.)

Another sighting by a military person took place just two days after that of Kenneth Arnold's. A flyer is listed as reporting: "26 Jun, 1947, by military pilot, 30 miles NW of Lake Mead (Nevada): 5–6 circular objects in

19. https://www.history.com/topics/paranormal/kenneth-arnold
20. *Aliens From Space.* Donald E. Keyhoe. Doubleday. Garden City, NY. 1973. pp.45-46.

formation, heading south, at 120 degrees." United States Air Force Project Blue Book[21] conclusion: "Balloon cluster." [22] [23]

At the end of this particular report, we see that the Air Force's own Project Blue Book (PBB) and/or a preceding and as yet unknown UFO reporting office thought a military pilot was too stupid and/or incompetent to be able to identify a balloon cluster; so already, at the start (before it, really), PBB exposed itself as being not a reporting center to honestly analyze UFO sightings, but to instead attempt to explain away such incidents, no matter how reliable the witnesses. Unfortunately, this was evidently largely if not almost entirely the primary purpose of PBB "investigations" – to look into UFO reports just long enough to find an excuse to dispense a word or phrase to spark even the slightest flicker of doubt, and to then promptly dismiss that incident, and as many other sightings as possible, then to immediately halt any further review of a particular incident and/or several of them – and to move on to attempts to debunk as many subsequent UFO observations as possible.

For this reason, among others, this investigation of a history of military encounters with UFOs will not repeat every ridiculous claim by government agencies; superficial media outlets; uninformed and ignorant scribblers who gloss over the facts and substitute irrelevant items such as witnesses being in an agitated state, etc.; and lifelong, professional skeptics whose psychological makeup prevents them from taking an honest look at UFO/UAP incidents. Instead, I will survey the facts, such as can be determined – including eyewitness testimony, physical evidence, and documentation – in a sincere effort to resort to cold logic to deduce what most likely occurred, unlike those who rely on government handouts, editorial prejudices, and perceived possible future personal and professional advancement to drive their versions – whether pro or con regarding UFOs/UAP – many of which are sensationalized absurdities about events reported to have occurred in our real world.

With regard to the lattermost point: I am once again reminded of astronomer Carl Sagan's attempt to deflate UFO reports by stating,

21. "From 31 December 1951, until 17 December 1969, the USAF conducted Project Blue Book to investigate UFO sightings. Centered at Wright-Patterson Air Force Base, Dayton, Ohio, PBB investigate 12,618 sightings, with 701 remaining without explanation." https://www.af.mil/About-Us/Fact-Sheets/Display/Article/104590/unidentified-flying-objects-and-air-force-project-blue-book/
22. https://archive.org/details/project-blue-book?&sort=-date&page=2
23. The problem here is that PBB was not yet in existence, and neither were the project's predecessors – Project Sign and Project Grudge. Evidently this report was resurrected and inserted into PBB to allow the Air Force to try to "explain," or, more properly, try to explain away the sighting with an "explanation" that is utterly absurd.

"Extraordinary claims require extraordinary evidence." Okay, then the same rule applies to one and all. If a pilot forthrightly, and without seeking money, attention, fame or glory, relays an account of five or six unidentified circular objects in the sky, then PBB and any prior or subsequent reporting agency must back up its counterclaim that an experienced, professional, military-trained aircraft operator instead could not identify a cluster of balloons – which is to me, *the* extraordinary claim. PBB, as well as previous and later analyzing agencies, must produce even a minimum – and not a necessarily extraordinary – item of evidence in the form of other witnesses who said he, she, or they, actually saw a cluster of balloons in this event; some radar returns depicting the balloon cluster; or the wreckage of the balloons themselves – along with details such as identifying serial numbers on weather-measuring instruments, and when and where they were launched – and found, if located at all. We cannot just meekly accept what PBB or anyone else says over the word of experienced military air crews and other personnel, commercial and even private pilots, people in law enforcement, and average citizens.

Moreover, with regard to the preceding point, as we have already seen in more than one instance, government clerks and spokespeople who hasten to try to just explain away reports by witnesses must not be automatically awarded more credibility than the plain-speaking eyewitnesses; and all the more so in that almost all of these often government-paid or professional debunkers have no military, law enforcement or air crew experience themselves. Their extraordinary claims must, once more, be buttressed by extraordinary hard evidence, not by mere empty and cynically written or spoken words of negativity.

Having addressed the relevant issues regarding the dependability of eyewitnesses over the writings and sayings of the perpetual naysayers, we can now focus on what may be the crucial event of this study: the possible crash of a UFO, or UFOs, in the interpretation of being one or more spacecraft of extraterrestrial origin, in New Mexico in the first days of July 1947.

The story of the New Mexico incident is complex, and is made unnecessarily more so by not just government secrecy but also evident efforts by the United States government and United States Army Air Forces – and in its later incarnation as the United States Air Force – to cover-up what actually happened there.

I will begin this part of the story with an outline of events as uncovered by two writers who spent a great deal of time, effort and expense investigating what is popularly known as the "Roswell UFO Crash."

Chapter 5

Roswell

UFO Incidents and Possible Crashes in New Mexico, 1947

In their 1994 book, *The Truth About the UFO Crash At Roswell,*[1] Lieutenant Colonel (Retired) Kevin D. Randle and Donald R. Schmitt list the sequence of events as follows below, with some minor variations; but, before commencing with their revelation of the story it is necessary to point out that Randle and Schmitt made numerous trips to the Roswell area, discovered and interviewed dozens of witnesses, made a huge volume of telephone calls, consulted innumerable documents, and undertook to personally investigate the Roswell incident at no small cost of time, energy and finances. Their exhaustive investigation is an invaluable guide to unraveling the mysteries surrounding the events of 1947 in New Mexico. There is no substitute for obtaining and reading that book, and its predecessor, *UFO Crash at Roswell,* which also contains the foundational material for understanding the entire Roswell incident. What follows does not even come close to revealing the entire story and is more of an overview of the Roswell UFO crash. Readers who wish to understand the full story, to the extent that it is known to us, are strongly urged to obtain and read both of these books by Randle and Schmitt.

Another key fact to point out is that the Roswell Army Air Field was then home to the 509th Composite Group – the only air unit in the world in 1947 trained, equipped and experienced in the delivery of atomic bombs. Here is the timeline constructed by Randle and Schmitt, with only minor clarifications and a few comments added by me:

Tuesday, 1 July 1947: Radars at three points in "the Roswell area"; overlooking the Los Alamos and Sandia Base nuclear research and production reservations, near the Alamogordo atomic bomb test site; and

1. *The Truth About The UFO Crash At Roswell* Kevin D. Randle, and Donald R. Schmitt. Avon. New York. 1994.

close to the White Sands missile assembly and testing grounds – detect an object that did not conform to the flight characteristics of a conventional aircraft. (These are approximate locations – the first two are not that close to each other, but relatively so.) Equipment checks uncovered no discernible technical problems with the radar units.[2]

Wednesday, 2 July: at 9:50 p.m., Mr and Mrs Dan Wilmot observe an oval-shaped object moving northwest at high speed as it passes above their house, near Roswell, New Mexico.[3,4]

Thursday, 3 July: a captured German V-2 research rocket launch fails, causing injury to several people at the White Sands Proving Ground. Steve MacKenzie was sent from Roswell Army Air Field to White Sands to monitor the radar scope there for twenty-four hours, where he observed a mysterious object on the display screen.[5] The object and many similar ones had been tracked flying over New Mexico for several days.[6]

Friday, 4 July: Warrant Officer Robert Thomas arrives at Roswell with a team aboard a plane from Washington, D.C. He is anticipating an immediate briefing on the situation.[7] Thomas had been sent there in response to the observations of numerous strange radar returns.[8] (Note that this assignment was *before* the subsequent reports by civilians of a crashed object. Also, it has been speculated in some ufology circles that he was actually a general officer operating undercover with an assumed rank and name.)

On the Foster Ranch, near Corona, ranch hand and foreman William "Mac" Brazel hears an unusually loud bang during a thunderstorm that sounds different from typical thunderclaps.[9]

---

2. *The Truth About The UFO Crash At Roswell* Kevin D. Randle, and Donald R. Schmitt. Avon. New York. 1994. p.196.
3. Ibid. p.196. And, *Need To Know: UFOs, The Military and Intelligence* Timothy Good. Pan Books. London. 2007. p.67.
4. https://thebkmag.com/2011/09/18/roswell-new-mexico-ufo-crash-abc-radio-origina-1947-broadcast/ Allegedly quoting from the "Original ABC Radio Roswell UFO Crash Report Broadcast."
5. *The Truth About The UFO Crash At Roswell* p.196.
6. Ibid. pp.5-6.
7. Ibid. p.196.
8. Ibid. p.6.
9. Ibid. p.196. Also: *Need To Know* p.67. But Good places the thunderstorm on 2 July, and writes that Brazel discovered the debris field, "the next morning," which would have been 3 July.

   And: *Open Skies, Closed Minds: For The First Time A Government UFO Expert Speaks Out* Nick Pope. Simon and Schuster. London. 1996. Pope also puts the thunderstorm on 2 July, and Brazel encountering the wreckage "the next day" – 3 July. p.15.

Those monitoring radars watch a strange object's on-screen image as it seems to pulsate, then explode. This is at 11:27 p.m. on 4 July.[10]

Jim Ragsdale and Trudy Truelove witness a bright flash of light; then an object roars overhead, convincing Ragsdale that something has fallen to Earth near their campsite.[11]

William Woody and his father see a white object with a red tail fall from the sky north of Roswell.[12]

So far, the progression of events is straightforward; however, now things start to become a bit complicated.

Saturday, 5 July: at about 5:30 a.m., military authorities, acting on their speculation that the object seen exploding on radar screens has fallen to Earth, organize a recovery team and dispatch it to the suspected crash site.[13] Again, this is prior to any civilian reports to anyone about a UFO or crashed objects.

Going out to inspect the lands of the Foster Ranch for possible damage to windmills, fences and outbuildings following the previous night's thunderstorm, Mac Brazel is accompanied by William D. Proctor, the young son of his neighbors and friends. Brazel and Proctor discover a large field of debris – shredded metal panels, tiny plastic-looking "I-beams," what appears similar to metal foil, and fine cables – or "strings." The sheep they are herding refuse to cross the thickly cluttered debris field, and Brazel and Proctor are forced to drive them around the materials to get the animals to drinking water.[14]

"J.R." – a substituted identity so the witness may remain anonymous – a friend of Mac Brazel, also encounters crash debris, but does not spend time investigating. He refrains from telling anyone about his discovery until many years after.[15] (The questions here include: was this the same "crash site," or another debris field? If this is a different location, is some of the debris still there?)

W. Curry Holden and others on an archeological expedition come across an impact site at a different location. One member of the group goes to find a phone and calls Chaves County Sheriff George Wilcox to tell him about

10. *The Truth About The UFO Crash At Roswell.* p.196.
11. Ibid. pp.196-197.
12. Ibid. p.196.
13. Ibid. p.197.
14. Ibid. pp.197-198.
Also: *Need To Know.* p.67. Again, Good places Brazel's finding of the crash debris on 3 July.
15. *The Truth About The UFO Crash At Roswell.* p.197.

the site of an apparent (conventional) aircraft accident. Wilcox alerts the local fire department, and firefighter Dan Dwyer is on the truck that heads to the site, about 35 miles north of Roswell. If this report is accurate, and I have no reason to doubt it, then, because the Foster Ranch site is about 75 miles from Roswell, this would have been a second crash site – "second" even though the "first," or initial, site had not yet been reported to Sheriff Wilcox by Mac Brazel.

Radio station KSWS reporter John McBoyle somehow hears of the downed object. He tries to reach the reported (second) crash site. McBoyle then calls to inform his parent station in Albuquerque, (KOAT), and tells Lydia Sleppy there that an object that looks like a "crushed dishpan" has crashed. Sleppy later said that it seemed at that point McBoyle got into an argument with someone on his end of the line, after which he told her over the phone to forget it because he had made a mistake. The call was reportedly made from about 40 miles north of Roswell.[16] (But Randle and Schmitt do not specify the location of the telephone. This was many decades before the general, civilian availability of mobile radio-telephones, and before the advent of cell phones.)

Sleppy attempts to send what little she knows of the story over the station teletype machine, only to be cut off by a message from the FBI office in Dallas, Texas, ordering her to stop the transmission. Timothy Good, in his book *Need To Know*, reproduces what was told to him as being the FBI message text: "ATTENTION ALBUQUERQUE: CEASE TRANSMISSION. REPEAT, CEASE TRANSMISSION. NATIONAL SECURITY ITEM. DO NOT TRANSMIT. STAND BY ..."[17]

Warrant Officer (or General?) Robert Thomas and his team from Washington, D.C. and other carefully screened personnel from Roswell Army Air Field move out and head toward the suspected impact location.[18] (Again, presumably, this would be the second site as, so far as we know, the military was as yet unaware of the first crash location on the Foster Ranch.)

The Army Air Forces (AAF) personnel find that there is a group of civilians already at the crash site. The civilians are escorted away from the area, and a security cordon is deployed. The military people discover five bodies at the site.[19]

---

16. Ibid. p.198.
17. *Need To Know* p.69 – citing *Crashed UFOs: Evidence in Search of Proof* William L. Moore. Moore Publications and Research. Burbank, CA. 1985. p.46.
18. *The Truth About The UFO Crash At Roswell.* p.198.
19. Ibid. p.197.

The bodies are first covered with sheets, then placed in lead-lined body bags. Guards remain posted to keep the curious out, while only personnel with the highest security clearances are allowed into the immediate area.[20]

One of the guards at the crash site, Melvin E. Brown, is ordered to escort duty aboard a truck. He climbs into the back and sees a tarp there. He is ordered to not look under the tarp. (So, naturally, he looks under the tarp as soon as everyone's backs are turned.) He sees bodies – small, with oversized heads, and with yellowish or orangish skins.[21] (There is an inconsistency here because it was earlier reported that the cadavers had been placed in lead-lined body bags.)

Mortician Glenn Dennis, of the Ballard Funeral Home in Roswell, is called by the Roswell Army Air Field mortuary officer (an administrator, not necessarily a medical or forensics expert) and asked about the availability of small caskets.[22]

Paleontologist C. Bertrand Schultz notices military guards along the west side of Highway 285 as he drives past.

The airfield mortuary officer calls Glenn Dennis again, and asks him about the effects that various chemicals would have on blood and bodily tissues, and also about preparing a body that has lain out in the elements. This causes Dennis to suspect that a very important person may have died.[23] (A dead alien would, indeed, have been a very important "person.")

Dennis, who is also employed by the funeral home as a local ambulance driver, is called to downtown Roswell to transport an injured airman accident victim to the army airfield hospital. He does so, and is waved through the front gate, then drives up to the base hospital loading-dock. There, he observes three other ambulances with odd-looking canoe-like objects and strange debris inside the vehicles.[24]

Meanwhile, the bodies have already been transported to the airfield hospital, and Dr Joseph Johnson pronounces them dead. Two other doctors begin an initial autopsy.

Mac Brazel takes William D. Proctor back to his parents, Floyd and Loretta. He brings along some of the debris he found, demonstrating to

20. Ibid. p.198.

21. *Alien Contact: Top-Secret UFO Files Revealed.* Timothy Good. William Morrow. New York. 1991. p.99. (Author's interview of Melvin Brown's daughter, Beverly Bean. Brown was extensively decorated by both the Army and the Air Force, and was a friend of Major Jesse Marcel and General Nathan Twining at the time. pp.100-101.)

22. *The Truth About The UFO Crash At Roswell* p.198.

23. Ibid. pp.198-199.

24. Ibid. p.199.

them on a sliver of it that he can neither cut nor burn the object. They suggest that he take the fragments to the sheriff.

Now inside the airfield hospital, Glenn Dennis is confronted by two officers. One, a red-haired captain, informs Dennis that the mortician has seen nothing, warning him that if he says anything his bones will later be found out in the desert.

Military bases along the West Coast have fighter planes on standby alert, and in Oregon and Washington the aircraft gun cameras are loaded with film. (This was a step not usually taken in peacetime, unless aerial combat was anticipated.)

In Circleville, Ohio, Sherman Campbell tells the local sheriff that he can explain the recent UFO sightings because Campbell found a crashed, metallic-looking weather balloon on his farm.

The balloon is exhibited and photographed at the local newspaper office, and Campbell takes it home with him. Later, his daughter Jean Campbell (Romero) says that Campbell stored the device in his barn for many years after. (As will be shown, this circumstance is in extreme contrast with how the Roswell debris was later dealt with.)

That evening, Mac Brazel removes a large panel of wreckage from the debris field and stows it in a ranch outbuilding about three miles north of the crash site.[25] (The Army Air Forces will later seize it.)

The extraterrestrials' bodies are stored in a large, sealed crate, which is placed in a guarded hangar. Evidently the cordon of Military Police guards is incomplete because an officer arrives that night and urges Melvin Brown to accompany him for a look inside the crate, but the packing and sealing prevent them from looking within it.

Sunday, 6 July: Mac Brazel rises early, as is his custom, takes care of his ranch chores, collects some of the debris, and drives the 75 miles to Roswell. When he shows the wreckage to Sheriff George Wilcox, the sheriff becomes excited about the find, and calls the Roswell Army Air Field.[26] While awaiting the arrival of Army officers, Sheriff Wilcox sends two deputies up to investigate the Foster Ranch crash site.[27]

William Woody and his father attempt to drive to the place where they believe the object they saw falling the night before came down, but they are stopped by the Military Police who won't allow them west of Highway 285.

---

25. Ibid. p.200.
26. *Need To Know* p.67.
27. *The Truth About the UFO Crash At Roswell* p.200.

Reporter and announcer for local radio station KGFL, Frank Joyce calls Sheriff Wilcox's office, asking if there is any news to report. Wilcox connects Joyce with Mac Brazel.

The commanding officer of the 509th Bomb Group, Colonel William Blanchard, orders the air intelligence officer, Major Jesse Marcel, to look into the Foster Ranch matter. Marcel drives to Sheriff Wilcox's office, examines the debris, interviews Mac Brazel, and decides to drive to the Foster Ranch crash site to investigate further. But first, the Major takes some of the debris back to the base, shows it to the Colonel and tells him what he learned from Mac Brazel. Colonel Blanchard now believes that whatever his unit is in possession of is very important, and possibly Soviet in origin, and he informs higher command levels of the situation. So far, no one has said anything about any type of balloon.[28]

Major Marcel, accompanied by the airfield's counter-intelligence officer, Captain Sheridan Cavitt, returns to Sheriff Wilcox's office; they escort Mac Brazel back to the Foster Ranch, and they continue on to the debris field.[29] However, they arrive near nightfall, have a can of beans, and spend the night in an outbuilding in their sleeping bags.[30] They return to the debris field the next day, which would be Monday, 7 July.

Major General Clements McMullen, deputy commander of the Strategic Air Command, orders Colonel Blanchard to send the debris on to higher headquarters. Blanchard retrieves more of the wreckage from Sheriff Wilcox's office, seals it in a courier's pouch, and sends it on a plane to Forth Worth Army Air Field, where Colonel Thomas J. DuBose receives it for further transport to Washington, D.C.[31]

The two deputies return after Marcel, Cavitt and Brazel have already left. They report that they could not locate the debris field but that they did run across a circular area in a pasture that had been blackened and burned, with the sand fused into glass – which is an effect of very high heat – where it appeared that a circular object had touched down.

Colonel DuBose and Colonel Alan D. Clark – base commander at Fort Worth, meet the aircraft dispatched from Roswell Army Air Field (RAAF) with the courier pouch containing a small amount of the crash debris (from

---

28. Ibid. pp.200-201.
29. Ibid. p.201.
30. Ibid. p.201.
Also: *Crash At Corona: The U.S. Military Retrieval and Cover-Up of a UFO.* Stanton T. Friedman and Don Berliner. Paragon House. New York. 1992. p.10.
31. *The Truth About the UFO Crash At Roswell* p.201.

the first site, at the Foster Ranch). Colonel Clark takes custody of the pouch and carries it aboard his command B-26 for a flight to Washington, D.C. to meet there with Major General McMullen.

Monday, 7 July: a special 2 a.m. flight leaves Roswell Army Air Field for Andrews Army Air Field, outside Washington, D.C. Aboard are crash debris and alien bodies (from the second crash site).[32]

Mac Brazel again leads Major Marcel and Captain Cavitt to the debris field.

The two RAAF military men walk around the wreckage, noting that it is scattered over three quarters of a mile lengthwise, and the debris field is about 300ft wide. It is oriented generally north to south, with a gouge in the earth in the same direction. The biggest bit of wreckage is at the southern end of the gash.

Marcel and Cavitt spend the remainder of the day gathering debris, loading it into Marcel's car and Cavitt's jeep carryall. As night falls they drive back toward Roswell.

Lieutenant General Nathan F. Twining, who is in charge of the Air Materials Command, which oversees operations at Wright Field, Ohio, cancels earlier plans and flies to Alamogordo – 90 miles from Roswell.

Mortician Glenn Dennis contacts a nurse he knows at Roswell Army Air Field and arranges to meet with her for lunch at the base. When they see each other, she tells him of the dead aliens and events at the hospital. When UFO skeptics attempted to track down this nurse without result, they declared Dennis a liar. But, on *Coast-to-Coast AM*, with host George Noory, 1–2 June 2022, UFO researcher Donald R. Schmitt revealed that Dennis was in fact having an affair with a nurse – not the woman in question, and that Dennis made up the fictitious nurse to cover the romantic-partner's true identity. Schmitt added that Dennis never recanted the rest of his story, and reaffirmed the particulars on his deathbed. However, UFO researcher Tom Carey and current co-investigator with Donald R. Schmitt insists that while Dennis's reports about being contacted by the RAAF mortuary officer are true, that Dennis fabricated the events concerning his taking the ambulance to RAAF and meeting with the nurse and being threatened by an Army officer there. I tend to agree with Carey in this regard, but I also agree with Schmitt about the validity of the calls from the base mortuary.[33]

32. Ibid. p.202.

33. https://www.coasttocoastam.com/

After his interest is aroused by Frank Joyce's phone conversation with Mac Brazel, Walt Whitmore Sr – owner of radio station KGFL in Roswell, locates Brazel and invites him to be his guest at his home. Brazel agrees and stays there overnight.[34]

Leo B. Spear, who is with the 195th Military Police Company, doesn't believe the stories other MPs are telling him about a flying saucer crash. He will later change his mind when he sees a news item about it in the newspaper.

Tuesday, 8 July: on the way to RAAF from the crash site, Major Marcel stops at his house at 2 a.m. He awakens his family and shows them some of the strange crash debris.[35] His son, Jesse Jr, later testifies that some of the debris has unusual symbols on it, and has an exotic appearance.[36] When he asked his father about the wreckage, Jesse Jr said Jesse Sr replied, "It's a flying saucer."[37]

Major Marcel would later testify that the debris included a foil-like metal with "memory," which, after being folded would unfold itself and assume its former shape. He would also describe a lightweight, plastic-looking, tan-colored I-beam-type of structural member that could not be broken, even with a sledge hammer. However, he would add that the small I-beams could be slightly flexed. Other strange wreckage included threads or wires that were tough and strong. Major Marcel would also later further describe the debris as "not of this Earth."[38]

At 6 a.m., Marcel and Cavitt brief Colonel Blanchard on their findings. Blanchard calls the Military Police commandant at RAAF and orders a cordon around the Foster Ranch debris field, and the exclusion of people without official business from an even wider area. He contacts Eighth Air Force headquarters, and then reschedules the base daily conference from 9 a.m. to instead begin at 7:30 a.m. that morning.[39]

After the base meeting, Colonel Blanchard checks by phone with Major General Roger Ramey, who orders Major Marcel to Fort Worth AAF.[40]

Walt Whitmore records an interview with Mac Brazel, convinces Mac to talk again with the military people, and delivers him to RAAF. Brazel

34. *The Truth About the UFO Crash At Roswell* pp.202-203.
35. Ibid. p.203.
36. Ibid. pp.43, 153.
37. Ibid. p.168.
38. Ibid. p.46, citing personal interview with Walter Haut.
39. Ibid. p.203.
40. Ibid. p.204.

is taken to the base guest house, where he will be confined – except for excursions under escort – for several days, and is interrogated by AAF officers. Meanwhile, Whitmore receives a call from Washington warning him that if he broadcasts his interview with Brazel, radio station KGFL will lose its license.

Lieutenant Walter Haut types a press release, which he said he had been ordered to prepare by Colonel Blanchard, and by noon has delivered it to both newspapers and the pair of radio stations in Roswell. The text of the official press release reads:

> The many rumors regarding the flying disc became a reality yesterday when the Intelligence office of the 509th Bomb Group of the Eighth Air Force, Roswell Army Air Field, was fortunate enough to gain possession of a disc through the cooperation of one of the local ranchers and the sheriff's office of Chaves County.
>
> The flying object landed on a ranch near Roswell sometime last week. Not having phone facilities, the rancher stored the disc until such time as he was able to contact the sheriff's office, who in turn notified Maj. Jesse A. Marcel of the 509th Bomb Group Intelligence Office.
>
> Action was immediately taken and the disc was picked up at the rancher's home. It was inspected at the Roswell Army Air Field and subsequently loaned by Major Marcel to higher headquarters.[41]

The captured flying saucer story goes out over the Associated Press wire service at 2:26 p.m. The base phone lines quickly become jammed as reporters from across the country and overseas attempt to learn more about the news.[42]

At 3 p.m., Major Marcel is ordered to take a small amount of the debris to Fort Worth AAF.

Major Marcel arrives at Fort Worth AAF and reports to General Ramey at his office. General Ramey asks Marcel to go with him to a map room to indicate exactly where the wreckage was found. When they return, instead of the crash debris, a wrecked weather balloon is on the floor.[43]

---

41. *Crash at Corona.* p.xiii.
42. *The Truth About the UFO Crash At Roswell* p.205.
43. Ibid. p.206.

General Ramey tells military personnel that the captured disc has been sent to Wright Field, in Ohio. Meanwhile, additional soldiers arrive at the Foster Ranch crash site and go over it thoroughly as they retrieve every scrap of wreckage.

At Forth Worth AAF, a small group of reporters is allowed to photograph the weather balloon debris, and they are given the public announcement that the balloon is what actually came to Earth near Roswell AAF. The story and photographs are widely circulated, and are reported on radio and later appear in newspapers around the country.

Wednesday, 9 July: people who know him see Mac Brazel being escorted around town by military officers. At the office of the *Roswell Daily Record*, Brazel – in the company of military men – says he found what he now calls a weather device, back on 14 June – and not in early July. He further says he has found weather balloons on two other occasions and can recognize them. Meanwhile, another military officer goes around town retrieving all copies of the press release that can be found, or coaxed – through requests or demands – from staffers at press outlets. Also at the same time, both crash sites are in the process of "sanitizing," and three to four large transport aircraft are being loaded with crates, at least one of which is escorted by armed guards.[44]

Mac Brazel tells reporter Frank Joyce his new story. Joyce points out the difference in the accounts. Brazel privately informs him it "would go hard on him" if he did not give out the latest version of events. Flight crews and witnesses are told to forget what they saw and to keep quiet about everything.[45]

Marcel tells Cavitt he wants to review his written report. Cavitt refuses to let him see it. The Major reminds the Captain that he has a higher rank. Cavitt tells him to take his request to Washington.[46]

Major Marcel had been told to pose with the wreckage of the weather balloon that General Ramey and other Army Air Forces officials declared to be the actual crashed unidentified flying object.

Subsequently, the press followed the new story line; military people finished cleanups, and interviewed and intimidated numerous witnesses.

For the next three decades the story of the crash of a UFO at Roswell was successfully suppressed, until 1978, when ufologist Stanton Friedman got in touch with a then uninhibited and talkative former Major Jesse Marcel.

---

44. Ibid. p.208.
45. Ibid. pp.208-209.
46. Ibid. p.209.

With regard to the incidents in and around Roswell, New Mexico, in 1947, I have listed just some of the scores of eyewitnesses, and second-hand testimony by those close to them, as revealed to us by Messrs Randle and Schmitt.[47] All of these people and others kept silent for decades out of loyalty to the government, and the people and the country of the United States – a weighty consideration in that era to a much greater degree than today. Or they remained quiet out of concern for career or legal repercussions – a deterrent for many people most of the time. The reluctance of some to testify stemmed to an even greater extent out of the fear of death for themselves or their family members (due to reported numerous threats delivered by people in the military and government) – always a decisive motivator at any time. To elaborate on the twenty-seven witnesses mentioned, we cite: Mr and Mrs Dan Wilmot – who saw an object fall to Earth and, when they went to investigate, were blocked by soldiers; Steve MacKenzie – who was ordered to White Sands Missile Range to track mysterious blips on radar screens; William "Mac" Brazel – who found the debris field on the Foster Ranch; Jim Ragsdale and Trudy Truelove – who also saw something tumble from the sky, and who were in turn prevented from investigating by military guards; William Woody and his father, who likewise observed something plummeting down, and who encountered roadblocks when they went to look for it; William D. Proctor – the young neighbor who was with Mac Brazel when wreckage was discovered; Sheriff George Wilcox – who received the crash news and coordinated reporting and investigating efforts for a short time early on; Dan Dwyer – who was on a fire truck and was among the first civilians to reach the crash area;[48] John McBoyle – who reported on the crash, and witnessed the suppression of the story; Lydia Sleppy – who attempted to relay the news via teletype, only to be blocked by the FBI; Melvin E. Brown – who saw the alien bodies; Glenn Dennis – who saw all of the commotion at the air base, and who heard from an unnamed nurse about the dead aliens; C. Bertrand Schultz – who observed the military men blocking access to one of the crash areas; Floyd and Loretta Proctor – parents of William D. Proctor, who handled some of the debris, and urged Mac Brazel to go and report it in town;

47. https://www.coasttocoastam.com/ Ufologist Tom Carey, during his appearance on *Coast-to-Coast AM* with George Noory, 1–2 June 2022, says his investigations have discovered 600 witnesses – first-hand and second-hand, to events at and near Roswell Army Air Field.
48. *The Truth About the UFO Crash At Roswell* p.197.

Jesse Marcel Jr – Major Jesse Marcel's son, who handled the debris; Frank Joyce – who also reported the story, and witnessed the beginning of the cover-up; Major Jesse Marcel – prime mover in revealing the story through his testimony as a key participant in the events; Colonel Thomas J. DuBose – who later testified and swore in an affidavit as to the reality of the events he was part of and observed; Captain Sheridan Cavitt – who refused to acknowledge but did not deny what had happened; Walt Whitmore Sr – who recorded an interview with Mac Brazel before he changed his testimony, and who was threatened into killing the story; Leo B. Spear – who heard about but initially disbelieved the reports of other military policemen about a crashed flying saucer; Lieutenant Walter Haut – who was ordered to draft the press release about the crash of a flying disc.

Of these twenty-seven people – some were direct witnesses, others second-hand – a few of them wished to be kept in the background even if they could not remain completely anonymous; others described what they saw personally and further testified that his or her spouse or companion had also been there; again, just one – Sheridan Cavitt – refused to acknowledge any of the events described in Randle and Schmitt's book.

The entire story of the events in New Mexico in the early days of 1947 is complex and extensive – too much to include in this analysis, which is focused on a general history of military encounters with UFOs. For more complete insights into the particulars surrounding the events at and near Roswell, readers are referred to the serious studies of the subject, some of which appear in the bibliography. My point in detailing as much as I have here is to provide a small sampling of the many reliable people who have assured us that yes, one or possibly two objects that are evident alien spacecraft, and also possibly up to five extraterrestrial beings – three or four dead and one alive, came crashing to Earth in early July 1947 in the arid grassland and desert of central New Mexico. (I will add my speculation here that the United States military may initially have thought that the debris from the "first" crash site, which was discovered later on the Foster Ranch, may have been from either an alien spacecraft or a conventional, Earthly aircraft, whether domestic or Soviet.)

Many learned people, including those who have conjectured on the probability of the existence of intelligent life forms not of this Earth, such as renowned astronomer Carl Sagan for example, dismiss without further consideration the possibility of alien visitors to our world.

Celebrated physicist Stephen Hawking is quoted as saying, "I am discounting reports of UFOs. Why would they appear only to cranks and weirdos?"[49] The people cited above, a very few among many others, are hardly "cranks and weirdos," and neither are Lieutenant Colonel Randle and Mr Schmitt.

Of course, on the official side of the subject of UFOs we will yet encounter numerous people spouting the skeptics' line that UFOs do not exist, even after the confirmation of the authenticity of the videos of them released by the United States Navy. Not only do their denials increasingly bounce off deaf ears, they tend to confirm the suspicions of an ever larger number of people worldwide, because they perceive the validity of the words of a well-known German statesman, "Never believe in anything until it has been officially denied." (Otto von Bismarck.)[50]

My own interpretation of the evidence (based in part on an alleged observation by Dr Lincoln LaPaz, to be presented later) is that an alien spacecraft experienced some problems during a thunderstorm in rural New Mexico. It apparently landed at the scorched and fused area discovered by the two Chaves County sheriff's deputies, possibly to effect repairs, then took off, only to careen out of control (in conjunction with a possible explosion), came to Earth in a grazing trajectory on the Foster Ranch – 75 miles from RAAF, became airborne once more, then fell back down again some 40 miles away – about 35 miles from Roswell, where the main portion of the craft, and possibly (even probably) crew members as well as wreckage were discovered, captured, and spirited away by military authorities.

Based on the testimony of just over a score of generally very reliable-seeming witnesses alone, I believe in the strong likelihood, if not the certainty, of a UFO crash near Roswell. This assessment is by necessity rendered in the absence of physical evidence because, as many of the witnesses tell us, the tangible proof was confiscated, removed and hidden away from us. If this case were in a court of law, as a juror I would be forced to vote in favor of the incident having actually happened, all the more so because in a legal proceeding one side is not permitted to withhold evidence from the other.

I would leave these findings to stand on their own, but there is evident, if currently incremental and somewhat oblique "confirmation" of the reality of UFO crashes and the retrieval of materials, in Major Marcel's words, "not of this Earth."

---

49. https://quotepark.com/quotes/1747706-stephen-hawking-i-am-discounting-reports-of-ufos-why-would-they-a/
50. https://www.forbes.com/quotes/10573/

In an internet article ("UAP — Crash Retrievals, Part 1") by Nick Madrid on 13 April 2022, citing a *New York Times* item from 23 July 2020, Madrid writes, "Numerous associates of the Pentagon program ['hypothetical' UAP crash-retrieval program], with high-security clearances and decades of involvement with official UFO investigations, told the NYT they were convinced such crashes have occurred, based on their access to classified information."[51,52]

Madrid's account cites Dr Eric W. Davis, who, "In an interview conducted by Alejandro Rojas on his Open Minds podcast, on 30 April 2019, Davis described an ongoing U.S. government UFO Program that is studying off-world vehicles of which he is a part."[53]

Madrid goes on:

> On July 23, 2020 Ralph Blumenthal and Leslie Kean published an article in the *New York Times* entitled, 'No Longer in Shadows, Pentagon's U.F.O. Unit Will Make Some Findings Public.' The article reported that Dr. Eric W. Davis provided a classified briefing to a 'defense department agency' as recently as March about retrievals from 'off-world vehicles not made on this earth.'[54]

Madrid points out that Dr Davis; scientific and engineering colleague Dr Harold Puthoff; Luis Elizondo, former Director of AATIP; and Christopher Mellon, former Deputy Assistant Secretary of Defense for Intelligence – all of whom have appeared on electronic media and/or made statements to the press regarding secret government studies of materials retrieved from UFO/UAP crashes – have not lost their government jobs or connections, and also have not had their security clearances revoked.[55] The implication is clear: the government is not opposed to this gradual release of confirmation of the reality of UFOs as alien spacecraft, some of which have crashed and left debris retrieved by at least the United States government and military, and possibly those of other nations. (It was stated by Dr Davis in the interview with Alejandro Rojas on his *Open Minds* podcast, 30 April

51. https://medium.com/@nickmadrid68/uap-crash-retrievals-49969d75fe42
52. https://www.nytimes.com/2020/07/23/us/politics/pentagon-ufo-harry-reid-navy.html
53. https://medium.com/@nickmadrid68/uap-crash-retrievals-49969d75fe42
54. Ibid. Also: https://www.nytimes.com/2020/07/23/us/politics/pentagon-ufo-harry-reid-navy.html
55. https://medium.com/@nickmadrid68/uap-crash-retrievals-49969d75fe42

2019, when he reported on the ongoing U.S. government UFO program studying off-world vehicles in which he is a participant. Davis also said all global superpowers have retrieved UAP crash debris, which they are trying to reverse engineer.)

Moreover, "[Christopher] Mellon appeared on *The Joe Rogan Show* in May of 2021, and was asked about the Roswell incident and said: 'I've been told by multiple people who have credentials and access that there is some truth to these stories, and I don't discount this.'" Further, Mellon also said:

> Curiously, president Trump himself indicated on air while being filmed that he did have classified information about Roswell, New Mexico, which is, as most people know, the legendary site of the alleged crash of a UFO. And when asked by his son about declassifying this information, he said: 'I'll have to think about it.'

There would be nothing to think about if only a weather balloon had been involved; neither would the information still be classified.

Yet many questions remain, among them: why would a spacecraft capable of traveling vast distances through the hostile environment of interplanetary or interstellar space just suddenly crash while cruising through the relatively quiescent atmosphere of planet Earth? Perhaps, just maybe, it was brought down by other than natural forces alone, whether intentionally or by accident.

Did The American Military, Perhaps Inadvertently, Cause the UFO Crash at Roswell?

In more than one book on the topic of UFO crashes it is asserted that powerful new-model radars installed to protect the many sensitive military sites in New Mexico after the Second World War could have distorted the electromagnetic and gravitic/anti-gravitic drives and navigation systems of UFOs/alien spacecraft, causing them to go out of control. This suggestion is based on speculation about how UFOs/alien spacecraft are operated. As this theory goes, when descending into Earth's atmosphere, being relatively safe from interstellar and interplanetary debris, and discounting the abilities of our planet's inhabitants to interfere with alien activities, the beings piloting these craft may have switched off their electromagnetic and gravitic/anti-gravitic shields, possibly due to power-consumption considerations. Such a move would have placed them and their craft in jeopardy should someone – such as people in one of Earth's military organizations – unexpectedly direct a strong energy beam such as a powerful radio or radar beacon at their spacecraft.

To bolster this theory, more than just one or even a pair of writers have cited the installation of new radar equipment at three points in New Mexico after the Second World War: at Continental Divide, El Vado, and Moriarty. These radar sites are, respectively, 258.27 miles, 214.23 miles (at Cebolla – near El Vado), and 141.04 miles from Roswell.[56] There is a major problem with this assertion: this complication concerns the radar equipment initially installed at these sites. The precise breakdown is as follows: at Continental Divide, AN/FPS-3 (Army-Navy, Fixed Position, Pulsed, Search) and AN/FPS-5 radar units, operated by the 769th Air Control & Warning Squadron; at El Vado, an ANKPS-5 (Army-Navy, Transportable, Pulsed, Search) radar device, staffed by the 767th AC&W Squadron; at Moriarty, AN/FPS-3 and AN/FPS-5 radar sets, crewed by the 768th AC&W Squadron.[57] Part of the problem is that some of these Second World War and early post-war radar sets did not have enough range even to detect objects in the air above or near the RAAF, and therefore would likely have also lacked the power to affect an ET electromagnetic, gravitic/anti-gravitic drive or navigation system. At Continental Divide, the AN/FPS-3 was a modified version of the ANKPS-5 long-range search radar,[58] which had a range of just 210 miles.[59] Likewise, the El Vado unit was also too far away. At the remaining (Moriarty) site, the radar could have detected anything flying over or near the RAAF; however, there is another major problem: the El Vado/Gallina Peak/Cebolla site was not activated until 1950, and the Continental Divide and Moriarty units were not set up and in use until 1952.[60] Even if we back up a bit to include the radars installed at Kirtland AFB, late 1949, to provide coverage for the Albuquerque-Los Alamos region, again their ANKPS-5 and ANKPS-4 radars could have seen UFOs over or near the RAAF, but were over two years too late to do so. Moreover, the AN/FPS-3 was not produced until 1 December 1950.[61] Nice theory, but wrong. Or is it?

---

56. https://www.distancefromto.net/
57. "Searching the skies: the legacy of the United States Cold War defense radar program." Prepared for United States Air Force Headquarters Air Combat Command. https://nuke.fas.org/guide/usa/airdef/1997-06-01955.pdf p.139.
58. Ibid. p.76.
59. http://usafunithistory.com/PDF/0600/661%20RADAR%20SQ.pdf p.2.
60. https://nuke.fas.org/guide/usa/airdef/1997-06-01955.pdf p.139.
61. https://web.archive.org/web/19991002024354/http://www.atlantic.net/~gschulz/bfectxt1.htm

The AN/CPS-5 (Army-Navy, Air-Transportable, Pulsed, Search) radar unit was of Second World War vintage. (Production began in January 1945.)[62] It was evidently in place at RAAF prior to 1950 when it was then part of an early Cold War makeshift radar warning net hastily patched together to provide for the defense of the entire United States.[63] Its initial function was to protect the approaches to RAAF. It had an output of 750kW.[64] The AN/TPS-1B was also Second World War era.[65] (Detailed information on this model could not be located, but the AN/TPS-1E, also Second World War era, radiated a power of 500kW; so, I will conjecture that the almost matching AN/TPS-1B unit had a similar output.) These units were evidently in place in mid-1947, to be replaced not until many years later.[66]

At Kirtland Army Air Field, and in the Los Alamos region (where the first atomic bomb was assembled) at West Mesa, the radar sets later used for the interim air-defense network in 1949 were also Second World War era.[67] The site used ANKPS-5 and ANKPS-4 radars at that time,[68] but they might have been in use earlier (my speculation here). The latter was often used in conjunction with AN/FPS-4 height-finder radars, with an output of 250kW.[69]

The SCR-270/1 (Set, Complete, Radio) radar was in use before December 1941. The SCR-270 was in operation at White Sands Proving Grounds from mid-1945 until mid-1947, or longer.[70] If the ANKPS-5 and ANKPS-4 units cited above were not installed until after July 1947, then these SCR-270-1 units were probably in use there instead (again, this is my speculation). I am being so thorough here because I expect UFO deniers to hastily assert that no such radar units were in the state of New Mexico at all in 1947.

I also suspect that one or more local commercial radio stations could have contributed to an electromagnetic cascade that may have crippled an intruding alien spacecraft. The first such broadcast outlet in Albuquerque,

62. https://nuke.fas.org/guide/usa/airdef/1997-06-01955.pdf p.73.
63. Ibid. p.139.
64. Radatutorial.eu https://www.radartutorial.eu/19.kartei/11.ancient2/karte001.en.html
65. https://web.archive.org/web/19991002024354/http://www.atlantic.net/~gschulz/bfectxt1.htm
https://nuke.fas.org/guide/usa/airdef/1997-06-01955.pdf p.73.Ibid. p.73.
66. Ibid. p.139.
67. http://usafunithistory.com/PDF/0600/661%20RADAR%20SQ.pdf p.2.
68. https://nuke.fas.org/guide/usa/airdef/1997-06-01955.pdf p.140.
69. Air Force Historical Research Agcy https://www.afhra.af.mil/
70. NADRM Online Radar Museum. https://radomes.org/museum/

KOB, had a radiating strength as of 1941 of 25,000W of power at night.[71] That would still only have been 10 per cent of the radiating power of the ANKPS-5 radar unit. There was another radio station in Albuquerque (KOAT) with an output of 250W.[72] KGGM in Albuquerque had a radiating power of 1kW, and eight other, smaller stations throughout the entire state of New Mexico in 1947 had an additional combined output of 2,750W (2.75kW).[73]

At cities in neighboring Texas, as close to Roswell as Albuquerque, were KROD and KTSM in El Paso, with a combined power of 1,000W at night. KFYO in Lubbock transmitted at 250W. KSEL, also in Lubbock, had a power of 1kW, but evidently did not broadcast at night. KCRS, in Midland radiated 250W. KIUN in Pecos also had an output of 250W.[74]

As for the two Roswell commercial broadcast stations, KGFL had an operating power of 250W,[75] and KSWS – which took to the air in May 1947 – even today broadcasts at just 1kW of power at night.[76] (The exact data for KSWS in 1947 could not be located.)

The first radio station on the air in the local area was KSVP, in Artesia, New Mexico, 38.71 miles south of Roswell,[77] which began broadcasting in 1946. Even today, it radiates a signal of just 1,000W (1kW) during the day, and only 250W at night, when the Roswell crash is thought to have happened.[78]

In spite of the fact that the more powerful radar sets were not installed yet, there would have been radar units at Kirtland and Roswell Army Air Fields in New Mexico: Biggs AAF at El Paso, Texas; and at the White Sands Missile Test Range. These would have been the earlier, Second World War designs such as the AN/CPS-5 and other units listed above.

It is not beyond the realm of possibility that such an occurrence as an electromagnetic bombardment – whether accidental or intentional – could have happened, just not in regard to a supposed UFO "crash" that was later revealed to be a hoax (at Aztec, New Mexico on 25 March 1948). Perhaps

71. https://www.oldradio.com/archives/stations/ccs/kob.htm
72. https://worldradiohistory.com/Archive-Radio-Annual/1947/Radio-All-RA-1947.pdf p.493 (201 on web.)
73. Ibid. pp.294-301.
74. Ibid. pp.625-633.
75. Ibid. p.296.
76. https://transition.fcc.gov/fcc-bin/amq?call=KSFX
77. https://www.distancefromto.net/
78. https://worldradiohistory.com/Archive-Radio-Annual/1947/Radio-All-RA-1947.pdf pp.493-495.

none of the radar beams and radio waves, or one or more lightning strikes, would have been sufficient, except in combination. It seems possible that it was a set of circumstances – fortunately for the people of Earth, and unfortunately for the ETs – that could have conspired to bring down an alien spacecraft in early July 1947. This is so whether due to human intervention, natural forces, or internal mechanical failure – or any of these factors together.

These suppositions depend on the reality of the electromagnetic and gravitic/anti-gravitic theory for spacecraft propulsion; they add another possibility in these particular instances – one a likely happening, and the other "crash" definitely hoaxed (at Aztec). There remains the prospect that ETs, either ignorant of or disregarding the power of Earthly thunderstorms, could have contributed to their own literal downfall by shutting off their spacecraft safety measures – perhaps because such systems may interfere with the aliens' ability to monitor our electromagnetic signals such as radio and radar transmissions – only to be felled by unexpected bolts of lightning. Moreover, even if a lightning strike did not in itself possess enough power to knock down an ET craft, perhaps even the older, Second World War radar equipment casting powerful beacons of radiation at the UFO while radio stations were also broadcasting just at the instant a random lightning bolt hit their craft brought them down to Earth.

Now, for the next scenes in the New Mexico saga. . .

Chapter 6

Going Deeper into the Cold War, and More Fireballs

Why Initial Fears of UFOs had more to do with the Russians than Extraterrestrials

To properly understand the concerns of people both in and out of the governments and militaries in the Western democracies after the Second World War, it is important to take a brief look at the international situation then. Here is a timeline of events during the latter half of the 1940s with regard to the expansion of Communism in the early years of the Cold War:

11 November 1945	Communist-controlled elections put their leader in power in Yugoslavia.
1945–47	Under Soviet military occupation, and through Soviet-rigged elections, Poland falls under the domination of the Communists.
31 May 1947	Hungary falls to a Communist coup.
4 December 1947	Bulgaria institutes a Soviet-style constitution.
30 December 1947	The Communist "Romanian People's Republic" is proclaimed.
25 February 1948	Czechoslovakia becomes Communist.
9 September 1948	North Korea declares a Communist state.
1 October 1949	Chinese Communist leader Mao Tse Tung announces the existence of the People's Republic of China.
7 October 1949	Soviet occupation forces oversee the creation of Communist East Germany.

With the exception of Communist China, all of these conquests were the result of the occupation of the then emerging Communist bloc countries by

Soviet military forces at the end of the Second World War; in China, armed forces gained control with the military, economic and political assistance of the Soviet Union. Likewise, the northern half of formerly Japanese-controlled Korea had been under occupation by the Soviet Red Army.

Just a few years previous to this, Imperial Japan had staged a series of surprise attacks that not only heavily damaged the United States Pacific fleet at Pearl Harbor, Hawaii but also seized the Philippines and Wake Island from the United States; ripped the resource- and oil-rich Netherlands East Indies from the Netherlands; occupied British outposts in Malaya, Hong Kong and Singapore; staged military surprise advances elsewhere all over Asia, the Pacific, and into the Indian Ocean. Moreover, the Nazi-Soviet Pact of 23 August 1939 had led to the temporary division of parts of Eastern Europe between Germany and the Soviet Union during the early days of the Second World War. Therefore, naturally, there was a great deal of suspicion and paranoia in the West, which was intense but justified. In such an atmosphere it is not surprising that many people in governments and militaries on both sides of the Atlantic suspected that UFOs and UAP could be the results of sinister Soviet military research projects more than the improbable to them at the time aliens from space.

The United States Government Takes Action

In addition to the first three of many countries to fall under Communist domination, the numerous UFO sightings by civilians and the world's militaries – far too many to list in this study – prompted the United States government to establish the Central Intelligence Agency on 18 September 1947, and to split-off the Army Air Forces as the independent United States Air Force on the same date.

I agree with UFO truth seekers, and not relying at all on the usual obdurate cynics, that the supposed memo from President Truman establishing the shadowy "Majestic 12" group is fraudulent. (The Majestic 12 hoax was thoroughly exposed by some UFO experts, including retired Lieutenant Colonel Kevin Randle.[1])

I also agree that while there was no Majestic 12 committee as such, there were likely one or more groups similar to it that would have been charged

1. *Case MJ-12: The True Story Behind the Government's UFO Conspiracies* Lieutenant Colonel Kevin D. Randle. HaperTorch. New York. 2002.

with investigating, analyzing and developing information, and even new technologies derived from UFO incidents. There is some relatively obscure, but I believe genuine, documentation to support this claim.

There was an interesting directive from Major General C.P. Cabell, United States Air Force Director of Intelligence, dated 8 September 1950. It was sent to "Commanding Generals, Major Air Commands, ZI (Zone of the Interior) and Overseas," and also to "All United States (diplomatic) Air Attaches."

The document states, (in part):

> 1… Air Force has a … requirement for … reporting and technical analysis of observations of unconventional aircraft … which might indicate an advance in technological progress of a foreign power. An unconventional aircraft … is … any airborne object which by performance, aerodynamic characteristics, or unusual features, does not conform to any presently known aircraft type. 2… a. A separate report of each incident will be forwarded. No information [except] … that bearing on the unconventional aircraft will be included … b. Priority of transmission … will be that appropriate in the judgment of the forwarding agency, according to its apparent authenticity and importance as intelligence … will be forwarded to Commanding General, Air Material Command … Reports forwarded … will include … . (1) A brief description … shape, size, color, number, formation if more than one, aerodynamic features, trail or exhaust, propulsion system, speed, sound, maneuvers, manner of disappearance, and other pertinent or unusual features. (2) Time sighted … (3) Manner of observation; visual or electronic, from air … or surface. Any type of optical or electronic equipment used should be described. (4) Location of observer during sighting… Location of object(s) with respect to observer … (5) Identifying information on observer(s) and witnesses, estimate of reliability and experience, and any factors bearing on estimated reliability of the sighting. (6) Weather … (7) Any activity or condition, meteorological or otherwise, which might account for the sighting. (8) Existence of any physical evidence; fragments, photographs (etc.) … (9) Interception or identification action … (… should be taken whenever feasible, complying with existing Air Force directives.) e. Reports

> … where feasible will include sketches and signed attested narrative statements of observers … g. Any physical evidence … will be forwarded … to Commanding General, Air Material Command … 3… no publicity (will) be given this reporting and analysis …

The document is signed by Major General Cabell, with the notice, "By Command of the Chief of Staff." And finally (and most interesting), this document was circulated to the director of intelligence of the army, the director of naval intelligence, the Commandant (Intelligence) of the Coast Guard, the special assistant for research and intelligence at the Department of State, the director of the FBI, and the director of the CIA[2] (It is understandable that readers will be skeptical regarding the frequent deletions necessary to shorten the directive herein. Doubters are referred to the online master copy for verification.)

We can see from the preceding that the above-cited military officers and civilian authorities were within the informational loop, which means they were also likely to be at least peripheral members of a committee or committees charged with analyzing and advising on activities not just dealing with "unconventional aircraft which might indicate an advance in technological progress of a foreign power," but also relating to a very foreign power – such as an extraterrestrial one. Further, the descriptions called for can apply just as easily to "unconventional aircraft" from either an Earthly or un-Earthly source. The Air Force had become quite adept at referring to UFOs without directly referring to them as "UFOs."

Also significant to note is that no special committee such as the fictitious "MJ-12" is on the c.c. list, and also possibly significant is the fact that neither anyone in the United States Congress nor at the White House is in this informational network. There may be a benevolent reason for this because both the Congress and the White House could maintain plausible deniability of any knowledge of this program. There is also the fact that these two segments of the American national government are the primary sources of many, if not most, intelligence and other secret information losses and leaks.

It is also interesting to note that this call for very detailed information was issued while the Air Force was publicly recommending (on 4 January

---

2. AFD-110719-005.pdf https://www.secretsdeclassified.af.mil/Portals/67/documents/AFD-110719-005.pdf?ver=2016-07-19-142520-690 pp.16, 17.

1950, just nine months earlier) that such reporting be discontinued, as is to be found on earlier pages of this same directive.[3] This document was also issued ten months after the termination of the UFO-reporting office of Project Grudge, on 27 December 1949. Moreover, the Air Force was advising its personnel, as of 18 October 1950, to tell the public that – I'm paraphrasing now: "The recent UFO report is being investigated, and there is nothing of substance in it."[4] In other words, just days after the directive to all Air Force commands to report in detail UFO sightings, another Air Force office was telling unit commanders how to give the press and public the brush-off, as we have by now come to expect. But, wait, there is even more…

Back on 23 September 1947, Lieutenant General Nathan F. Twining, Commanding the Air Materials Command at what was then Wright Field, Dayton, Ohio, sent a letter to the Commanding General of the Army Air Forces, in Washington, D.C.[5]

The subject line of the letter reads: "Subject: AMC Opinion Concerning Flying Discs."

After the Salutation, the letter states:

> 1. As requested by AC/AS-2 (Air Force intelligence) there is below the considered opinion of this Command concerning the so-called 'flying discs.' This opinion is based on interrogation report furnished by AC/AS-2 and preliminary studies by personnel of T-2 and Aircraft Laboratory, Engineering Division T-3. This opinion is arrived at in a conference between personnel from the Air Institute of Technology, Intelligence T-2, office, Chief of Engineering Division, and the Aircraft, Power Plant and Propeller Laboratories of Engineering Division T-3. 2. It is the opinion that: a. The phenomenon reported is something real and not visionary or fictitious. b. There are objects probably approximating the shape of a disc, of such appreciable size as to be as large as man-made aircraft. c. There is a possibility that some of the incidents may be caused by natural phenomena, such as meteors. d. The reported

3. AFD-110719-005.pdf https://www.secretsdeclassified.af.mil/Portals/67/documents/AFD-110719-005.pdf?ver=2016-07-19-142520-690 p.1.
4. Ibid.p.2.
5. Yes, the United States Air Force had just branched off only five days before, but the Army ranks, titles and procedures were still in place.

operating characteristics such as extreme rates of climb, maneuverability (particularly in roll), and action which must be considered evasive when sighted or contacted by friendly aircraft and radar, lend belief to the possibility that some of the objects are controlled either manually, automatically or remotely. e. The apparent common description of the objects is as follows – (1) Metallic or light-reflecting surfaces. ~~SECRET~~ U-39552 Basic Ltr fr CG, AMC, WF to CF, AAF, Wash. D. C. subj "AMC Opinion Concerning "Flying Discs." (2) Absence of trail, except for a few instances when the object apparently was operating under high-performance conditions. (3) Circular or elliptical in shape, flat on bottom and domed on top. (4) Several reports of well-kept formation flights varying from three to nine objects. (5) Normally no associated sound, except in three instances a substantial rumbling roar was noted. (6) Level flight speeds normally above 300 knots are estimated. f. It is possible within present U.S. knowledge – provided extensive detailed development is undertaken – to construct a piloted aircraft which has the general description of the object in subparagraph (e) above which would be capable of an approximate range of 7000 miles at subsonic speeds. g. Any developments in this country along the lines indicated would be extremely expensive, time consuming and at the considerable expense of current projects and therefore, if directed, should be set up independently of existing projects. h. Due consideration must be given the following – (1) The possibility that these objects are of domestic origin – the product of some high security project not known to JC/AS-2 or this Command. (2) The lack of physical evidence in the shape of crash recovered exhibits which would undeniably prove the existence of these objects. (3) The possibility that a foreign nation has a form of propulsion, possibly nuclear, which is outside of our domestic knowledge. 3. It is recommended that: a. Headquarters, Army Air Forces issue a directive assigning a priority, security classification and Code Name for a detailed study of this matter to include the preparation of complete sets of all available and pertinent data which will then be made available to the Army, Navy, Atomic Energy Commission, JRDB (Joint Research and Development Board,

Vannevar Bush, Chairman, established 7 October 1946.[6] This is after the "Ghost Rockets" wave but prior to the Roswell incident.), the Air Force Scientific Advisory Group, NACA, (National Advisory Committee for Aeronautics),[7] [8] and the RAND (Research and Development – "R and D" – RAND – Corporation.), and NEPA (Nuclear Energy for the Propulsion of Aircraft) projects for comments and recommendations, with a preliminary report to be forwarded within 15 days of receipt of the data and a detailed report thereafter every 30 days as the investigation develops. A complete interchange of data should be effected. 4. Awaiting a specific directive AMC will continue the investigation within its current resources in order to more closely define the nature of the phenomenon.

---

6. https://www.cia.gov/readingroom/docs/Joint_R&D_Board_Rules_of_Organization_and_Procedure_7_Oct_1946.PDF "JOINT RESEARCH AND DEVELOPMENT BOARD RULES OF ORGANIZATION AND PROCEDURE" document approved for release by the Central Intelligence Agency, 2001.
7. https://www.google.com/search?q=NACA+government+acronym&oq=NACA+government+acronym&aqs=chrome..69i57j33i160.8431j0j7&sourceid=chrome&ie=UTF-8
8. The National Advisory Committee for Aeronautics, whose Director was Hugh L. Dryden from 1947 until the creation of NASA in 1958. Alfred J. Eggers joined NACA in 1944 as an aerospace scientist. Robert Gilruth was the first manager of NACA's guided missile range. Harry J. Goett became a project engineer at Langley Aeronautical Laboratory in 1936, and Ames Aeronautical Laboratory in 1940 as Chief of the Full-Scale and Flight Research Division from 1948 to 1959. Jerome Hunsaker served as a member of NACA in 1922 and 1923, then NACA in 1939. He became chairman in 1941, and served until 1956. Eastman Jacobs helped create the Second World War airfoil "bible" for the design of the P-51 Mustang. John F. Parsons joined the Langley Aeronautical Laboratory as a junior aeronautical engineer, transferred to Ames in 1939, and from 1943 to 1947 served as the Chief of the Full Scale and Flight Research Division while also Chief of the Construction Division, then served as Assistant to the Director of the Center until 1949. I. Irving Pinkel joined Langley Aeronautical Laboratory in 1940 and transferred to the Lewis Laboratory in 1942. In 1949 he became Associate Chief of the Physics Division. Henry J. Reid joined NACA's Langley Aeronautical Laboratory in 1921 and became Director of the Center in 1926, and presided over its development as a leading aeronautical and space research facility. He served until 1960. Russell Robinson joined NACA in 1939 at Langley Aeronautical Laboratory. In 1939 . . . he supervised the first construction of the Ames Aeronautical Laboratory, was called back to Langley in 1940 and returned to Ames in 1950. Robert C. Seamans served on technical committees of NACA from 1948 to 1958. Edward R. Sharp became manager and was appointed Director of the Aircraft Engine Research Laboratories in 1947. John Stack joined the Langley Aeronatucial

> Detailed Essential Elements of Information will be formulated immediately for transmittal thru [*sic*] channels.[9]

So again, if we dig just a little bit deeper we find that Vannevar Bush, as chairman of the Joint Research and Development Board, was on the circulation list, and was likely involved with the committee or committees charged with investigating UFO sightings, and even retrievals of crashed or landed "unconventional aircraft." This does not confirm the validity of the MJ-12 documents, which place him on that fictitious committee, but it reconfirms that they were very clever frauds.

In response to the Twining letter, the commanding general of the new Air Force established "Project Sign" to investigate UFOs.[10] Also known to the public as "Project Saucer," when the "Project Sign" name became generally known, it was changed to "Project Grudge."[11]

After these developments it is easier to understand the detailed investigation of subsequent unusual and unexplained aerial phenomena within the context of the government's heightened interest following what I now believe was a crash (or crashes) of one or more extraterrestrial

---

Laboratory as an aeronautical engineer in 1928. In 1939 he became director of all high-speed wind tunnels and high-velocity airflow research at Langley. He was named chief of the compressibility research division and was promoted to assistant chief of research in 1947, and then assistant director of the research center. John F. Victory was the first employee of NACA, in 1915. He became its secretary in 1921 and its executive secretary in 1948, in general charge of its administration. Walter C. Williams joined NACA in 1940 as a project engineer to improve Second World War fighter planes, and went to what is now Edwards Air Force Base to set up flight tests for the X-1. Demarquis D. Wyatt joined the Lewis Laboratory in 1944, where he specialized in supersonic research in propulsion system installations and later became the Associate Chief of the Propulsion Aerodynamics Division. The source of this information is NASA's Biography Page. https://history.nasa.gov/naca/bio.html

In my opinion there is a strong likelihood that some, many, most or even all of these individuals would have been at least peripherally involved with a high-level committee or committees assigned to work on the many mysteries of the UFO phenomenon. Again, there is no reference to the fictitious MJ-12 Committee or its supposed members.

9. Twining Letter https://www.documentcloud.org/documents/20797978-twining-memo
10. *The Report On Unidentified Flying Objects*. Edward J. Ruppelt. E-artnow. No city listed. 2020. pp.20–21.
11. "Sightings of unidentified aerial phenomena increased, and in 1948 the U.S. Air Force began an investigation of these reports called Project Sign. The initial opinion of those involved with the project was that the UFOs were most likely sophisticated Soviet aircraft, although some researchers suggested that they might be spacecraft from other worlds, the so-called extraterrestrial hypothesis (ETH). Within a year, Project Sign was succeeded by Project Grudge." Britannica https://www.britannica.com/topic/unidentified-flying-objects#ref985171

spacecraft in New Mexico in July 1947. (The idea has come to pass that perhaps the possible electromagnetic interference suggested to be involved in the Roswell crash caused two alien spacecraft flying close together in formation to accidentally collide with each other. I prefer the single-UFO solution, based on the evidence apparently discovered in New Mexico in 1947, and the numerous eyewitness accounts.)

Green Fireballs

Following the UFO crash incident in New Mexico in July 1947, a mystifying series of sightings occurred, concentrating once more above that state.

For the initial source cited regarding the "Green Fireballs" I now turn to *The Report On Unidentified Flying Objects*,[12] by Captain Edward J. Ruppelt. My earlier disparaging remarks about Project Blue Book (PBB) do not apply, or do so to a much lesser degree, to Captain Ruppelt. I write "to a much lesser degree" because, despite his even-handedness and honest efforts to investigate and report on UFO incidents, I argue that he remained too much of an "organization man," which is understandable as he was part of a powerful military organization. I further believe that while he struggled to remain completely objective in his investigations, analyses and reporting, at times I feel he tended to skew too much toward conventional explanations by the United States Air Force when certain incidents were of a more ambiguous nature. After leaving PBB, Ruppelt did not hesitate to make his feelings known about people whom he believed were taking advantage of interest in the UFO phenomenon for personal gain and not to relay true facts as they found them.

In late November 1948, people in the Albuquerque area reported seeing "green flares" in the sky at night. Military officials at Kirtland Air Force Base, at Project Sign, and ATIC (Air Technical Intelligence Center)[13] all

12. *The Report On Unidentified Flying Objects*. By Edward J. Ruppelt. E-artnow. No city listed. 2020.
13. "The establishment of Air Materiel Command's T-2 Intelligence at Wright Field in July 1945 began the move toward a balanced integration of engineering and intelligence. T-2 was responsible for the creation of air intelligence; identifying foreign aircraft and related equipment needed for study; receiving, translating and distributing foreign language documents; and distributing air intelligence products... The Air Force established the Air Technical Intelligence Center (ATIC) at Wright-Patterson Air Force Base as a field

agreed, in a way: they thought that the fireballs were standard military flares fired by veterans who had "liberated" flare guns when they came home after the Second World War.[14] Over the next few days the reported flares were more numerous and bigger until, on 5 December a Captain Goede was flying an Air Force C-47 transport plane at 18,000ft east of Albuquerque when he, his co-pilot and flight engineer all saw a large, bright-green fireball shoot across their flight path. It did not arc downward as do most meteors. They reported that the orb had instead arced upward from near the Sandia Mountains, leveled off and continued on. They called-in their report to Kirtland AFB tower, considering it very important as they had already seen an identical green fireball twenty-two minutes earlier near Las Vegas, New Mexico.

Shortly after, at 9:53 p.m. the pilot of a Pioneer Airlines DC-3 also called Kirtland tower to inform them that he had seen a green fireball earlier, again near Las Vegas, New Mexico. He told them he would file a full report upon landing at Albuquerque. At the airport he found several military intelligence officers waiting for him. He told them the object had approached at 9:35 p.m. and had flown in a low and flat trajectory, changing from orange-red to green as it seemed on a collision course. He said he took evasive action as the fireball pulled alongside, then dropped away, gliding toward the ground as it grew dimmer and disappeared. He stated that it looked to be as big as or bigger than a full moon.[15]

From that momentous night of 5 December, sightings of green fireballs followed near the Atomic Energy Commission's facilities at Los Alamos, New Mexico. There were more, on 6, 7, 8, 11, 13, 14, 20 and 28 December, according to a memo from the San Antonio office of the FBI, which was sent to Director John Edgar Hoover.[16]

We now turn to a key player in the "Green Fireball Mystery," who unexpectedly proved able to throw some light on earlier UFO incidents.

A treasure-laden sea chest of enlightening information has been brought to us by researcher Joel Carpenter, and the facts are contained in his

---

activity of the Assistant Chief of Staff for Intelligence 21 May 1951." https://www.nasic.af.mil/About-Us/Fact-Sheets/Article/611728/national-air-and-space-intelligence-center-heritage/

14. *The Report On Unidentified Flying Objects*. Edward J. Ruppelt. E-artnow. No city listed. 2020. p.41.
15. Ibid. p.42.
16. *Clear Intent: The Government Coverup of the UFO Experience* Lawrence Fawcett and Barry J. Greenwood. Prentiss-Hall. Englewood Cliffs, NJ. 1984. p.160.

"Green Fireball Chronology."[17] (While attempting to obtain biographical information on Joel Carpenter, I encountered an interesting article related to "Time reversed optical waves by arbitrary vector spatiotemporal field generation," by Joel Carpenter, among others.[18] This item will be placed within the proper context later.) Carpenter introduces the specifics of the record by informing us that they were found in the personal correspondence and memoranda of Dr Lincoln LaPaz.

On 9 December, special agents of the Air Force Office of Special Investigations (AFOSI) interviewed Army Colonel William Hayes at Kirtland Air Force Base. He told them that in the latter part of 1947 he saw a bright light near Vaughn, New Mexico on Highway 60 that drifted lower from 500ft, only to silently explode in a shower of red sparks about 200ft above the ground. He also said that on either 3 or 4 November and again on the 23rd, 1948, he had seen a similar phenomenon, adding that all of the incidents occurred around 10 p.m.[19]

One of the AFOSI special agents flew a light aircraft to the area where the sightings had occurred while another went to the University of New Mexico to confer with Dr Lincoln LaPaz. LaPaz said the phenomena were not meteors, that there had also been mysterious "meteorite falls" near Memphis, Tennessee and in Russia, as well as in New Mexico. He told the AFOSI man the unexplained incidents should be investigated for positive identification.

LaPaz then consulted with colleagues and learned that similar green lights had been observed near other defense establishments, including the nuclear materials production site at Hanford, Washington.

Army and Air Force representatives informed AFOSI agents that no secret or confidential maneuvers or experiments were being undertaken in the area by either military service.

Dr LaPaz apparently enlisted the aid of the Civil Air Patrol as he undertook a survey of the skies. At first he suspected some connection with the annual Geminid meteor showers but quickly concluded they could not be linked due to their flight paths and behavior, as well as the fact that in all of his observations since 1915 he had never seen the Geminids produce even a single green fireball.

While on a scouting drive on 12 December LaPaz and two AFOSI agents saw a green fireball gliding near the horizon until it "burned out."

17. Green Fireball Chronology. http://www.project1947.com/gfb/gfbchron.html
18. https://www.nature.com/articles/s41467-020-19601-3
19. http://www.project1947.com/gfb/gfbchron.html

Upon reporting the sighting to the security chief of the Los Alamos nuclear installation, LaPaz was relieved to learn that perimeter guards there had also seen the green fireball. LaPaz then watched the Geminids all night; none were green, and all proceeded almost straight down, not even close to parallel with the horizon.

LaPaz calculated the trajectory of his sighting and determined that the green fireball he and the others had seen on 12 December traveled horizontally at about 50,000ft altitude and at 36,000mph for nearly 25 miles, passing almost directly above the Los Alamos high-security site. He was deeply affected by these events and abandoned all ideas that the green fireballs were natural phenomena.

At his next meeting with security officials at Los Alamos, Dr LaPaz brings letters from other scientists who support his theory that the green fireballs are artificial objects. He asks the Atomic Energy Commission to help in the investigation.

LaPaz experiments in his lab and discovers that incinerated copper salts produce almost an identical color to the green fireballs. Meanwhile, security agencies assist by setting up special cameras to capture green fireball events on film.

Between 21 and 27 December an SK-1M (Search, Transportable) mobile radar site is set up to hunt for green fireball images.

(The SK-1M was a land-based trailer-mobile version of an early naval air search radar operating with a peak output of 1MW, but was usually set with a signal strength of 250kW.[20] It had a range of 186.4 statute miles.[21] It had been in use since 1944 in its naval, ship-borne version. It is interesting to note that this mobile radar unit, and possibly others, was available in the central New Mexico area about seventeen months after July 1947, indicating that additional such radar units could have been in use nearby at the time of the Roswell incident.

These possible sources of directed radiation with a relatively high peak output were electromagnetic beacon sources that could easily have been deployed at the time of the Roswell crash, giving added credence to the notion that perhaps radio and radar electromagnetic signals, with or without added input by lightning, could conceivably have caused a spacecraft to lose navigation and propulsion control.

20. http://www.navweaps.com/Weapons/WNUS_Radar_WWII.php
21. https://www.theunitconverter.com/nautical-miles-to-miles-conversion/162-nautical-miles-to-miles.html

There is some speculation that this was part of an intentional effort hatched by Secretary of Defense James Forrestal to disable, trap, capture a UFO – not beyond the realm of possibility, but I still think it probably was an accident.)

On 20 December patrols spot green fireballs near Los Alamos; security chiefs think they resemble rocket or vehicular exhaust plumes.

On 29 December the Associated Press reports that Defense Secretary James Forrestal announced plans for an armed satellite to orbit the Earth some nine-tenths of the way to the moon – about 200,000 miles distant, to potentially launch missile attacks against any point on our planet.[22]

On the same day, Dr LaPaz interviews witnesses at Los Alamos to the 20 December sightings. He calculates that the green fireball descended from 50,000ft at a 45° angle to 12,000ft, traveling at 13,000 to 27,000mph. This is many times faster than either the German V-1 or V-2 rockets, then fastest and most advanced in the world. The object had come to within about 6 miles from the Los Alamos installation. It made no sound.

On 13 January 1949, Colonel Eustis Poland of Army Intelligence sent a memo to the Director of Army Intelligence in which he stated, "Agencies in New Mexico are greatly concerned over these phenomena." He added that the competing theories then being aired included possible "'sensing shots' [by, presumably, a foreign power] with some super-stratospheric" objects designed to self-destruct; and that it was expected that after the technique had been perfected the self-destruct mechanism would be replaced by a warhead. Another theory was that green fireball events were part of radiological warfare tests by a foreign power; and that, further, the rays could cause death and may also have been responsible for recent plane crashes. Yet another conclusion was that the United States itself was conducting the tests. Finally, in view of the many "sensitive installations" in the area, Colonel Poland suggested that a "scientific board" be set up to resolve the problem.

On 30 January near Gaedheim, West Germany, a pale-blue, luminous object described by several witnesses as looking and sounding like a missile, glides in from the northeast and falls with a loud explosion near the Main River. "A U.S. military investigation begins on 9 February, including chemical analysis of the debris." This is the fourth incident of this type since October 1946. This item was filed by LaPaz as "USAF 'Gaedheim, Germany' case file," 18 February 1949.

22. Green Fireball Chronology. http://www.project1947.com/gfb/gfbchron.html

This curious item seems to confirm that the events of the ghost rockets of 1946 and after were not all figments of imaginations, because debris had been subjected to "chemical analysis"; the object had evidently come from the "northeast" – in the direction of the then Soviet-occupied East Germany, including the former Nazi rocket testing site at Peenemünde, Soviet-occupied and controlled Poland, the Baltic Sea, and Sweden; and, moreover, this was the fourth such incident.

The same evening, a green fireball described as "the brightest yet" is seen by more than 1,000 witnesses, many of whom were personally interviewed by Dr LaPaz. They include military people who were waiting outside to see an open-air screening of a movie. Other eyewitnesses include perimeter guards, oil workers, air crew and control tower personnel. The object made no sound. LaPaz affirmed that it was a green fireball, but people who saw it toward the end of its course over Texas said it looked to be blue, red, orange or purple.

On 31 January the commander of the Air Force Office of Special Investigations (AFOSI) at Kirtland AFB, Colonel Doyle Rees orders an "all-out search on the ground for material from the fireball."

On 1 February, Dr LaPaz is provided with a staff car and he undertakes a field survey, hoping to find where the green fireball of two nights before fell to Earth. He and the AFOSI teams canvas the New Mexican communities of Moriarty, Etanoi, Vaughn, Ramon, Mesa, Roswell, Caprock, Tatum and "other towns in New Mexico." They also visit Lamesa, Brownsfield, Plains, Lubbock, Muleshoe and other sites in Texas. Some places are visited more than once. At Roswell, the Walker AFB (formerly Roswell Army Air Field) AFOSI team officer, Lieutenant Paul Ryan assigns Special Agent Bill Rickett to the search party. (Special Agent Rickett will reappear momentarily in our investigation.)

On 4 February 1949, an AFOSI air crew circles an area west of Cedar Lake, Texas, between the towns of Seminole and Lamesa, where it is believed the green fireball fell to Earth, while an AFOSI ground party, led by Lieutenant Paul Ryan – from Roswell – conducts a careful search "from Lamesa, through Amherst, Texas, and to Clovis, New Mexico." They find nothing.

On 21 February 1949, Dr LaPaz returns to teaching full-time as the head of the University of New Mexico mathematics department, ending his field work with AFOSI on the green fireball phenomenon.

In an item listed as being on 24 February 1949, at Schweinfurt, West Germany (near Gaedheim), American authorities remained puzzled by the four mysterious projectile crashes that had occurred since October 1946. The most recent fall was listed in this memo as 31 January 1949, yet in

LaPaz's earlier document it was recorded as occurring on 30 January; but that is a minor discrepancy. Eyewitnesses said the objects came from the northeast and had flaming tails about 20ft long. The report also said, "Experts so far have been unable to reconstruct the projectiles from the small bits recovered from the craters." So, here we learn that not only had at least four ghost rocket-like missiles been recovered (as debris), that they left craters, and that they were being subjected to "reverse assembly."

As is usual with the UFO phenomenon: There's more ...

Re-enter Bill Rickett, who had been assigned to assist Dr LaPaz in the search for the green fireball impact site. Rickett also detailed another mission he conducted: helping Dr LaPaz in trying to locate the exact fall-location of the crashed disc near Roswell.[23]

Rickett said the professor was fascinated by the fact that when he (LaPaz) interviewed Mac Brazel, the ranch foreman reported that his animals behaved strangely after the incident.

Rickett arranged an aircraft so the doctor could conduct an aerial survey of the local terrain. Evidently, LaPaz found the spot where the craft had briefly touched down before later crashing. Rickett said the sand had been fused into a glass-like substance; (confirming the discovery by the two Chaves County sheriff's deputies); that LaPaz gathered soil samples, and recovered some of the foil-like metal there (verifying the testimony of other witnesses regarding the characteristics of some of the crash wreckage). Rickett went on to say that LaPaz sent the soil and metal debris to be tested, but that he, Rickett, did not know to where it had been dispatched. I suspect that would have been ATIC, at Wright-Patterson AFB.

Bill Rickett further explained: "LaPaz was very good at talking to people." He elaborated that Dr LaPaz, using his command of the Spanish language, spoke to many of the local people who had limited English skills, and learned that "a day or two" after the UFO "had blown up," (as was indicated on military radar images at the time – early July 1947) a couple of people reported their animals behaving strangely when two equally unusual-looking objects were seen slowly cruising over the area.[24]

Rickett concluded with the revelation that Dr LaPaz thought the crashed object had gotten into trouble, landed to effect repairs (supporting what the two deputies from Sheriff Wilcox's office had found – "a circular area in a pasture that had been blackened and burned, with the sand fused into

---

23. *Crash At Corona: The U.S. Military Retrieval and Cover-Up of a UFO.* Stanton T. Friedman and Don Berliner. Paragon House. New York. 1992. p.102.
24. Ibid. pp.102, 103.

glass").[25] It had then taken off, and subsequently exploded. LaPaz told him he thought the other two cruising aerial vehicles had been searching for the missing craft. When Rickett said he posited to LaPaz that the objects were from a higher civilization, the professor said he would leave any such speculation out of his report.[26] (But, obviously, not out of his conscious awareness.)

While looking into what may at first seem to be a diversion into the green fireball mystery (which was never solved), we found additional information, though not irrefutable confirmation and certainly not the whole truth, but rather hints and clues regarding the possibility of electromagnetic interference from more transportable radar units contributing to, or causing, the Roswell crash; an added insight into some of the hidden aspects of the ghost rocket phenomenon; that reports on the Roswell crash from different angles – this time from Dr Lapaz and local Spanish-speaking eyewitnesses – and recollections support one another; and also the possibility that the aliens may have sent out a search party to locate one of their craft that went missing in the Roswell, New Mexico region, in July 1947. I also stumbled across the scholarly article, "Time reversed optical waves by arbitrary vector spatiotemporal field generation," which could illuminate how certain optical distortions during UFO observations might be created, even without resorting to technological extremes.[27]

25. *The Truth About the UFO Crash At Roswell.* p.201.
26. *Crash At Corona: The U.S. Military Retrieval and Cover-Up of a UFO.* Stanton T. Friedman and Don Berliner. Paragon House. New York. 1992. p.103.
27. https://www.nature.com/articles/s41467-020-19601-3

Chapter 7

The "Tipping Point" – USAF Decides to Shoot Them Down

The Loss of Captain Mantell

This section will review descriptions of the following incident as brought to us by Captain Edward J. Ruppelt in his book, *The Report on Unidentified Flying Objects*.

On 7 January 1948, the control tower at Godman Air Force Base, outside Louisville was called by the Kentucky State Police to check on aircraft activity after receiving numerous calls from people who reported a strange object in the sky. The tower operators said their radar screens were clear, and checked with the not-very-distant Wright-Patterson Air Force Base, in Dayton, Ohio (166.62 miles).[1] The staff there also said there was no air traffic in the area. The unusual object was described as being circular, and about 250 to 300ft in diameter. The witnesses' observations made it evident the UFO would soon pass directly over Godman AFB.[2]

At first, the assistant tower operator had been reluctant to make a UFO report, so he delayed telling his superior what he saw. After both men observed the UFO, they called upper echelons, and soon several higher-ranking base staff, including the intelligence officer, were in the tower and utilizing its 6x50 binoculars to look at the object. No one could account for it, so they decided to contact approaching military planes to have them take a closer look.

The Godman tower called the flight leader, 25-year-old Captain Thomas Mantell, who was leading four planes on an aircraft-ferrying mission to a nearby airfield. Mantell's group was directed toward the south to intercept the UFO; but one of the pilots reported that he was low on fuel and would

1. https://www.distancefrom to.net/
2. *The Report On Unidentified Flying Objects*. Edward J. Ruppelt. E-artnow. No city listed. 2020. p.31.

be landing. Mantell and the two remaining pilots, all flying F-51 propeller-driven fighter planes, set off in search of the object.

According to Captain Ruppelt, giving the exact time – 2:45 p.m., Mantell was heard to say, "I see something above and ahead of me and I'm still climbing." Ruppelt reported that everyone in the tower heard this, and a wingman's following question, "What the hell are we looking for?" Ruppelt goes on to write, "Odd as it may seem, no one can remember exactly what he answered," although Ruppelt vaguely credits "some UFO historians" with Mantell's subsequent communication: "I've sighted the thing. It looks metallic and is tremendous in size … Now it's starting to climb." Ruppelt then says "not everyone in the tower could agree" on his words up to that point. I was willing to leave Captain Ruppelt's report at that – accepting that Captain Mantell's words were misremembered, until later, when combing through a different document that, as is often the case, seemed at first to deal with other aspects of the UFO phenomenon.

The document I read was called: "Air Intelligence Report No. 100-203-79. Analysis of Flying Object Incidents in the U.S. Air Intelligence Study No. 203. 10 December 1948. Directorate of Intelligence and Office of Naval Intelligence." (Posted by NICAP [National Investigations Committee on Aerial Phenomena[3]] on the internet.) The joint Air Force and Navy document was originally stamped "Top Secret." There was a warning notice that it contained classified information. On page 12 the report stated:

> On 7 January 1948, a National Guard pilot was killed while attempting to chase an unidentified object up to 30,000ft. While it is presumed that this pilot suffered anoxia, resulting

3. National Investigations Committee on Aerial Phenomena. "NICAP was founded on 24 October 1956, by inventor Thomas Townsend Brown. The board of governors included several prominent men, including Donald Keyhoe, Major USMC (Retired), and former chief of the Navy's guided missile program RADM Delmer S. Fahrney USN (Retired) … (And) "Keyhoe's Naval Academy classmate Vice-Admiral Roscoe H. Hillenkoetter, USN (Ret.). He had been Director of Central Intelligence and first head of the Central Intelligence Agency. Another important name on the letterhead was that of General Albert Coady Wedemeyer USA (Retired) …

"The organization had chapters and local associates scattered throughout the United States. Many of their members were amateurs, but a considerable percentage were professionals, including journalists, military personnel, scientists and physicians. One of NICAP's prime goals was thorough field investigations of UFO reports. They would eventually compile a significant number of case files and field investigations which (Jerome) Clark characterizes as 'often first rate'." Air Intelligence Report 100-203-79.pdf - NICAP.orghttp://www.nicap.org › airintelrpt100-203-79PDF http://www.nicap.org/index.htm

> in his crash, his last message to the tower was, 'It appears to be metallic object … of tremendous size … directly ahead and slightly above … I am trying to close for a better book [*sic*].'[4]

So, despite the typo at the end, I am prepared to accept that a joint-force, top-secret internal military report probably gave more complete facts regarding classified information than that allowed for either Project Blue Book at the time or Captain Ruppelt in his later book.

Mantell's wingmen had fallen behind as he aggressively pursued the object. They called to him when they were at 15,000ft because they were concerned about his well-being as none of the planes were equipped with high-altitude oxygen supplies; but their calls went unanswered.[5]

Mantell's wingmen landed at a nearby airfield. One of them had his plane refueled and took to the air in search of his missing commanding officer. Mantell had not been heard from again. The tower had by then lost sight of the UFO, and soon afterward received a report that Captain Mantell's plane had crashed, and that he was dead.[6]

Initially after reading Captain Ruppelt's account and analyses by others recounting UFO incidents, I agreed that there was no discernible evidence that a UFO (that was not a research balloon) had anything to do with Mantell's crash and his death. However, after reading the Air Intelligence Report cited above I have changed my view to leaning heavily toward the object being a UFO, meaning a possible alien spacecraft. This does not mean that I necessarily believe the UFO directly caused Captain Mantell's accident.

The Air Force at first claimed that Captain Mantell had chased the planet Venus, then changed the story to have him attempt to intercept a high-altitude research balloon. To assert that Captain Mantell was chasing a balloon means the Godman tower personnel and higher-ranking officers all could not recognize the UFO as such, despite resorting to 6x50 binoculars. This casts serious doubt on the competence of U.S. Air Force officers of lower and higher ranks, some of whom had the responsibility of identifying and controlling air traffic. This assertion is so unlikely as to be absurd.

---

4. Air Intelligence Report 100-203-79.pdf - NICAP.org http://www.nicap.org › airintelrpt100-203-79PDF
5. *The Report On Unidentified Flying Objects* Edward J. Ruppelt. E-artnow. No city listed. 2020. p.31.
6. Ibid. pp.31-32.

The main problem with the Venus story is the fact that Mantell was headed south, but Venus follows the plane of the ecliptic which, though it shifts north and south to a limited degree, generally runs from east to west, and not low in the sky to the south, far from the path of the sun. Another problem is that Venus, again being on the ecliptic, would only be that high in the sky in high summer, and in January is never almost straight overhead[7] – because Mantell, the people in the Godman AFB tower, and other eyewitnesses, only indirectly mentioned here who called the state police, all said is where the UFO was seen. In any event, it is likely that he had lost consciousness due to oxygen deprivation, causing his plane to go out of control and plunge to the ground, apparently without any external interference. However, to me there remains a slight chance that Captain Mantell's plane was brought down by hostile extraterrestrial action. If the facts change I shall reassess.

While the Mantell incident does qualify as a military encounter with a UFO – of whatever nature – the event is probably not a case of an extraterrestrial spacecraft attacking a human-piloted flying machine, even if the UFO originated beyond our Earth. The top-secret Air Force-Navy report would most likely convince military people in all the branches – and also those in foreign militaries who likewise knew of this and similar events that have been held secret – that Captain Mantell had perhaps fallen victim to hostile alien action. That suspicion would have future political, bureaucratic and military consequences.

The Intelligence People Report While There is a Reversal on High

Captain Ruppelt advises us in his book *The Report on Unidentified Flying Objects* that at the close of the "Green Fireball" wave there was a sudden shift in attitude at the top levels of command.[8] The change coincided with an unsuccessful effort to capture the green fireballs on camera, and also with the name-change from Project Sign to Project Grudge. Ruppelt speculated on what was to become a major (unofficial) excuse: if UFOs were confirmed to be alien spacecraft there would be widespread public panic, like that which

7. "Venus would rise at 09:10 am and set at 07:15 pm. 85% of Venus would be illuminated by the Sun… The angular distance in the sky between Venus and the Sun would be 31° 13' 07.4"." https://takemeback.to/astronomy/07-January-1948 .

8. *The Report On Unidentified Flying Objects*. Edward J. Ruppelt. E-artnow. No city listed. 2020 pp.47-48.

supposedly followed the Halloween-night 1938 radio broadcast adaptation of H.G. Wells's science fiction classic, *War of the Worlds*. (Listeners tuning in late to the drama did not hear the opening announcement that it was a work of fiction. Subsequent dramatized "news" bulletins seemingly interrupted a musical presentation with "news" that Martian invaders had landed in New Jersey, defeated army units, and were massacring civilians. How many people actually panicked has been disputed since the broadcast, although its creator, Orson Welles, hastily attended a press conference to offer apologies.) I have a more bureaucratic and political interpretation, which I will get to shortly.

Following the loss of Captain Mantell, on 24 July 1948 a DC-3 airliner captained by Clarence S. Chiles and co-piloted by John B. Whitted, when near Montgomery, Alabama, was confronted by a UFO rushing at them at high speed from straight ahead. To avoid a collision, Chiles steered his plane in a tight left turn. The UFO whizzed by about 700ft to the right, leaving behind turbulent air as the object went into a steep climb. "It was [like] a B-29 fuselage … the underside had a 'deep blue glow.' There were 'two rows of windows from which bright lights glowed,' and a '50-foot trail of red-orange flame' shot out the back." A crew chief at Robins AFB, one passenger on the airliner, and the crew of another airliner also saw UFOs either nearby or heading toward the Montgomery area.[9]

Ruppelt reported that the UFO-DC-3 near-collision had a profound effect at the Air Force's Air Technical Intelligence Center (ATIC). "This report shook them worse than the Mantell incident." Not wanting to seem out of step and behind unfolding events, especially after the Twining letter of 23 September 1947, the people at ATIC compiled an "Estimate of the Situation."[10] Captain Ruppelt explained: "In intelligence, if you have something to say about some vital problem you write a report that is known as an 'Estimate of the Situation.'" When the Estimate reached the Air Force Chief of Staff, General Hoyt S. Vandenberg on 5 August 1948, he rejected it, and ordered all copies destroyed.[11] Yet Captain Ruppelt states: "The estimate died a quick death. Some months later it was completely declassified and relegated to the incinerator. A few copies, one of which I saw, were kept as mementos of the golden days of the UFOs."[12] With this remark we come upon yet one more mystery in the continuing saga of a history of military encounters with UFOs.

9. Ibid. p.36.
10. Ibid. p.48.
11. *Aliens from Space*. By Major Donald E. Keyhoe. p.17.
12. *The Report On Unidentified Flying Objects*. Edward J. Ruppelt. E-artnow. No city listed. 2020. p.39.

While all copies of the Estimate of the Situation were reported to have been destroyed, we find that a man who was none other than the director of the renamed Project Sign as Project Grudge informing us that a few copies did survive. Moreover, while it was supposedly held to be top secret (but later declassified before it was "destroyed"), Captain Ruppelt at times obliquely reveals some of the report's contents. He says of the genesis of the analysis: "the situation was the UFOs; the estimate was that they were interplanetary!" (Punctuation in the original)[13] This is an important revelation of a key conclusion. Ruppelt also wrote that there were several other UFO incidents, including those just described and more, a few of which involved military planes pursuing interception and identification assignments that resulted in aerial games of "chicken," in soaring, rolling, turning, diving "dog fights" with the UFOs, which included some possible attempted or feigned ramming attacks by the unidentified objects.[14] Yet despite the fact that different, experienced, military pilots all described prolonged interactions with unidentified flying objects that often accelerated at high speed, engaged in complex maneuvers, and would streak past them, Ruppelt seemed ultimately to agree with official conclusions that all of these pilots had been fooled by lighted weather balloons.[15] (Really?)

In addition to Captain Ruppelt's information about the "Estimate of the Situation" we find the curious fact that the Air Force denied to UFO researcher Major Edward Keyhoe that it ever existed. But then former Major Dewey Fournet, who worked closely with Captain Ruppelt, affirmed in a letter to a UFO research group in 1958 that the Estimate of the Situation had existed, along with another report that Major Keyhoe had been seeking from the Air Force. In his letter Fournet wrote,

> At the request of Major Keyhoe I would like to confirm the existence of two USAF documents which were recently denied by an official USAF representative. They are: 1. An intelligence summary on UFOs prepared in 1948 by the organization which later became the Air Technical Intelligence Center at Wright-Patterson AFB. 2. An intelligence analysis on specific aspects of UFO data which I prepared in 1952 while acting as UFO program monitor for Headquarters USAF, Washington, D. C.[16]

---

13. Ibid. p.37.
14. Ibid. pp.37-39.
15. Ibid. p.39.
16. NICAP http://www.nicap.org/reports/eots_vitello-ridge.htm

Fournet also stated that with regard to the subsequent report, he further wrote: "The important point should be, therefore, that such a document had existed – not that it did or did not establish anything about UFOs." He evidently made this clarification because "Since both documents were classified when I last saw them, I am not at liberty to reveal their contents." This lattermost remark is a bit curious because Captain Ruppelt has divulged some of the contents of the Estimate of the Situation; but perhaps Major Fournet took his secrecy oath more seriously than Captain Ruppelt, or just decided that despite the Estimate of the Situation becoming declassified prior to its demise, his oath was still in effect, as stated in his declaration. Despite official denials, both Ruppelt and Fournet said they saw the Estimate of the Situation before it was dropped into the memory hole. However, we are not going to be left completely uninformed about the contents, or rather the likely substance of the Estimate of the Situation.

The Estimate of the Situation, in addition to those aspects of the UFO phenomenon that Captain Ruppelt described above, would likely have included information to be found in the summary of the Project Sign Report, issued in February 1949, regarding the different types of UFOs being discussed: "1. Flying disks i.e., very low aspect ratio aircraft. 2. Torpedo or cigar shaped bodies with not wings or fins visible inflight. 3. Spherical or balloon shaped objects. 4. Balls of light."[17] The report also states:

> The possibility that some of the incidents may represent technical developments far in advance of knowledge available to engineers and scientists in this country has been considered. No facts are available to personnel at this command that will permit an objective assessment of this possibility. All information so far presented on the possible existence of space ships from another planet or propelled by an advanced type of atomic power plant have been largely conjecture.

Of course, but I find it interesting that the summary states that such speculation of UFOs as extraterrestrial spacecraft was "largely conjecture," but not entirely so; but perhaps I am reading too much into the use of the words, or maybe not.

---

17. http://www.nicap.org/docs/SignRptFeb1949.pdf

The Project Sign Report goes on to say:

> Reports of unidentified flying objects are not peculiar to our present time. In *The Books of Charles Fort*, by Tiffany Taylor, published in 1941 by Henry Holt & Co., New York, similar phenomena are described as having been sighted during past centuries. In the last war, numerous sightings of "balls of fire" in the air were reported by bomber crews.

(Author's note: Originally, this book included a handful of incidents going back to ancient times; but, due to necessary publishing word limitations, these were omitted in favor of the many events having a more direct impact on modern military and other considerations. Those UFO sightings from ancient and medieval times had little to no relevance to military and related considerations of a lasting, influential impact.)

In its conclusions, the summary of the Project Sign Report states the unlikelihood of the ability to prove the existence of UFOs "without the examination of the remains of crashed objects." Also: "Proof of non-existence is equally impossible to obtain unless a reasonable and convincing explanation is determined for each incident." Here the summary does not state that there had been found "the remains of crashed objects," but only that proof of the existence of UFOs (as alien spacecraft) was not possible without the admission of facts into evidence after "examination of the remains," which makes this doubtful (or cynical) observer suspect that the writers of the document were having a bit of fun with those of us who are not in the know while also giving a wink and a nod toward those who do know, but do not say. With regard to the lattermost: "a reasonable and convincing explanation … for each incident" certainly cannot be found in either official government statements or press "coverage" due to the fact that so many attempts to explain away UFO incidents are absurd on first hearing. Moreover, "unexplained" reports in general overall amount to about 20 per cent of the total even by official estimates, which are heavily skewed toward "explanations," no matter how ridiculous they are in fact.

In the main body of the Project Sign Report, and in an appendix, the possibility that UFOs could be extraterrestrial spacecraft is not sincerely explored but is instead somewhat arrogantly dismissed by a "scientist" who accurately describes Mars and Venus as being unsuitable for life (as we now know it), then asserts that interplanetary travel within our solar system is given the odds of 1,000-to-1 against (which we Earthlings are now engaged in with probes, and likely no-too-distant future trips by humans again to the moon, and beyond). He further explains that based on our then (1949) human knowledge, interstellar travel just would not work either, and he concludes with the ignorant statement that the possibility of UFOs being extraterrestrial spacecraft will not be further considered. How "open-minded," "healthily curious" and "scientific" of him!

Despite the intention to dismiss UFOs being possible alien spacecraft, the Project Sign Report inadvertently admits it as the only alternative; in the section elaborating on the fact that UFOs seem to demonstrate a mastery of technology far in advance of what was available in the United States in 1949: other nations were ruled out, except the Soviet Union; but then the qualifier was added that almost all of the most modern technologies possessed by the USSR were copied from other countries – which would leave only the United States and, unlikely, the then defunct Nazi Germany. (Because the United Kingdom, France, Italy and Japan, among a handful of other technologically adept countries, were in severe economic, social, political distress or ruin following the war.) Moreover, the complete collapse of the Third Reich had left almost all of its state records – and secrets – behind for the Allied powers to seize and examine. Also, the United States had launched "Operation Paperclip," which delivered the majority German scientists, engineers and technicians who had worked on the most modern technologies for the Nazi regime to America to develop advanced aeronautical and space research applications in the United States. Therefore, we knew the Russians could not create such technologies, could be sure the Germans had not, were certain the West did not possess them, which to me left only the extraterrestrial possibility intact. (I am excluding the interdimensional and time-travel hypotheses as too improbable and lacking in sufficiently strong evidence, barring future changes of facts.)

It is curious that the report mentioned a crash of a UFO as providing confirming evidence as a hint that such an event was postulated, or even known about, behind the scenes; of course I am speculating here, but the conjecture is based on what I believe is the compelling evidence presented by dozens of known witnesses to the Roswell UFO crash, as revealed to us by retired Lieutenant Colonel Kevin D. Randle and Donald R. Schmitt, among others now.

Also, if we harken back to the Twining letter we can recall the statement in paragraph 2.b. that "There are objects probably approximating the shape of a disc, of such appreciable size as to be as large as *man-made* aircraft." So, whether intentionally or not, General Twining was indicating that at least some UFOs are of about the same physical dimensions as "man-made aircraft," which leads, inexorably, to the conclusion that the objects in question were considered to be *not* 'man-made aircraft,' by which it logically follows that they are of some sort of alien, non-human origin. (To those who advocate in favor of the interdimensional theory: any beings from beyond our time-space continuum would also qualify as non-human. Time travelers could or might not be human.)

In addition, General Twining's opening statement that "The phenomenon reported is something real and not visionary or fictitious," already refutes the later Project Sign Report's suggestion that UFO observations can be invalidated by "reasonable and convincing explanations." (Actually, they were ill-conceived attempts to merely dismissively explain away.)

Captain Ruppelt stated that the attitude within the Air Force had suddenly undergone a reversal, and many were questioning why that was the case. He provided the response by illustrating the new outlook: "The answer was simply that the official attitude toward UFOs had drastically changed in the past few months. They didn't exist; they couldn't exist."[18]

Ruppelt went on to declare that the "drastic change in official attitude is as difficult to explain."[19] He wrote that everyone in Air Force intelligence chose sides between the extraterrestrial hypothesis (ETH) and the new view from on high that UFOs did not exist. Of the former he informs us, "These people weren't a bunch of nuts or crackpots either. They ranged down through the ranks from generals and top-grade civilians. On the outside their views were backed up by civilian scientists." Of the latter group who denied the existence of UFOs he reported, "many of them could see the 'I don't believe' bandwagon pulling out in front and just jumped on."

Ruppelt further wondered why the change was so pronounced; if there was a hidden reason for the sudden reversal; if the UFO investigations were going underground to keep them secret and, if so, why? Was it to prevent a mass panic? The switch in operating philosophy troubled the Captain as he speculated, "Maybe I was just playing the front man to a big cover-up … if somebody up above me knew that UFOs were really spacecraft, I could make a big fool out of myself if the truth came out."

Captain Ruppelt further analyzed the situation: the Twining letter asserting that UFOs were real meant that the intelligence people were suddenly committing themselves to the belief that they were not real, which could not as yet be proven. Senior officers were becoming uneasy, and the press and public were demanding answers that the people in intelligence did

18. *The Report On Unidentified Flying Objects*. Edward J. Ruppelt. E-artnow. No city listed. 2020. p.47.

19. Ibid. p.48.

not have, despite another year and a half of effort. They tried floating the "Estimate of the Situation," which still failed to prove the extraterrestrial hypothesis, but that was kicked back. So they switched tacks to the "UFOs don't exist" line, which suited the top brass just fine, because: according to a conclusion I had already reached prior to encountering the same hypothesis that echoed among UFO researchers, UFOs could not exist because the Air Force was powerless to stop them.

I had already reached this conclusion and my reasoning dovetails exactly with that of others, although we have slightly differing takes on the "ignore the UFOs and they will go away" philosophy, so, to save space and time I'll just present mine: these strange objects came and went at will, violating our airspace whenever and wherever their crews wished. They engaged in odd antics, and potentially dangerous aerial maneuvers that forced pilots of more than one airliner or other aircraft, including military planes, to take drastic evasive action, causing injuries to crew members, flight attendants and passengers. Even without the injuries, the reckless "games" of "chicken" caused stressful moments for air crews – civilian and military – as, again, pilots climbed, twisted, dove, rolled and turned in efforts to avoid collisions with UFOs. Here was the United States Air Force, just created and hungry for enough in the way of tax dollars to meet the new Soviet threat, with just one job – control of the air; and the USAF could not do it, and didn't know how to do it because they had no idea with what they were dealing. The best course, for careers and the service itself, was just to explain as many UFOs away as possible, leaving the remainder for future explaining away when "more facts were known." In Captain Ruppelt's words, "UFOs don't exist." From that point on, instead of the old answer of "We think they are real, but can't prove it," the new reply became "It was a balloon."

Unfortunately for the Air Force, the UFOs would not always cooperate.

Why Don't They Land on the White House Lawn? They Almost Did, in 1952

For a summary of what happened in the skies above Washington, D.C. in 1952, I will rely once more on the report by Captain Edward J. Ruppelt, who was director of Project Blue Book that year.

The month of June and the first three weeks of July were very active as far as UFO sightings and attempts at interceptions by military jets were concerned in the state of Virginia and the outer reaches of Washington, D.C. Then, at 11:40 p.m. on the night of 19 July 1952, at one of the three radar stations regulating air traffic for the area around the nation's capital, several radar returns intensified the Washington, D.C. UFO wave.[20] These were on both of the radars at Washington National Airport, now known as Ronald Reagan Washington National Airport, in Arlington, Virginia. When several civilian airliners in the area were contacted, their crews confirmed mysterious lights in the skies at the same locations as the radar echoes; so jet fighters were called in.

Three miles east of Washington National was Bolling AFB, and 10 miles farther east was Andrews AFB. All four of the radars (Washington National had two – one with a 100-mile range; the Air Forces bases' and the remaining airport radars were all short-range units) were linked via an intercom system. At first, seven targets appeared on a screen being monitored by one operator who watched as the UFO cruised at between 100 and 130mph, then zipped away at very high speed. No aircraft were expected in the area, so he shouted to his supervisor, who also called over other radar observers; they all agreed that the on-screen blips could not be airplanes – because of their extreme maneuvers and high velocities. A technician was summoned, and the unit was certified as being in good working order.[21]

Airline pilots were radioed again, and two affirmed observing lights at the same locations where radar echoes were seen; others did not admit to seeing anything, "but the senior [air] controller knew airline pilots and knew that they were very reluctant to report UFOs."[22]

After UFOs played tag with an airliner, and other air crews confirmed visual observations of the radar targets, controllers at the Washington National tower asked that military jets investigate. For some reason, the first request produced no results; but a fighter was finally dispatched as daylight approached, and the military pilot failed to see anything unusual in the skies.

Captain Ruppelt admitted that in processing the UFO reports of 19–20 July the investigation, reporting and response had not been handled well by the Air Force. He and USAF intelligence officers had learned most of the early information from the press and had little to nothing to add. Worse, Ruppelt himself had been denied any funds or transportation assets to investigate in the Washington, D.C. area, so he returned to his PBB base office at Wright-Patterson AFB near Dayton, Ohio. The entire government and Air Force bureaucratic infrastructure seemed almost paralyzed. In

20. Ibid. p.112.
21. Ibid. pp.112, 113.
22. Ibid. p.113.

Ruppelt's words, "To say the least, the sighting at Washington National was a jolt."[23] But there would be more to come.

On the night of 26 July at 10:30 p.m. – almost exactly a week to the hour since the earlier sightings – the same radar operators who had been on duty the previous weekend picked up nearly identical radar returns again; but this time they were arrayed in an arc extending from Herndon, Virginia, to Andrews AFB. The unit at Andrews also picked up the same unknown radar returns.[24]

At 11:30 p.m. jet fighters were requested; but again there was a delay. Just after midnight, two F-94 interceptors took to the air from New Castle County AFB in Delaware and were on the way.

Reporters and photographers who had been in the air traffic control center were ushered out on the excuse that classified defense procedures were being followed. Ruppelt commented that this was absurd as any good ham radio operator could build the equipment to eavesdrop on aircraft intercepts. He added that it was anticipated by some that this could be the historical event when Air Force planes finally closed with and positively identified UFOs for what they really were, "and [they] didn't want the press to be in on it."[25]

However, as the two F-94s appeared on the scene the UFOs immediately disappeared. No one could observe either a radar blip or make a visual sighting. After an optical and airborne-radar search for a few minutes, the jets returned to base. A few minutes after the F-94s departed, the UFOs reappeared on the ground-based radar screens. At the same time, people near Langley, Virginia, AFB called the tower there to report strange lights with shifting colors hovering above and over the nearby town of Newport News, Virginia. An airborne F-94 in the area was called in. The plane's radar locked on (*) a target. But the lock was broken when the UFO sped away. The pilot had briefly seen the UFO, but reported that it had almost instantly become invisible, as if a switch had been thrown. Over the next few minutes the jet's unit achieved two more lock-ons, but both were broken as the target quickly departed.

(* A radar set can have a search mode, sweeping the sky with its beacon, or some can be switched to a tracking function (lock-on), where the transmission stays on a certain target by aiming its signal at that specific radar echo.)

23. Ibid. p.114.
24. Ibid. p.115.
25. Ibid. p.116.

A few minutes after the F-94 searching the Langley and Newport News area had acquired its final radar lock-on, the blips reappeared on radar screens at Washington, D.C., but this time the images stayed on as interceptors returned. When pursued by the Air Force planes, the group of UFOs darted away – except for one. The pilot gave chase, and, just as at Langley, the light winked out. Ground controllers kept directing the plane, but the UFO continually outmaneuvered the F-94. The pilot of the pursuing jet later said, "I saw several bright lights." After about twenty minutes, the Air Force planes, low on fuel, returned to base. By then, daylight was approaching.

Ruppelt was advised later that the radar operators had also seen weather images on their 2-ft-wide displays but had ignored them. The radar observers were convinced the UFO blips represented solid, metallic objects.[26] Ruppelt wrote that he had recognized at the time that these solid targets could poke along at 100mph, then outrun a jet – an impossibility for weather phenomena.[27]

What is seldom if ever reported about is the fact that these were far from the only UFO incidents in the Washington, D.C. area at about that time. At approximately 8 p.m. the previous 23 May no fewer than fifty UFOs appeared on local radar screens; they were tracked until midnight. For four hours! On the Wednesday night between the Saturday-Sunday sightings of 19 and 26 July – which would be 23 July; again on the night of a UFO-related press conference by General John Samford, USAF intelligence chief (29 July); and on the following Sunday – presumably 3 August, but this

---

26. "Why doesn't weather radar display airplanes and other non-weather images?" https://wgntv.com/weather/weather-blog/why-doesnt-weather-radar-display-airplanes-and-other-non-weather-images/ Also: "temperature inversion images on radar screens"
https://www.google.com/search?source=univ&tbm=isch&q=temperature+inversion+images+on+radar+screens&fir=Fs0RE5kMOx-kzM%252CVFiya-spgqiOsM%252C_%253BiE1XhbGZzu-hvM%252C85gAdSfmnnxLdM%252C_%253BCxrv76_fTt8E9M%252CoFhN8ZBTyKW0XM%252C_%253BtzYYDA4a1eh1yM%252C6nC5MwZGCkpeTM%252C_%253BAuLV6QfDpN51FM%252C5QtGNa7lHYERWM%252C_%253BJKox_jXDlHy16M%252CjyTyyZYN_70VXM%252C_%253BLF2yvos65fTxLM%252CaasZX9OdnNI-uM%252C_%253BzAM7mTwkQRqLpM%252C8YmMxArxIgRUuM%252C_%253BhZLS3_6pTNjkPM%252CoFhN8ZBTyKW0XM%252C_%253BGmGUlLeiPx4HSM%252CApOMcCN2sKEcNM%252C_&usg=AI4_-kQRqx8ks_kVVR3OV0wdLXyFfHjOqA&sa=X&ved=2ahUKEwjS69Shkfj1AhV4l2oFHRBGCEgQjJkEegQIAhAC&biw=1309&bih=688&dpr=1.1
27. *The Report On Unidentified Flying Objects*. Edward J. Ruppelt. E-artnow. No city listed. 2020. p.117.

lattermost date was not made clear; and also during other times in August, 1952 there were eight more sightings. In many cases, civilian and military pilots made visual observations of UFOs in the same locations where the radar echoes showed them to be.[28]

While Captain Ruppelt also wrote that a few – a very few – people later changed their eyewitness accounts about some of the sightings, including the tower operators at Andrews AFB, he also observed: "I heard from a good source that the tower men had been 'persuaded' a bit." (Quotation marks in the original.)

At the aforementioned 29 July press conference, General Samford at times seemed at a loss for words regarding UFO reports as he groped for careful, measured, reserved language before settling on "There have remained a percentage of this total [of UFO sightings], in the order of 20 per cent of the reports, that have come from credible observers of relatively incredible things."[29]

Shoot-Down Order Re-Stated to Interceptor Pilots

Despite the 29 July press conference by General Samford, and General Ramey – who had also been involved in the Roswell incident – and assurances by the Air Force that UFOs posed no threat to national security, several newspapers reported on the same day as the press conference that USAF jet fighters were on twenty-four-hour standby alert with orders to intercept UFOs, attempt to communicate with them by radio, direct them to land, and if those orders were ignored, to shoot them down. Reproductions of the newspaper stories appear at the RoswellProof.com website. The newspapers include: *The Fall River, Massachusetts News*; *The Seattle Post-Intelligencer*; *The San Francisco Examiner* – all on 29 July 1952; and in *The Albuquerque Journal* on 30 July 1952. One of the items is credited to Barry Greenwood's newspaper clipping collection.[30] A link at that site reproduces an item from the *Charleston Gazette*, also of 29 July, which cites a release by the International News Service of the previous day confirming the shoot-down order, and also repeating the Air Force's insistence that UFOs did not pose a national security threat.[31]

28. Ibid. p.120.
29. https://www.saturdaynightuforia.com/html/articles/articlehtml/samfordpctanscript.html
30. http://www.roswellproof.com/ShootDown_INS_72952.html
31. http://www.paradigmresearchgroup.org/Charleston_Gazette-July_29_1952.htm

So, while intercepting UFOs – whether of an extraterrestrial or Earthbound nature; and inquiring of them, or directing them to land, under threat of the use of force – is a standard operating procedure, combining these potential actions with a twenty-four-hour standby alert and issuing new orders reiterating this policy indicates to me that the incursions above the United States' capital by unidentified flying objects that were likely extraterrestrial spacecraft was a tipping point, beyond which the United States was in a technical, if not formal, state of war against the UFOs.

There are numerous reports from various sources stating that pilots in the Soviet Union were also ordered to attack unidentified intruding aircraft. Of course, due to the secrecy imposed by the Soviet government, and re-imposed by the authorities in Russia today, it is impossible to verify almost all of these accounts. However, given the nature of the Soviet system, and in view of the traditional governmental tendencies toward official paranoia and aggression – often posited as "defensive" aggression – in that part of the world (central-western Eurasia), such a policy is highly probable. Therefore, despite the absence of documents or corroboration from official sources, I believe the few Russian and East European pilots who have been courageous enough to submit testimony that they were ordered to intercept and shoot down unidentified flying objects that appeared to be not conventional aircraft but likely artifacts of an exotic and unknown nature – or were potential alien spacecraft.

I do not see how it is possible to insist, as the USAF has for three-quarters of a century, that the radar images seen during the D.C. wave were the product of temperature inversions. (Temperature inversion images generally appear as slow-moving blobs; aircraft images are sharper, and faster than weather systems.)

Likewise, with so many of the most expert radar operators regulating air traffic and directing the air defense of America's capital, it is impossible for me to agree that these well-trained and experienced people were easily fooled by a weather phenomenon that is common in the region. Moreover, only the best pilots are selected to fly jet fighters – to defend not only the nation's capital but also the important military and industrial assets in the area. To disbelieve the testimony of such people makes no common sense. Airline pilots also make up a special class of people who are trusted with the lives of thousands of passengers each year; they, too, comprise a select element of aviation professionals whose eyewitness accounts must not be dismissed lightly, if at all. The same applies to military pilots making attempted interceptions and seeing the objects visually and on their aircraft radar. To conclude that the D.C. wave of 1952 was a case of unfortunate weather effects, incompetence, mistaken perceptions, lack of experience and poor training is not only an affront to many classes of dedicated professionals, such a stance also insults the intelligence of average people in the general public.

As should be obvious to one and all by now, I believe that the D.C. wave of 1952 was an occurrence of numerous UFOs behaving as if they were under intelligent control; even though their aerial antics defy an easy explanation as to motives and objectives. I am forced to conclude that the events in the skies above Washington, D.C., in July – and also May, June and August, if not other months not covered in this inquiry – reflect the activities of aerial objects not manufactured on our planet, whether they were piloted by alien beings on board, were operated by remote control, or acted as independently directed autonomous vehicles such as our most advanced drones of today.

Further, I believe the D.C. wave was so traumatizing to senior military and government officials charged with defending the airspace of not just the United States but the nation’s capital that they reacted out of shock, fear (including fear of disgruntled taxpayers and voters) and anger in deciding that if they could not cure the problem of UFOs, or hope they would go away by ignoring them, it was imperative to instead damage, ground, or destroy them. Finally, to declare that unknown aircraft violating the airspace around and over the capital city of the United States presented “no threat to national security” is completely ridiculous, which is why I, among others, am forced to ridicule Air Force and government officials making such absurd claims.

Over England, a UFO “Shoot-Down Order” was Radioed to a USAF Pilot

On the night of 20 May 1957, U.S. Air Force Lieutenant Milton Torres, flying out of RAF Manston, was ordered to intercept and shoot down a UFO.[32]

The story, widely reported in UFO literature, is also presented to us by the *History of Manston Airfield*, published 20 May 2021.

According to Ministry of Defence files released between October 2008 and June 2013, two F-86D fighter jets were scrambled from Kent to

32. https://www.manstonhistory.org.uk/usaf-f-86d-manston-ordered-fire-ufo-may-20th-1957/

intercept a UFO above East Anglia. The pilots were from the USAF's 406th Fighter Interceptor Wing, based at RAF Manston. Milton Torres, then a Lieutenant, said he was ordered by RAF ground controllers to intercept a UFO at 32,000ft altitude, and to do so at maximum power. Torres recalled, "Then the order came to fire a full salvo of [twenty-four] rockets at the UFO. I was only a Lieutenant and very much aware of the gravity of the situation." He continued, "I asked for authentication of the order to fire, and I received it."

After confirming the command and making adjustments to his armament controls, Torres scanned the sky as his plane hurtled toward the reported position of the UFO.

> The final turn was given, and the instructions were given to look 30 degrees to port for my bogey… There it was, exactly where I was told it would be … at 15 miles. The blip was burning a hole in the radar with its incredible intensity … it was the best target I could ever remember locking on to.

Torres added that as he attempted to close with the UFO it gained speed, then zoomed away. After landing, Torres said he was told "The mission was considered classified," and that he would be contacted by an investigator, who arrived the following day.

Thus, we have a confirmation by a pilot involved in the interception of a UFO that at least one direct shoot-down order had been given in the mid-1950s, in this case by the Royal Air Force.

Chapter 8

The (UK) Flying Saucer Working Party

A High-Level Association Urges Investigations of UFOs, and a Possible Landing at Broadlands

On 1 October 1950, the *London Sunday Dispatch* published a letter to its editor from Lord Louis Mountbatten, "one of the most powerful military leaders of the twentieth century."[1] In his communication, Lord Mountbatten cited the many reports from all over the globe about "some new thing definitely exists which is capable of flying at very slow speed or even perhaps hovering and accelerating at an unheard of speed several times the speed of sound."

Lord Mountbatten was a "British statesman, naval leader and the last Viceroy of India. He had an international royal family-background; his career involved extensive naval commands, the diplomatic negotiation of independence for India and Pakistan, and the highest military defense leaderships."[2] Lord Mountbatten was far from being the only member of peerage and prestige to be a firm believer in UFOs as a reality, if not extraterrestrial spacecraft. Yet he was not a "believer" in the sense of having an almost religious devotion with regard to accepting the UFO phenomenon as real (but which, in my opinion, has lately been proven as factual); he did believe, however, that the phenomenon should be the subject of a rational study.[3] Others who were enthusiastic about research to discover the secrets of UFOs included Lord Mountbatten's nephew, Prince Philip.

1. *Out of the Shadows: UFOs, the Establishment and the Official Cover-Up* David Clarke and Andy Roberts. Piatkus. London. 2002. p.59.
2. Britannica. https://www.britannica.com/biography/Louis-Mountbatten-1st-Earl-Mountbatten
3. *Out of the Shadows: UFOs, the Establishment and the Official Cover-Up* David Clarke and Andy Roberts. Piatkus. London. 2002. p.59. (Citing *Mountbatten: The Official Biography* Paperback – 1 December 2001, by Philip Ziegler.)

The Prince's military duties included being "on active service with the Royal Navy, commanding the frigate *Magpie*." In 2011, to mark his ninetieth birthday, Queen Elizabeth conferred on him the title and office of Lord High Admiral – the titular head of the Royal Navy.[4]

These distinguished gentlemen were part of a circle of aristocrats and military leaders who included Sir Hugh Dowding – mastermind of the brilliant air defense in the Battle of Britain; Sir Frederick Browning – British Army general; and Sir Arthur Barratt – RAF wartime pilot. As of 1952 this slice of the United Kingdom's upper crust had become convinced that our planet was under surveillance by extraterrestrial beings.[5]

In the case of Lord Mountbatten, in 1950 he started to amass a file of information relating to UFOs. He, along with government and military officials on both sides of the Atlantic, was concerned that UFOs and the belief in them could pose a threat to the West, either as secret Soviet weapons or just as part of a Soviet-inspired scheme to jam Western defenses with false UFO reports, allowing an actual surprise attack to gain headway before an effective response could be redirected.[6] Like many others who initially took the UFO phenomenon seriously, accepting the testimony of reliable witnesses eventually gave way to doubts as physical evidence seemed to elude investigation, and eyewitness accounts were questioned. He was also appalled at the unscrupulous schemers and confidence men who soon took advantage of the most gullible (and even, over time, experienced researchers) for personal gain. Then, retired British Army Sergeant Frederick Briggs, while working as a bricklayer at Mountbatten's Broadlands estate in Hampshire, reported that on 23 February 1955, a strange craft had briefly almost touched down there.[7]

The Broadlands Incident

The account is cited Timothy Good's work, *Above Top Secret*.[8] In that book, Good reported that Frederick Briggs had been riding his bike to a Broadlands

4. Britannica. https://www.britannica.com/biography/Philip-duke-of-Edinburgh
5. *Out of the Shadows: UFOs, the Establishment and the Official Cover-Up* David Clarke and Andy Roberts. Piatkus. London. 2002. p.60.
6. Ibid. pp.60-61.
7. The Royals and UFOs – Some tantalizing facts behind the hype. https://www.openminds.tv/the-royals-and-ufos-pt-i-669/9453
8. *Above Top Secret* Timothy Good, William Morrow, NY, 1988. p.40.

work site when he saw an object, "shaped like a child's huge humming-top and half-way between 20 ft and 30 ft in diameter." He said the incident occurred about 8:30 a.m. and that there was "an overcast sky and light snow on the ground." Briggs then reported that he dismounted from his bicycle and watched as a tube descended from the center of "the Saucer" where a helmeted, human-like figure in dark overalls stood on a platform within it. He further reported that the UFO was hovering about 80ft above the ground, which sloped away from him, and was at a distance of about 100 yards.

Briggs said that a bright blue light from one of a row of portholes seemed to shine in his general direction and at the same time he felt himself knocked over and held to the ground by some force as the cylinder withdrew into the craft. He said that after he had lain there "for more than a few seconds, he felt dizzy, as if he had been hit on the chin." After a partial recovery, Briggs described the incident to his supervisors on the estate, who had seen nothing.[9]

Lord Mountbatten took the report, and interviewed the witness while Brigg's wife and daughter were in attendance. Mountbatten went to the site, saw the tracks in the snow of Briggs' bicycle tires, foot prints, and the impressions where Briggs had fallen. Mountbatten then went down to the area below where the craft was said to have hovered, seeing only partially melted snow there. In his written comment, Lord Mountbatten stated, "Mr. Briggs was dazed … and worried that no one would believe his story." Mountbatten also wrote that Briggs had said that he had never believed in flying saucers previously and was amazed at the appearance of one. Lord Mountbatten said that Briggs seemed sincere and offered to deliver a sworn statement, but that Mountbatten did not think that step was necessary.[10] Did a UFO almost land at Lord Mountbatten's Broadlands estate? I don't know. There was only one witness, but a very credible source – Lord Mountbatten himself – observed that the witness seemed sincere. We could theoretically join in the many attempts to belittle Sergeant (Retired) Briggs's. account, but I will not do so. It is possible that a single witness could have had a delusion, was somehow mistaking another object such as a helicopter for a top-shaped craft, or was lying, but in a court of law I would give this man the benefit of the doubt and find that while he could have been mistaken, at the very least he was sincere, based on the estimation of Lord Mountbatten, who, due to his life experience, could be expected to be a very good judge of people.

9. Ibid. p.41.
10. Ibid. p.42.

Assuming this account is true, what could an extraterrestrial being have had in mind by making an appearance at the estate of a prominent member of the English aristocracy and military? Was the intention to be diplomatic, as in making friendly contact; sinister, as in an effort to be threatening or intimidating; was the purpose to embarrass and discredit a well-known person intent on investigating the UFO phenomenon; or was the event, if it occurred, merely coincidental? When analyzing incidents of potential political or military significance it is imperative to try to understand who and what are the driving forces behind actions. I am mystified about possible alien motivations, but, once more, I am keeping an open mind pending the discovery of new facts in this case.

Did Aliens, or Others, Try to Meet with Prince Philip?

This was not the only instance of a potential, if implausible, attempt at some "exopolitics" (interplanetary or interstellar diplomatic relations). Royal Equerry and later Assistant Chief of Air Staff (Operations), Sir Peter Horsley had a keen interest in studying secret military and government files regarding UFOs. Gentleman Usher to the Sword of State at Buckingham Palace, Sir Arthur Barratt introduced Sir Peter to a mystery man called "General Martin." Martin was of the belief that alien beings were here to warn us of the danger of nuclear weapons.[11] General Martin in turn brought Sir Peter together with a "Mrs Markham" in a meeting at a flat in Chelsea in 1955. He was shown to a second-floor drawing room on Smith Street, where he met a man identified only as a "Mr Janus." Janus asked Sir Peter to tell him all he knew about UFOs, and Sir Peter complied, then asked Janus what his purpose was, to which the mysterious man replied, "I would like to meet the Duke of Edinburgh."

This statement put Sir Peter on guard, and he told the man that arranging such an audience was far from simple and easy. After discussing esoteric subjects such as a possible extraterrestrial expedition to Earth to warn humanity of the perils and pitfalls of technological progress, Sir Peter went away with the strange feelings that Mr Janus was himself a visitor to our world. Further, the Royal Equerry reported the equally odd apprehension that during the meeting Sir Peter suspected that his thoughts were being

11. *Out of the Shadows: UFOs, the Establishment and the Official Cover-Up* David Clarke and Andy Roberts. Piatkus. London. 2002. p.71.

monitored and analyzed.[12] (As we shall learn later, this is not as outlandish as it seems at first, as our current level of technology allows humans to monitor brain waves and to analyze and harness them for medical rehabilitation and even attitude-detection purposes.)

While being acutely aware of safety concerns, Sir Peter nevertheless refrained from reporting the bizarre interlude to security organizations, based on his apprehensions regarding potential developments if he took that obvious step. So, instead, he consulted with UFO and ET believer Sir Frederick Browning. Browning wanted to meet with Mr Janus himself. Sir Peter attempted to arrange such a get-together, but General Martin was suddenly evasive and distant, Mrs Markham had disappeared; and when he went to the flat in Chelsea he found it empty, with neighbors reporting that Mr Janus had quickly cleared out.

Was this an elaborate setup by British security services to test the Royal Equerry? Was it some sort of weird plot by a foreign power or terrorist group? Could these people have been hoaxers, whether pro, con or in the middle of the UFO/ET controversy? Or, just maybe, could Mr Janus have been in fact an envoy from an alien civilization? Anyone's guess is as valid as my own; all the more so for those really in the know, as I am not. What do I think? Sir Peter was obviously being sincere, and I think it is more likely – much more so – that this was some sort of Earthly plot, conspiracy, operation or prank than the extreme unlikelihood that alien beings would take the time and trouble to haltingly stumble through such an awkward process to meet Prince Philip.

Yet another well-known member of the British elite also revealed his beliefs regarding UFOs…

A Member of Peerage Instigates an Official Inquiry

Lord Peter Hill-Norton worked his way up through the ranks from a junior officer in the Royal Navy until he "became Chief of Defence Staff, Britain's most senior serving officer, with the rank of Admiral of the Fleet, in April, 1971. His final active post was as Chairman of NATO's Military Committee from 1974 to 1977."[13] Further: "Enobled in 1979, Baron Hill-Norton became an active member of the House of Lords."

12. Ibid. p.72.
13. Britannica. https://www.theguardian.com/news/2004/may/20/guardianobituaries1

Over time, and while a member of the House of Lords, Lord Hill-Norton asserted in writing his belief that "there is an official cover-up of the investigations which governments have made of UFOs, certainly in the United States, probably in our own country though not in France."

With the interest in the UFO phenomenon due to well-publicized reports in the press, it is no surprise that in response to numerous accounts by the military and civilians of UFOs, the "Flying Saucer Working Party" was established in June 1950. Probably the primary motivating factor was the story of an RAF pilot, flying a Gloster Meteor, twin-engine jet fighter out of Tangmere, Sussex, who said he had seen a shining, rotating disc. A press report stated that there had also been a radar image, but the Air Ministry said that could not be (or would not be?) confirmed.[14] Newspaper reports asserted that "a curtain of secrecy" had descended on the subject.[15]

As for the Flying Saucer Working Party itself, it was chaired by the Deputy Director of Intelligence and included the major scientific and technical departments of the Ministry of Defence, as well as the Secret Intelligence Service, and the technical intelligence branch of the Air Ministry. The key component was the Directorate of Scientific Intelligence. Also represented were the intelligence branches of the Admiralty and War Office, Air Ministry consultants from the Operational Research section of Fighter Command, and the ministry's Meteorological Office. This was in response to a request by Sir Henry Tizard – who had been a prime mover in the development of radar, and who was very influential in Whitehall (Britain's "Pentagon"). Sir Henry had asked for "a small … working party,"[16] but, judging from the eventual membership listed above, the Flying Saucer Working Party was probably not "small."

The Flying Saucer Working Party final report, issued in June 1951, is short and dismissive, with almost no substantial information included due to heavy input by the USAF and CIA, which allowed for the holding back of all except very little of substance. In fact, the MoD held for years that no copies had survived; until uncovered by researchers (Dr David Clarke and Andy Roberts) filing disclosure requests.[17]

---

14. *Need To Know: UFOs, The Military and Intelligence.* Timothy Good Pan Books. London. 2007. p.148. Citing the *Daily Herald* and the *Daily Mail*, both on 7 June 1950.
15. Ibid. p.148. Citing the *Daily Mail*, 7 June 1950.
16. *Out of the Shadows: UFOs, the Establishment and the Official Cover-Up* David Clarke and Andy Roberts. Piatkus. London. 2002. pp.77-79.
17. Ibid. pp.80-84.

Meanwhile, across the Atlantic, both Project Sign and Project Grudge reached similar, inconclusive "conclusions" that most UFO reports could be "explained" (away), while analyzing a small sample of low-grade accounts – a single witness, no corroborating indications such as radar returns, lack of information, etc. – and resorting to simplistic and even ridiculous "explanations" that relied on discounting or ignoring witness testimony and other supporting evidence such as radar blips.

An example of this type of "investigation" in the UK was that conducted in the case of an experienced test pilot at the aircraft research facility at Farnborough, Hampshire. First Lieutenant Stan Hubbard observed a saucer-shaped craft on 14 August 1950. As if that had not been enough, on 5 September 1950, Lieutenant Hubbard was on a watch tower with five other airmen when another disc-shaped object appeared. A Scientific Intelligence team interviewed Hubbard at length, and did so separately for all of the witnesses to the second incident. The SI team concluded that in the first case Lieutenant Hubbard had been the victim of an optical illusion, and that in the second sighting all of the witnesses had been "influenced" by the earlier sighting.[18] One of the other witnesses, Wing Commander Frank Joliffe, in 2001 when he was finally presented with the subsequent official account, said, "The conclusions reached in the MoD report are ludicrous."[19]

18. Ibid. pp.87-92.
19. Ibid. p.93.

Chapter 9

More American Planes Downed

Air Force Jet Disappears While Intercepting UFO

For the facts concerning the following as they are known, I am indebted to The Computer UFO Network – CUFON.[1] The good people at that organization contacted the USAF, up to and including Secretary of the Air Force, for the official version of what happened.

On 23 November 1953, radar operations ground controllers ordered an intercept mission from Kinross Air Force Base, near the tip of Michigan's Upper Peninsula. The responding aircraft, an F-89C "Scorpion" two-seat interceptor, crewed by First Lieutenant Felix Eugene Moncla Jr, pilot; and Second Lieutenant Robert L. Wilson, radar observer, took off at 11:22 p.m., Zulu (Greenwich Mean Time), or 5:22 p.m., Central Standard Time.[2] I now quote from a report to CUFON by Colonel John R. Clapper, United States Air Force:

> Aircraft took off at 2322 Zebra (Zulu) 23 Nov 53 on an active Air Defense Mission to intercept an unknown aircraft approximately 160 miles Northwest of Kinross Air Force Base. The aircraft was under radar control throughout the interception. At approximately 2352 Zebra the last radio contact was made by the radar station controlling the interception. At approximately 2355 Zebra the unknown aircraft and the F-89 merged together on the radar scope. Shortly thereafter the IFF (Identification, Friend or Foe) signal from the Air Force

1. CUFON The Computer UFO Network http://www.cufon.org/ SYSOP - Jim Klotz. Webmaster - Chris Lambright UFO Reporting and Information Service. Director - Dale Goudie.
2. Ibid. From the Air Force unit reports up and down the chain of command found at the CUFON website.

> plane disappeared from the radar scope. No further contact was established with the F-89 … [Approximately sixteen characters followed by one whole line (of approx. eighty-three characters including spaces) excised] … An extensive aerial search has revealed no trace of the aircraft. The aircraft and its crew is [*sic*] still missing.

The cited communique tells most of the story; however, a key point was omitted, but provided to CUFON in another message by the office of the Secretary of the Air Force, which reads, in part:

> At 1847 EST, at the request of "Pillow" [a ground controller's code name], the aircraft descended to 7,000ft to begin the interception. Location of the aircraft was then approximately 150 miles northeast [this should be "northwest," as in the previous report] from Kinross AFB and over northern Lake Superior. At 1851 EST, the interceptor pilot was requested to turn to a heading of 20 degrees to the cut-off vector. After the turn was completed, the pilot was advised the unidentified aircraft was at 11 o'clock, 10 miles distant. Radar returns from both aircraft were then seen to merge on "Pillow's" radar scope. The radar return from the other aircraft indicated it was continuing on its original flight path, while the return from the F-89 disappeared from the GCI (Ground Control Intercept) station's radar scope.
>
> The unknown aircraft being intercepted was a Royal Canadian Air Force Dakota (C-47), Serial No. VC-912, flying from Winnipeg to Sudbury, Canada. At the time of interception, it was crossing Northern Lake Superior from west to east at 7,000ft.

This set of official reports seems to make the analysis of the situation straightforward and clear, and they do just that – up to a point, and that point is where the objects seemed to merge; but one continued on. Major Donald E. Keyhoe, in his book, *Aliens from Space*, informs us that the USAF contacted Lieutenant Moncla's widow and told her that her husband had closed with and identified the UFO as a Canadian airliner before Lieutenant Moncla experienced vertigo and crashed.[3] Keyhoe further wrote

3. *Aliens from Space* By Major Donald E. Keyhoe. p.202.

that the Air Force later said the airline company in question had denied the report; so, according to the retired Marine Major, the Air Force then asserted that Moncla's plane had exploded at "high altitude" (actually only 7,000ft). Keyhoe stated that after that, "a headquarters spokesman, Major William T. Coleman, said the F-89 had intercepted a Royal Canadian Air Force transport – presumably the same one mentioned in the CUFON record above; and, according again to Keyhoe, the lattermost version was given out over a year later.[4] However, Major Keyhoe, who was a senior official for the National Investigations Committee on Aerial Phenomena (NICAP), further stated that when his group queried the RCAF, that military organization denied that any such flight had taken place on that date.[5]

We have in this case a fairly convincing set of official U.S. Air Force reports, followed by some counter-assertions by the former head of a UFO advocacy group; however, writer Darryn King of history.com seems to bolster Keyhoe's argument with a story at that website from 7 January 2020: "This Air Force Jet Was Scrambled to Intercept a UFO—Then Disappeared. The Air Force offered the pilot's widow conflicting explanations."[6]

After the above photo caption, the story at History.com continues: "The night an Air Force jet mysteriously disappeared over Lake Superior—November 23, 1953—was a stormy one. The Air Force flip-flops in its explanation.

"The Air Force's official news release about the disappearance, delivered to the Associated Press, stated that the vanished jet 'was followed by radar until it merged with an object 70 miles off Keweenaw Point in upper Michigan.'" The statement appeared in a story in the *Chicago Tribune* with the headline, 'Jet, Two Aboard, Vanishes Over Lake Superior.'"

> The Air Force soon retracted the statement and changed its story. According to the new statement, the ground-control radar operator had misread the scope … the F-89 had successfully completed the mission, intercepting and identifying the UFO as a Dakota—a Royal Canadian Air Force C-47 aircraft—flying some 30 miles off course. Lieutenant Moncla, probably stricken with vertigo, crashed into the lake during the return to base. Canadian officials refuted the account—no flights had taken place in the area that night.

4. Ibid. pp.202-203.
5. Ibid. p.203.
6. https://www.history.com/news/ufo-fighter-jet-disappears-over-lake-superior-kinross-incident

The History.com account then goes on to quote Keyhoe, as I did above. However, yet again … wait, there's more …

The NICAP page coverage – accessed 9 February 2022, in a report by Richard Hall, in an item produced by Francis Ridge, says that both radar blips disappeared, yet the Air Force version shown above contended that the UFO continued on without changing course. The NICAP page describes the weather that fateful evening: "There were several layers of scattered clouds (one with bottoms at 5,000 to 8,000ft) and some snow flurries in the general area. Official records state, however, that the air was stable and there was little or no turbulence."[7] These relatively mild atmospheric conditions are confirmed in the numerous documents posted by CUFON.[8] The Air Force records displayed by CUFON also confirm that Moncla and Wilson's F-89 had passed inspection certification and re-checking after being scrambled earlier that same day, and that the flight crew described no problems with the plane.

The NICAP page further states:

> In answer to queries from … NICAP in 1961 and again in 1963, RCAF spokesmen denied that one of their planes was involved. Squadron Leader W.B. Totman, noting that the C-47 was understood to be on a flight plan over Canadian territory said, 'this alone would seem to make such an intercept unlikely.'[9]

A well-known UFO habitual debunker accepted the Air Force's vertigo story, adding that radar operators were fooled by atmospheric conditions (which were cold, gloomy, and with light snow, but without turbulence, as cited above) and saw a "phantom image." (Here we have a professional debunker asserting more expertise than experienced Air Force radar operators.)

While the NICAP account is mistaken in claiming both radar images disappeared – according to the Air Force – Hall and Ridge cite some unanswered questions, including: "If [the debunker's] explanation is accepted and there was no actual intercept, why did the Air Force invoke a Canadian C-47, which RCAF spokesmen later stated was not there?" Further, the NICAP page concludes with the observation: "No intelligence document has yet surfaced that reports the radio communications between

7. http://www.nicap.org/reports/kinross.htm
8. http://www.cufon.org/
9. http://www.nicap.org/reports/kinross.htm

the pilot and radar controllers, and what each was seeing. Without this information, it is impossible to evaluate the 'true UFO' versus the false radar returns and accidental crash explanations." Indeed, and this problem permeates the entire field of ufology. However, in one of the official Air Force reports delivered to CUFON we find: "At approximately 2355 Zebra the unknown aircraft and the F-89 merged together on the radar scope. Shortly thereafter the IFF signal disappeared from the radar scope. No further contact was established with the F-89. [Approximately sixteen characters followed by one whole line (of approx. eighty-three characters including spaces)] excised)." So, "approximately" ninety-nine characters from the actual official record were excised by the Air Force. Perhaps there is pertinent information therein, or maybe not; but, once again, there is more …

In an effort to explore the Moncla-Wilson disappearance from more than one or two angles, I ran across some interesting information at the website "UFO*BC." There, in an item by Gord Heath, I found that he had contacted a serious UFO researcher, Dr Richard Haines. Gord credits the good man: "Mr. Haines was kind enough to search through his files for relevant information which he photocopied and mailed to me."[10] That information involved some fascinating press reports, including "a copy of a newspaper article printed in the *Sault Star* on October 30, 1968." The article was headlined "Do aircraft parts belong to missing F-89?" The news then was that a pair of prospectors had found aircraft debris in the woods near Cozens Cove, Alona Bay, on the eastern shore of Lake Superior. The article explained that the wreckage had been found the day before the prospectors' discovery by the Ontario Provincial Police, who had been to the site and had gathered and taken away an aircraft tail section. Later inspection discovered that the tail section was fashioned from heavier metal for most aircraft, indicating that it had been from a jet plane.

Mr Heath said the news item piqued his curiosity, so he contacted Transport Canada to inquire about any possible positive identification of the wreckage with regard to a particular aircraft. He was told the agency had no records regarding the debris in question. Heath said he thought that if the aircraft parts had come from a private or commercial plane, then Transport Canada would have information on file about the crash. He further deduced that since this was not the case, it suggested the debris was very likely from a military aircraft. When Heath submitted an "Access to Information"

10. https://www.ufobc.ca/kinross/otherAccounts/aircraftParts.html

request, he was informed that the Department of National Defence had no records concerning the wreckage.

Heath went on to further note that it was very odd that both the agency required to look into civilian aircraft mishaps and the DND – charged with investigating military airplane crashes – had no information concerning physical evidence indicating that a plane had gone down in the area. Heath wondered if there had been a failure by one or both agencies to investigate, or whether they had in fact conducted a probe and then classified the information as secret. He also put forth the possibility that the relevant government files had been "lost," or "misplaced."

Heath also posted two other news items that he had uncovered while performing research at the Sault Sainte Marie, Ontario public library in 2004. The first of these articles appeared on 31 October 1968. The article states that a vertical stabilizer from a military jet had been found, and that a Major J.H. Parker, of Kincheloe Air Base (formerly Kinross AFB) had positively identified the wreckage as such. However, the news item concludes that it "appeared unlikely" that it was from the missing F-89 Scorpion. Yet, as Heath points out, it is not stated exactly why or how it was that the Moncla-Wilson aircraft had been eliminated from further consideration.

In a *Sault Daily Star* article of 31 October 1968, writer Richard Plaunt speculated that the "Parts of plane found may be any of seven lost." However, in the article (which is rife with factual and typographical errors) it is revealed that almost all of the seven missing aircraft went down on land, not in Lake Superior, and some of these crashes occurred in Michigan, and Lake Huron. The two incidents that could be related involved T-33 military trainer aircraft. However, a tail section should reveal identification markings, or if those had been eroded away, then the numerous manufactured components would have disclosed serial numbers which could have been backtracked to their source, and then forward to which aircraft they eventually became a part. This was partially ceded near the end of the article in a short paragraph, which read: "No paint was left on the section but flecks of yellow primer paint were apparent. An unexplainable maroon color could also be seen which could have been a second color changed by the weather, or by heat." The final sentence of the quoted follow-up news item again made a concluding statement without supporting facts: "Earlier there was some conjecture it could have been wreckage from an F-89 Scorpion interceptor downed in 1953 but this later appeared unlikely."

After relying on serious historians, ufologists, dedicated researchers, and official sources, I decided to do a little digging on my own.

The lost jet and its missing crew disappeared from view just about in the middle of Lake Superior, approximately 70 miles off the tip of Keweenaw Peninsula. I checked the patterns of the currents at some websites with that information posted by the National Oceanic and Atmospheric Administration.

The F-89 disappeared from radar screens near the center of Lake Superior, at Global Grid Coordinates 48° N 86° 49' W. Surface currents would generally have driven any floating wreckage north.[11] In November (when the jet vanished) and December, the currents at the surface would push everything toward the south.[12] Those two months showed stronger currents, with a swirling action just east and southeast of the point where Moncla and Wilson's aircraft went missing from radar screens.[13] What all of this lake-current information suggests is that there is an almost equal chance that drifting wreckage from the missing aircraft, whether floating or partially submerged, could have ended up on the northern, southern, or eastern shores of Lake Superior, with a much smaller chance such debris would have moved westward. Or it could have all settled to the bottom of the lake (this is very unlikely due to many parts being buoyant) and remained there ever since.

But there is yet another complication, which only occurred to me later: the wreckage discovered by the prospectors, while near a bay was "found in the woods," which tends to rule out the F-89 as a source for the debris. However, the aircraft tail section could have been from one of the missing T-33 training aircraft, or the F-89 if it plunged below radar coverage, and ended up crashing on land.

As is so often the case when investigating UFO incidents, the picture becomes obscured by government agencies, including militaries, conceding precious few facts while giving out a great volume of what is often irrelevant information and (as is usually the case) by a massive overreliance on excessive secrecy. However, to be fair, I feel compelled to include the Air Force's side of the story with regard to one aspect of the secrecy issue. Again, I am reliant on the research performed by CUFON, and now quote

11. NOAA/GLERL Great Lakes Surface Currents Map. https://www.glerl.noaa.gov/res/glcfs/currents/
12. NOAA/GLERL Great Lakes Depth-Averaged Currents Map. https://www.glerl.noaa.gov/res/glcfs/currents/glcfs-currents-avg.html
13. NOAA/GLERL Great Lakes Monthly Depth-Averaged Currents Map. https://www.glerl.noaa.gov/res/glcfs/currents/glcfs-currents-month.php?mon=11&year=2013

from the communication sent to CUFON's James Klotz from the Secretary of the Air Force:

a. The safety investigating board's analysis, findings, and recommendations are exempt from disclosure under the United States Code… and Air Force Regulation… Release of this information would have a stifling effect on the free and frank expression of ideas and opinions of Air Force officials.
b. The statements of witnesses giving unsworn testimony before the safety investigating board, as well as any direct or implied references to such testimony, are exempt from disclosure under the United States Code… and Air Force Regulation… In order to promote full disclosure, witnesses are promised by the mishap investigation board that their testimony will be used solely for mishap prevention and for no other purpose. This promise of confidentiality is made in order to encourage witnesses to disclose to the investigating board everything they know about the mishap even though the statements they make may be against their personal interest or possibly incriminating.
c. Information from the Life Sciences Reports are exempt… United States Code… and Air Force Regulation… Disclosure of this information would result in an unwarranted invasion of personal privacy. However, release of the factual portions of the medical data (Life Sciences Report) is made only to the next of kin and only upon their written request.

Release of these portions of the safety report, even though the report is old, would jeopardize a significant government interest by inhibiting its ability to conduct future safety investigations of Air Force aircraft mishaps. Disclosure of this information would be contrary to the promises of confidentiality extended to witnesses and investigators. There was no time limit placed on this promise, and such a disclosure could set a precedent that would result in a weakening of the process whereby the Air Force gathers and evaluates safety information in future aircraft mishaps. Witnesses and investigators would be less candid if they knew that at some future date what they said would be released outside of safety channels. The decreased ability of

> the Air Force to gather and evaluate safety information would result in the increased loss of aircraft and crewmembers and ultimately have a detrimental effect on National Security.[14]

In this case, what do I think? The Air Force itself admits that an F-89 jet fighter flew an air-defense mission to intercept a UFO. When the jet approached the object, the radar images of both the plane and the UFO merged, after which the jet's radar return (and transponder signal) vanished, while the other radar echo continued on its former course. It is possible that the jet could have flown below or above the object, and that the pilot could have lost control of his plane and crashed. This could also have occurred if the interceptor suddenly came upon the UFO – for example, if one or both were emerging from a cloud or a snow flurry at the same altitude. Lieutenant Moncla could have tried emergency evasive action, leading to a crash, or, both the plane's pilot and that of the UFO could have attempted to evade each other, but in so doing they may have mutually engaged in the same maneuver, such as diving, climbing, or turning in such a way as to accidentally collide anyway.

However, again, the UFO continued on its way and, upon completing the evasive maneuver, or at the least upon landing, the human pilot of an Earth-manufactured aircraft would have filed a radio or in-person report of the incident; but no such reports were made. Moreover, both the (incorrectly implicated) Canadian airline and the RCAF denied having planes in the area. While there is a chance that an aircraft engaged in smuggling, for example, did not file a flight plan and was not on a legally approved journey (in the manner of complying with air traffic regulations), it is a very small chance, particularly in the early 1950s when smuggling activity was at a minimum. Likewise, a pilot could have neglected to file a flight plan. Again, this is a very unlikely occurrence. More probable, in view of the hundreds or thousands of accounts by commercial airline and military pilots of UFO encounters – the vast majority of which have almost certainly been withheld from the public – the likelihood is great that the unfortunate Lieutenants Moncla and Wilson collided with, or were brought down by, a UFO, in this instance being an extraterrestrial spacecraft. In the event – provided that such a craft would have some sort of electromagnetic or gravitic/anti-gravitic force field to protect itself from space debris – such a collision would have left the extraterrestrial vehicle

14. http://www.cufon.org/

undamaged while the Earth-manufactured aircraft would have been heavily damaged or destroyed. This is what I think happened in this case. There is also the disturbing possibility that an extraterrestrial spacecraft's pilot, knowing that its vehicle was protected by a force-field shield, could have intentionally rammed the F-89, bringing the Air Force plane down while the alien vehicle continued on its way.

As for the debris found and removed by the Ontario Provincial Police, it seems to have, as in so many other cases, disappeared into the official memory hole of evidence that evaporates from public view with little or no explanation. To speculate: perhaps the paint or other residue on the salvaged tail section could reveal what, if anything, collided with the missing jet, possibly even exposing the fact that exotic metals or other materials adhered to the wreckage, providing some indirect "proof" that this incident involved an encounter with an extraterrestrial spacecraft. Of course, future discoveries could invalidate my conclusion that this was likely an accidental collision between an Air Force jet and an alien spacecraft, in which case my opinion will change.

Was an Air Force Jet "Shot Down" by a UFO?

Let us now take a look at just one military encounter with a UFO (or not) that did not end well for an aircraft crew, and was even worse for others on the ground.

I was informed about the Walesville, New York tragedy while doing some preliminary research for this examination on the internet and found out more in the book *Aliens from Space*, by Major Donald Keyhoe. So, I thought I "knew" the story; but, of course, with regard to the UFO phenomenon, things tend to get complicated. This became evident when I started doing some last-minute looking around as I began to write this section. That is when I came across an article by a heavyweight pioneer and UFO researcher – to whom latecomers such as I am are deeply indebted – Lieutenant Colonel (Retired) Kevin D. Randle, who threw more light on the incident, and added some contention, and a resolution to the puzzle.

According to Major Donald E. Keyhoe's account, just prior to noon on 1 July 1954, a United States Air Force F-94C Starfire jet fighter was directed by radar operators at Griffiss Air Force Base in New York state to intercept and investigate an unknown aircraft – a UFO. Keyhoe reported that when the jet approached the UFO, which he described as "a gleaming disc-shaped machine," the flight crew suddenly experienced extreme heat in the cockpits of their aircraft. Keyhoe wrote that the pilot was "stunned," and "gasping for breath" as he popped open the jet's canopy and, after seeing that his radar operator had safely bailed out, he, too, ejected from the aircraft, and they both parachuted to safety.[15]

However, the then pilotless jet continued on, gradually, then ever-more-steeply, arcing down toward the small town of Walesville, New York. When the plane fell to Earth it demolished a building, then struck a car, killing all of the occupants of the vehicle – a husband and wife and their two infant sons. Several people elsewhere on the ground were also injured.[16]

As the flight crew parachuted to a landing, a reporter immediately showed up and the pilot mentioned the extreme heat in the cockpit; but before he could continue an Air Force car arrived and the aviators were taken to Griffiss AFB. The press was prevented from further access to the pilot and radar man and, after the news story was published – remarking on the heat the airmen had felt – headquarters denied it, claiming engine trouble. This stance by the Air Force led to a great deal of friction with residents of the town, who recalled the many flyers who had stayed with their planes, some dying in the process, to prevent their damaged aircraft from falling onto local communities.

Keyhoe added later that because he investigated the crash in 1954 he was not aware until 1968 that the pilot said he had also briefly blacked out. The Major also contended that as of 1973, when his book was published, the Air Force report on the crash was still being held secret.[17] We shall return to Major Keyhoe's observations regarding this incident shortly.

Enter retired Lieutenant Colonel Kevin D. Randle, who during his army career served as helicopter pilot and intelligence officer, among other duties.

Lieutenant Colonel Randle tells us that he was dragged into the Walesville case through a miscommunication by two other UFO researchers – Barry Greenwood and Larry Fawcett – who Randle said had misreported him as the source of some information that should properly have been attributed to ufology giant Jacques Vallée. As Randle himself asked of readers at his blog, "Convoluted enough for you yet?" Then, after doing some further research on the Walesville crash, Randle (the renowned authority among students of the UFO phenomenon for his exhaustive studies of the then

15. *Aliens from Space: The True Story of Unidentified Flying Objects* by Major Donald E. Keyhoe. pp.26-27.
16. Ibid. p.27.
17. Ibid. p.28.

postulated crash of an alien spacecraft at Roswell in July 1947) relayed his take on the story.

Randle notes that the F-94 was already airborne when it was diverted to intercept the unidentified aircraft.[18] He then goes on to cite substantial errors by two others reporting on the incident: Otto Binder, writing in *What We Really Know about Flying Saucers* (1967) and the aforementioned Jacques Vallée. Randle informs us that Binder omits a material fact: that the source of the heat experienced by the interceptor's crew could have been from one or more faults in the aircraft itself and not necessarily, as Binder states, from a UFO attack. The other source cited is Jacques Vallée, who, according to Randle, reported in *The Edge of Reality* (1975) a book he co-wrote with J. Allen Hynek – another longtime UFO authority, "that *two* jets had been 'scrambled' to intercept a UFO." (Instead of, as Randle insists, just the one dispatched fighter plane, and who also states that the single plane was diverted while in flight, and not "scrambled," which is an emergency take-off by a crew and plane on readiness alert.)

Randle then goes on to inform readers that the co-authors Hynek and Vallée differed over the documentation of the case: Hynek said there was no documentation; but Vallée insisted, "Yes, it is documented. It was even mentioned in the *New York Times* the next day." This brings us to another complication in the story, as revealed by Randle: *The New York Times* did report on a wave of at least 1,000 UFO sightings in the Utica, New York area – on 2 July, not 1 July. An Air Force spokesman informed everyone that the reported UFO of 2 July 1954 was evidently a partially collapsed, large balloon.

Citing the official Air Force report, which was not released until many years after the fact, Randle informs us that, yes, Griffiss AFB controllers had diverted the already airborne jet to intercept an unknown aircraft at 10,000ft altitude. (A Mohawk Airlines pilot, reporting the next day, 2 July, had estimated the object to be at 20,000ft, and said that a light shined from it.) Further, while the interceptor was searching for the UFO, Griffiss controllers contacted the pilot of a second UFO. This (temporarily) "unidentified" aircraft, it was later discovered, was an Air Force C-47 cargo plane. Randle quotes the report as stating that neither the F-94 nor the C-47 experienced or observed any problems with the fighter jet's performance.

---

18. http://kevinrandle.blogspot.com/2009/03/walesville-ufo-jet-chase.html

Randle told his readers that there were "broken clouds" at different altitudes, which could sometimes obscure an aircraft, but probably not for very long as most of the sky would be visible at any one time. (He would definitely know this, in view of his military piloting experience.)

We are also informed that, according to the Air Force report, the original UFO was now in a traffic pattern, bound for Griffiss AFB. Meanwhile, the diverted jet had been vectored to intercept what had been, and possibly still was, an unidentified aircraft. While the fighter pilot was doing as instructed, an engine-fire warning indicator activated, and both crew members felt intense heat, and believed the plane was on fire. After idling the engine, pausing and unlocking the canopy, first the radar operator then the pilot ejected.

Randle explains that due to mysterious causes, the tower at Griffiss AFB was unable for a time to identify the C-47, or another plane also bound for their airfield. Randle theorizes that this is where the mistaken notion by Vallée originated about two UFOs. Further, Randle also reports that the belatedly released Air Force investigation revealed that the pilot of the plane that crashed had earlier that day been forced to repeatedly adjust the cockpit temperature settings, which indicates a possible problem with its air-conditioning, pressurization and heating systems. Moreover, the report states, according to Randle, that for unknown reasons the engine fire-detection circuit was faulty, and that the crew followed established procedures in executing a bail-out. In addition, Randle told his readers that the accident report also concluded that inspection procedures for engine fire-warning equipment required improvement. He also cites physical evidence gleaned from the wrecked aircraft that indicated there had been no on-board fires before the plane hit the ground.

Randle continues, and cites the fact that since the accident report had not been made public at the time Major Keyhoe wrote of the event, he had been forced to rely on supposition in his determination that the Walesville incident had involved a flying disc. (Despite the fact that no one, in any report other than Kehoe's I have seen, had imagined the presence of a metallic flying saucer.) Then there was the complication of the many UFO reports in the area the following day; but, as is too often the case, the Air Force assessment was that what had been seen was a large, plastic balloon, consistent with research and weather balloons, and its potentially deceptive appearance. (Recalling that the Mohawk Airlines pilot thought that "a light shined from it," which instead was likely a reflection of the sun.)

While the real tragedy here is the fate of the victims (who, Randle also observed, had been misidentified by Major Keyhoe).

This case illustrates the problem we encounter when trying to separate fact from fallacy when so much information regarding UFOs/UAP is, in the opinion of most observers, unnecessarily and excessively classified as secret. I do not mean to suggest that the public should immediately be made aware of everything. As Lieutenant Colonel Randle affirms, military accident investigators have "understandable confidentiality requirements." (As was stated in the communication sent to CUFON's James Klotz from the Secretary of the Air Force regarding the Moncla-Wilson disappearance above Lake Superior, which was reproduced earlier.) However, suppressing relevant information such as that contained in even the very sensitive accident reports for several decades is, by almost any measure, disproportionate. Randle also reveals that the accident report was declassified and released at the request of Jan Aldrich, who worked with the National Investigations Committee on Aerial Phenomena (NICAP).

Later, when the infamous Condon Report[19] performed what may have been a cursory "investigation" of the events above New York state on 1 July 1954, the finding was in agreement with Randle's assessment, namely: the first object was probably a balloon, and there was no "UFO" (as opposed to a failure to immediately identify one or two conventional aircraft) involved in this aircraft accident case.

However, Kevin Randle did not (quite) get "the last word" on the Walesville tragedy.

While the National Investigations Committee on Aerial Phenomena (NICAP) became defunct, its files remained and were preserved and updated by subsequent investigators. One of those people, Francis Ridge, disputed Randle's conclusions, and that side of the controversy can be viewed in full on the internet. In Ridge's reply, he challenges the idea that there was no engine fire, referring to newspaper coverage that cited Undersecretary of the Air Force James H. Douglas as having expressed his "sympathy and sorrow" to the affected families, adding, "preliminary reports indicate that a fire developed in the forward section" of the plane, and that intense heat in the cockpit forced the crew to bail out.[20] (I feel compelled to observe here that "preliminary" reports are sometimes in error.)

19. "In 1966 the Air Force sponsored a project, directed by University of Colorado physicist Edward U. Condon, to conduct what was billed as an "independent" study. In fact it was part of an elaborate scheme to allow the Air Force, publicly anyway, to get out of the UFO business." https://science.howstuffworks.com/space/aliens-ufos/ufo-government7.htm
20. http://www.nicap.org/reports/540702walesville_ridge.htm

However, in Ridge's rebuttal, the news account presented there also states an interesting fact: it specifies one Richard L. Carner as a "member of the Utica Astronomy Club," who viewed the mystery object through a 250-power telescope, allowing him to identify it as "a weather balloon."

Jan Aldrich, whom Randle acknowledged as being the person who persuaded the Air Force to declassify and release the aircraft accident report, also took issue with the retired Lieutenant Colonel.

In his telling of the story, Aldrich states, "It is obvious to me, but maybe I am an idiot conspiracy theorist, that the report was obfuscated." He goes on to write that the plane was on a training missions but was diverted to an air-defense mission, yet there were no documents to describe what that mission would have been; the narrative is that the crew was forced to leave the plane when a fire-warning indicator came on, but also that, according to the report, no heat was felt or smoke detected. Aldrich further points out that in other cases crews will stay with a failing aircraft to be certain it clears populated areas before they bail out; however, in Aldrich's words, "This portion of the narrative seems strange" because the Air Force did not fault the pilot, stating that he had "followed proper procedures" when, again according to the Air Force, the engine-fire warning light was later determined to be defective.

Aldrich declares that "Something is obviously wrong with this story," because if a warning light were the only indicator, the pilot would have stayed in the plane – with or without the radar operator – and that newspaper accounts state that there was a fire, not just in the engine compartment but in the cockpit. He then cites the Condon Report. However, the text from that document quoted is in error regarding the dates and times of the attempted interception – which had been a few minutes after 11 a.m. on 1 July and the observations of a UFO, which were made on the evening of 2 July. It is alleged that the UFO looked like a weather balloon; and that an Air Force officer said that if it were still being seen the next day, (which would have been 3 July), he would investigate. Aldrich parenthetically interjects: "I don't understand how any kind of balloon could stay in the area until the next day, or why the officer made such a ridiculous statement." (However, failing balloons can slowly lose buoyancy and stay aloft and remain in one area – due to counteracting winds – for not just hours but days. Also, the high-altitude Japanese "bomber balloons" of the Second World War had stayed in the air long enough to be wind-driven all the way across the North Pacific Ocean.)

Aldrich further relates that the Condon Report's coverage of this incident goes on to say that the F-94C in question – identification number 51-13559 –

then located and identified the C-47 by its tail number, which air controllers had placed at an altitude of 10,000ft; and that they then vectored the interceptor to investigate a second, low-flying unknown aircraft that was apparently making a landing approach at Griffiss AFB. According to his reading of the report, as the F-94 was descending the pilot felt the cockpit temperature suddenly increase, which caused him to scan his instrument panel, where he saw the fire warning light was on. He told the radar operator and idled the engine – effectively shutting it down, after which the crew ejected.

Aldrich then details what the Condon Committee's account said about the crash, adding that it explained that its information came from "the official USAF accident report ("Summary of Circumstances"), adding that "There is no Blue Book file because no UFO was involved." He also presents the Condon Report's "Conclusion: The first UFO was a weather balloon." There was no UFO involved in the crash of the interceptor.

I must now necessarily digress to explain that during this early part of the Cold War, fearing a Pearl Harbor-style sneak attack by the Soviet Union, the United States embarked on a crash program to set-up a network of radar stations to provide warning of incoming possible enemy aircraft – modeled on the world's first and foremost air-defense system developed and emplaced by Great Britain just prior to the Second World War, and which was responsible in large part for Britain's victory in the aerial Battle of Britain. However, building and installing that radar network took considerable time – years, really. So, in the meantime, the Air Force resorted to a system of civilian volunteers recruited into the "Ground Observer Corps." GOC people stood atop wooden platforms and watchtowers where, aided by binoculars, they could spot any potential intruders – "unidentified flying objects," or UFOs as they were to be known from that time forward. Upon spotting suspicious aircraft, the GOC volunteers would telephone communications hubs, known as "filter centers" to provide their code phrases and give reports, which would be passed on to Air Force air controllers, allowing them to scramble or divert planes to intercept the UFOs.

Returning to Aldrich's account of the concluding remarks in the Condon Report: at the White Plains, NY GOC Filter Center, an Air Force spokesman said there had been no GOC reports of strange aircraft; however, Aldrich points out, this is far from conclusive because almost all GOC stations were understaffed due to a shortage of enough volunteers to provide complete geographical or twenty-four-hour coverage.

To summarize, here are Aldrich's objections: the Condon Report insists there was no UFO; but the Air Force diverted the F-94 because of a UFO.

By the time the plane had crashed there were then two identified flying objects – IFOs (the weather balloon and the C-47.)

The report lists Leonard Stringfield as a witness. Stringfield had been involved with the GOC in Cincinnati at the time, and later went on to become a long-time UFO investigator and researcher. Aldrich speculates that perhaps Stringfield's GOC contacts in New York had reached him by phone in Ohio, and he may have relayed the information about UFO reports to the Air Force. Aldrich goes on to detail the printed press coverage, almost exclusively eyewitness reports – which, by my count, consisted of 1,053 words of precious newsprint in just one example alone – emphasizing the value placed on such testimony in what was the golden age of the newspaper medium. He then concluded:

> Something still isn't right. Blue Book should have had a hayday [*sic*] with this UFO that quickly became an IFO. But there is no [Project Blue Book] file on the incident. And the accident report is among those in the AF HQ Operations Top Secret files. Apparently the pilots didn't have time to bail out over better terrain. I certainly would not call this a successful bailout. And somewhere there are files, involving Leonard Stringfield, I bet, and the GOC, about what happened that day.

As we can see in our complicated and sometimes convoluted look into just one mysterious, UFO-related event, such situations are all too often far from conclusive – beyond all reasonable doubt. However, unfortunately, in order to sensationalize and to support a given position, too many UFO investigators, ufologists, UFO/UAP advocates, other writers merely interested in stimulating book and print or internet magazine sales will just recite an incident found in other written works or lists and promote them as if they had been carefully vetted in their efforts to depict the UFOs/UAP in a certain light, whether for, against, or somewhere in between. That is exactly where I find myself regarding this incident – somewhere in between.

I am inclined to accept Jan Aldrich's and Lieutenant Colonel Randle's take on the story; there are enough in the way of complicating factors (such as Air Force deception, as I learned about in researching this topic), mistakes, and indications of possible concealment of material facts by the Air Force and the Condon Committee – the former in being far too secretive, the latter with regard to referring to Leonard Stringfield as being a witness when, in fact, he worked with the GOC not in New York, or even in neighboring Pennsylvania, but at the far end of yet another state away, in Ohio. Why drag him into it without explaining the connection, if any?

While I tend to lean away from the Walesville crash as having anything to do with hostile action by a UFO, I am pulled back in that very direction by disturbing reports in other places of UFOs resorting to a "heat ray" as a weapon. Yet, despite those contrary indications, I agree with Jan Aldrich and Lieutenant Colonel Randle and, based also in large part on the input of the amateur astronomer who viewed the "UFO" through his telescope, identifying it as a weather balloon, as cited by NICAP.[21] It is evident that the Walesville incident was the result of a series of equipment failures and unfortunate coincidental developments that led to a tragic aerial mishap that had nothing to do with aggression on the part of a UFO – as in an alien spacecraft.

21. http://www.nicap.org/reports/540702walesville_ridge.htm

Chapter 10

A UFO "Attack" off the California Coast

Strange Events: Bizarre Incident Described in Uruguay

Having found contentions that the Walesville tragedy was the result of an alien attack are lacking in substance, it is time to look elsewhere for valid reports of the suspected use of heat or other energy as weapons by UFOs.

This next case was presented to readers in the United States by Major Donald Keyhoe. It involves a Uruguayan pilot of a private plane, but he evidently had been a former military man, and there are also two other tenuous but extant military connections.

Ten minutes after taking off in his biplane, on 5 May 1958, Carlos Alejo Rodríguez was flying past the Capitán Curbelo Naval Air Base (the first military connection – reflecting the apparent attraction of UFOs to Earth's military sites) when he observed at 3:40 p.m. local time a UFO about 2km (1.25 miles) farther out over the South Atlantic. He said it looked like a child's musical top (more or less saucer- or spindle-shaped). He stated that in his decades as a pilot he had never seen anything else like it.[1]

Señor Rodríguez, described in the initial report as a private pilot and paratroop instructor (our next connection with the military), also said he had experience in biplane-flight only, but he had flown them for decades. He told the Uruguayan Research Center for Unidentified Flying Objects (CIOVI) that within his enclosed cockpit he suddenly felt extreme heat, so he took off his jacket and opened the aircraft's window. Señor Rodríguez further declared that, believing he had been attacked, his plan then was to fly over to the UFO and bail out after crashing into it. (I have made this albeit indirect connection with the armed forces because Señor Rodríguez displayed military thinking in his planned response to perceived aggression.)

1. https://www.angelfire.com/va/CIOVI/Alejo.htm English Version.

His determination to use his plane as a ram is not quite as extreme as it seems, although it is a drastic action. (Some Allied – Royal Air Force and Soviet – pilots during the Second World War were taught how to "flip" German V-1 "Buzz-Bombs," with a wing tip,[2] or shred horizontal stabilizers on enemy bombers with their propellers; and that they could then, if necessary, safely bail out and survive while the rocket bomb or bomber crashed.)[3] Señor Rodríguez said that before he could accomplish his goal the UFO sped away.[4]

After taking his report, CIOVI investigators set up a second interview. Meanwhile, Señor Rodríguez achieved his lifelong goal of owning an all-metal monoplane. However, on his first take-off attempt in the unfamiliar aircraft, apparently not allowing for the need to attain the greater air speed required for an all-metal mono-winged flying machine before getting completely off the ground, he evidently tried prematurely to gain altitude and his plane immediately crashed, killing him. There would be no second CIOVI interview.

As is often the case in many preliminary UFO and other types of accounts, the initial information contains at least one substantial error: the CIOVI report stated that his aircraft was a Piper Cub; but that model is not a biplane, although it is constructed on a metal frame – with a metal covering for the Super Cub, or fabric covering in standard Cubs. Biplanes were also fabric-covered, but on a wood frame to save weight.

The UFO investigators in their later internet report self-criticize their own performance in conducting what they admitted afterward was an incomplete initial investigation.

In the self-criticism from CIOVI we learn that the organization had been founded just six days prior to the Rodríguez UFO incident. In their self-critique, CIOVI concedes that they erred in not contacting the Uruguayan naval air base for radar or other confirmation regarding air traffic in the area at that time on that date. After landing in Melilla at the Ángel S. Adami civil airport, Señor Rodríguez reported his observation to a Señor Piacenza, then Inspector of the Civil Aeronautics Directorate; but CIOVI investigators also failed to follow up with him either. Moreover, CIOVI neglected to contact that airport for any air traffic, radar or other information.

---

2. https://www.forces.net/heritage/wwii/how-spitfire-pilots-really-rammed-v1-bomb-out-sky
3. https://www.quora.com/Did-allied-pilots-in-WW2-ever-deliberately-ram-enemy-planes-ships-vehicles-or-buildings-after-being-shot-down-knowing-that-they-will-die-anyway/answer/Rustam-Muginov
4. https://www.angelfire.com/va/CIOVI/Alejo.htm English Version.

The CIOVI self-critique, published on the internet on 7 April 2008 by Milton W. Hourcade of Montevideo may now be viewed at the UAPSG-GEFAI website.[5]

However, not able to benefit from the half-century-later CIOVI subsequent report, Major Donald Keyhoe and others picked-up the Rodríguez story and published it as it was presented at that time.[6,7]

CIOVI went on to state in their 2008 follow-up that the case received worldwide acceptance and congratulations due to the described approximate saucer shape of the object, the heat-effects – which were by then recognized as a general characteristic of UFOs, and the fact that the witness was a seasoned aviator and parachute instructor.[8]

The CIOVI 2008 *mea culpa* concludes:

> [The steps] necessary to complete the investigation were never taken, and therefore the conclusion was rushed. Inexperience in the matter took its toll. The case therefore has to be classified as 'insufficient data' or perhaps as 'inconclusive investigation,' but not as corresponding to the observation of an Unidentified Flying Object.

Once more we find ourselves in a situation where a report and its effects, while publicized globally, may not be all that they seem at first, one way or the other. Yet again we must attempt to reach a conclusion based on evidence that is unconfirmed and therefore equivocal.

Personally, I lean heavily toward accepting Señor Rodríguez's word and keeping this incident on the list of likely actual events as far as an encounter of a (semi-) military nature with a UFO.

It is time to take a brief look at the Fort Itaipu story.

UFO "Attack" in Brazil

After an internet search, none other than UFO researcher retired Lieutenant Colonel Kevin Randle's blog reappears to yet again save us from being

5. https://www.uapsg.com/
6. *The UFO Evidence: (unidentified Flying Objects.)* By National Investigations Committee on Aerial Phenomena. Clayton Smith; Richard Hall. Washington, 1964.
7. *UFOs and Anti-Gravity: Piece for a Jig-Saw*. By Leonard G. Cramp. p.153. Adventures Unlimited Press. 1997. p.37.
8. https://www.angelfire.com/va/CIOVI/Alejo.htm English Version.

taken in by an exciting but completely unsupported story posing as reported fact.

Lieutenant Colonel Randle informs us of what he cites as an often to almost always little-known (because it is overlooked) aspect of events in southeastern Brazil in the de Beyssac sighting in the early hours of 4 November 1957. A cargo plane pilot, Jean Vincent de Beyssac, spotted a red light, which seemed to grow large. He turned his plane toward it, and the light suddenly grew even bigger, as if approaching. At that point the plane's automatic direction finder, right engine generator and radio all quit. The red UFO then vanished.[9] It is here that the UFO story is diverted – hijacked, really – and becomes much more dramatized.

According to a Dr Olavo Fontes Teixeira, later that night two Brazilian army sentries spotted a bright orange light that drew near, hovering above the Fort Itaipu military base. Up close, it was described as looking like a flying saucer bathed in an orange glow. The account says that as the UFO hovered the sentries were hit by high heat, injuring them. What follows in the dramatized yet poorly written account is the usual stuff – the base was locked down, all troops were sworn to secrecy, high-level Brazilian and even "North American" military officers arrived to investigate. Nice story, but there is no corroborating evidence, and all subsequent reports on the supposed incident, at NICAP and in Major Keyhoe's book, *Aliens from Space*,[10] and others, all trace their origin back to the same Dr Fontes, who did not, as it turns out, enjoy a reputation for complete dependability among reputable ufologists in Brazil.[11] So, without going into all of the details of this story, thanks again to Lieutenant Colonel (Retired) Kevin Randle, and also to investigator Edison Boaventura, we can accept as fact that the "Fort Itaipu Incident" never occurred. In Senhor Boaventura's exhaustive investigation it was revealed that neither the supposed victims nor any other direct witnesses were ever located, and also the imagined physical evidence (a partially melted and twisted rifle barrel) was never found; there was no documentation whatsoever of the fictional occurrence.

Taken altogether, we have a situation that ranges from ambiguous to doubtful. My vote is for the view that this incident was the invention of a single hoaxer.

In the case of the Walesville incident (thanks in large part to the observations of retired Lieutenant Colonel Kevin Randle), to me, the majority of the evidence leans away from a UFO using a heat ray on the

9. http://kevinrandle.blogspot.com/2016/06/fort-itaipu-and-olavo-fontes-revisited.html

10. On pages 26-27 (in my copy of the book, pages 23-25.)

11. http://kevinrandle.blogspot.com/2016/06/fort-itaipu-and-olavo-fontes-revisited.html

F-94 jet that day. This forces me to conclude that yet again by omitting material facts and/or misinterpreting them, some commentators have apparently misled their readers, whether or not they meant to do so, by overly dramatizing the events of 1 July 1954, or because they did not perform their own due diligence in looking a little bit deeper behind what others had written. They thereby unintentionally furthered a myth, causing others – including, I must admit, this writer at first – to accept as fact what may be at best a misunderstanding of the situation and at worst an intentional effort to sensationalize a non-event into something significant.

The story of the unfortunate pilot Carlos Alejo Rodríguez is slightly more convincing, despite the fact that the investigation was not adequately undertaken, and the tragic aspects of the story are saddening. In Señor Rodríguez's case, I am more inclined to accept his account, even with some of the more doubtful aspects such as his expressing a disposition and willingness toward taking an extremely dangerous course of action in evidently deciding to ram the mysterious flying object with his small airplane. (The irony being that many UFOs have simulated or attempted ramming attacks of their own.)

As for the Fort Itaipu incident: to me, again, it is an evident hoax by an insecure individual seeking to make a reputation for himself as, ironically, a reliable ufologist. Once more we all must thank retired Lieutenant Colonel Kevin Randle, and now also investigator Senhor Edison Boaventura, for exposing the truth.

UFO Zaps Missile Warhead Test off the California Coast

Former U.S. Air Force 1st Lieutenant Robert Jacobs attests that a UFO followed and then destroyed an ICBM dummy warhead during a test launch from Vandenberg Air Force Base – now Vandenberg Space Force Base – off the California coast on 14 September 1964.[12]

Jacobs made the announcement at a mock Congressional hearing at the National Press Club. The story was originally covered in *The Sun*, but merited enough attention for the editors of the *New York Post* to reprint the report on 21 October 2021. Jacobs said, "I was part of a US Airforce [*sic*]

12. https://nypost.com/2021/10/21/former-air-force-chief-claims-he-once-saw-ufo-firing-at-nuke-missiles-launched-from-secret-base/
Also: https://www.military.com/daily-news/2021/10/19/air-force-veterans-who-are-ufo-true-believers-return-newly-attentive-washington.html

cover-up. It was shaped like a flying saucer and was firing a beam of light at our [dummy, test] warhead.”

In his announcement Jacobs reported that he had been in command of a 100-person monitoring unit whose job was to track the ascent of a then state-of-the-technology Atlas-D missile launched from the Vandenberg test facility on California’s pristine Pacific coast near Lompoc.

The observation teams utilized high-speed and ultra-long-distance cameras to film every instant of the missile’s flight as it went up in a suborbital trajectory to the edge of space, where the simulated warhead was to separate from the launch vehicle.

Jacobs, later a PhD and professor at Bradley University, says that on the day after the test launch he was summoned to the office of a Major Florenze Mansmann where three men who announced they were from the CIA awaited him.

The former Lieutenant said Major Mansmann invited him to sit and then activated a motion-picture projector that displayed a film of the previous day’s test launch. Jacobs said the brief movie was an amazing film record in perfect clarity of the launch, which had been 160 miles away from the high-powered cameras set up on the mountaintops just inland from Big Sur.

Then the unexpected, as a saucer-shaped UFO followed the missile, which had reached a velocity of 8,000mph; the strange craft “homed in and fired four beams at the warhead.”

Dr Jacobs reported, “Then it flew out of the frame the same way it had come in. At that point the warhead tumbled out of space.” He added that it was then that the Major lit up the room and he and the three CIA men watched his reaction as Mansmann demanded to know, “‘[W]ere you guys screwing around up there (at [the] camera site?)’ I said, ‘No, sir.’”

“And he said, ‘What was that?’ and I said, ‘It looks to me like we have a UFO.’”

Professor Jacobs then reported that after his remark, “He escorted me to his door and said, ‘I don’t need to remind you of the seriousness of the security breach.’ I said, ‘No, sir.’”

But that wasn’t the end of the ordeal for the man who was then a young Lieutenant because as he left the room Major Mansmann leaned close and whispered so the CIA men could not hear while he issued a final threat: “‘Lieutenant, if you were ever tortured in the future, somebody has you up against the wall and they’re frying your privates with fire, you can tell them this: it was laser tracking.’”

Yet Dr Jacobs explained by noting, “But we never had laser tracking in 1964.”

Jacobs's final comment to the press gathered at the meeting was, "What we (several military witnesses to UFO incidents) are here today to tell you is this is a real event that is the most important event in the history of mankind. We are not alone."

Great story; but, it is reported by a single source who, despite the fact of his PhD and apparent pure service record, had initially no supportive information. But, is there now?

In the same story, Dr Jacobs also said that the film showed with "amazing clarity" how the missile went through all three stages of its powered flight, even from 160 miles distance. He further explained that the nose cone then opened to dispense radar-baffling aluminum foil strips – known as "chaff" – to interfere with enemy defenses by disrupting anti-missile detection and guidance systems.

I checked the Vandenberg AFB (SFB) history log: "Vandenberg SFB Launch History," posted on 23 May 2021, to find:

"Date	Launch Time	Vehicle	Pad/Silo	Comments
1964 SEP 14	Unknown	TAT/Agena D	PALC-1-1	AFSC launch. Quit Claim"[13]

We do find an Atlas (Agena D) launch on that date and at that place.

Next, located at the National Security Archive website is a publication titled, "USAF Ballistic Missile Programs: 1964–1966." Within is the remark, "In 1963 the ABRES [Advanced Ballistic Missiles Re-Entry Systems] program became a national effort to investigate the characteristics of the optical and radar wakes left by re-entry vehicles, the forces acting upon those vehicles and penetration aids including chaff,"[14] In this paragraph we confirm that the Air Force was indeed then testing chaff as a penetration aid for warheads.

The history of the ballistic missile program goes on to state, "[at] the end of 1964 two sites were being used for ABRES launchings. The Ballistic Systems Division decided in September of that year to transfer to Vandenberg AFB."[15]

The report continues with, "Large boosters, such as surplus Atlas missiles, hurled instrumented re-entry vehicles from Vandenberg toward Kwajalein Atoll." In this passage from a separate document is further

13. https://www.spacearchive.info/vafblog.htm
14. https://nsarchive2.gwu.edu/nukevault/ebb249/doc04.pdf p.32.
15. Ibid. p.33.

verification that Atlas launchers were hauling experimental "re-entry vehicles" (a euphemism for dummy warheads) toward the test range at Kwajalein Atoll.

The USAF missile test history continues:

> Activities within the ABRES program changed as new problems arose … for example … light-weight vehicles (warheads, as opposed to heavier spacecraft) proved their feasibility but also demonstrated their susceptibility to roll resonance … believed caused by uneven melting of the ablative shield – that set up vibrations capable of wrenching the vehicle apart. An inquiry into the causes of roll resonance and the ways it could be prevented became part of the ABRES program.

Here we find that "uneven melting" of the heat shield could cause the warhead package to vibrate, roll and tear apart. Perhaps such uneven melting could be the result of being hit by some sort of high-energy electromagnetic ray, as Dr Jacobs said happened during one of these tests.

The same report later goes on to summarize the four basic causes of missile booster and warhead failures:

> prompt gamma rays, neutrons, electromagnetic pulse, and "soft" and "hot" X-rays. Prompt gamma rays emanating from nuclear blasts introduced currents that caused false guidance signals, while neutrons could damage the components of electronic subsystems. Electromagnetic pulses burned out wires and transistors by causing violent surges of electrical current that might also confuse the guidance system. Soft X-rays could cause the peeling or buckling of heat shields. Hot X-rays could vaporize a heat shield, erase memory drums that carried arming information, or burn out circuits within the vehicle and thus cause false guidance commands. During 1965–1966 the Air Force was most concerned with protection against hot X-rays which, when caused by nuclear bursts outside the atmosphere, were believed effective for hundreds of kilometers.[16]

16. Ibid. pp.39, 40.

In this paragraph we find a clue as to what type of "rays" could cause a missile test (or actual) warhead to tumble and be destroyed as it re-entered Earth's atmosphere: "soft X-Rays" and "hot X-Rays." The major suspected culprit here to me would be "soft X-Rays," which "could vaporize (in whole or part) a heat shield." This lends added credence to Dr Jacobs's story because just a relatively short set of bursts from a "milder" form of X-radiation could have caused the destruction of the test vehicle as Dr Jacobs described. We will get back to other methods of interference, damage or destruction later.

Based not just on the testimony of a witness whom I consider very credible, a couple of short searches on the internet have quickly uncovered if not confirming evidence then at least corroborative indications convincing me that, yes, an alien spacecraft did indeed interfere with one of our weapons systems tests. The remaining question in my mind is whether the aliens were issuing some sort of warning regarding the danger of our arms races or were showing off their ability to render ineffective efforts on our part to resist the extraterrestrials' programs.

Discounting the Walesville crash as a tragic accident not caused by a UFO, and dismissing the hoaxed event in Brazil, and even if we disbelieve the story of Señor Rodríguez concerning the supposed wave of heat he felt, causing him to contemplate a kamikaze-style attack on a UFO, I cannot disbelieve the testimony of former 1st Lieutenant and later Dr Robert Jacobs. It is not only likely but probable that, given the extraterrestrials' apparent mastery of electromagnetic forces and waves, they do have access to at least one high-energy electromagnetic ray in their potential arsenal. The reality of such a weapon is borne out by the fact that we humans have also developed heat rays utilizing microwave energy to, for example, disperse unruly crowds, and for combat applications.[17]

17. https://interestingengineering.com/us-militarys-active-denial-system-is-a-95-ghz-heat-ray

Chapter 11

A Prime Minister, and a President, "Kept in the Dark"

Operation Mainbrace

In September 1952, an international force from eight NATO nations, plus New Zealand, held exercises in the North Sea off the coasts of Norway and Denmark. Known as "Operation Mainbrace," it included 200 ships, 1,000 planes and 80,000 personnel. The operation began on 13 September 1952 and was under the command of British Admiral Sir Patrick Brind. It had been the largest of NATO drills conducted by then so far.[1]

The first night of maneuvers the Danish destroyer *Willemoes* was cruising north of Bornholm Island in the western Baltic when Lieutenant Commander Schmidt Jensen and several crew members spotted a triangular UFO. It streaked past toward the southeast, emitting a blue glow. Commander Jensen estimated its speed at over 900mph.

On 20 September a news reporter and photographer aboard the aircraft carrier USS *Franklin D. Roosevelt* was shooting color photos of a plane taking off when his attention was drawn to a group of pilots and sailors near the ship's fantail. He went there and they observed a large, silvery sphere flitting along behind some other ships. He took several photos, which were inspected by naval intelligence, but never released to the public. Judging from the rate of progress between each photo, it was estimated that the object was moving very rapidly. A check with all ships found that no weather balloons had been launched.[2]

The following day, six RAF pilots flying their planes in formation over the North Sea spotted a shiny, spherical object coming from the direction

1. http://www.nicap.org/ncp/ncp-mainbrace.htm
2. *The Report On Unidentified Flying Objects* Edward J. Ruppelt. E-artnow. No city listed. 2020. p.137.

of the Mainbrace fleet. They pursued it, but it sped away. Then, one of the pilots noticed the object was following his plane, a jet-powered Gloster Meteor, so he turned toward it, but the UFO outdistanced pursuit once more.

The next day, 22 September a UFO was detected above (RAF) Topcliffe Aerodrome, and another twin-engine Meteor jet was scrambled to chase it. That pilot radioed back that the object was "round, silvery and white," and that it seemed to rotate vertically with a wobble. Before he could close it accelerated away. Captain Ruppelt reported, "It was these sightings, I was told by an RAF exchange intelligence officer in the Pentagon, that caused the RAF to officially recognize the UFO."[3]

However, despite the official recognition, the RAF seemed not to take either the public or even its flight crews all that seriously with regard to sharing the facts, or even affirming the existence of UFO reports. Case in point: in the skies above and near the Central Flight School, RAF Rissington, one month later, 21 October 1952, Flight Lieutenant Michael Swiney was instructing student pilot Royal Navy Lieutenant David Crofts in a Gloster Meteor VII jet when, just ahead, he saw three round objects. Thinking they were parachutists, he took control of the plane from his student and immediately pitched it into a tight, climbing turn. When the Meteor rose to the same level as the round objects they seemed to flatten into saucer shapes.[4]

According to Air Marshal Sir Peter Horsley, Swiney radioed Rissington ground control; he was ordered to pursue the UFOs. Swiney intercepted at full power, reaching Mach 0.8 (613.815mph), and flew at one of the UFOs until it grew to about the size of a dinner plate on his windscreen. Then, the object seemed to stand on its side, and sped away.[5]

Meanwhile, radar operators at Rissington simultaneously alerted Fighter Command and Air Traffic Control at Gloucester. Two Meteors on twenty-four-hour standby alert were scrambled from RAF Tangmere in Sussex, under the control of radars at Rudloe Manor, Wiltshire. The planes gave chase, but the UFOs disappeared over the Atlantic.

Sir Peter said the RAF launched an investigation, interrogating the flight crews and radar operators, then fell silent.

Swiney heard nothing more, so when on assignment at the Ministry of Defence in the mid-1970s he decided to look into the official records of the

3. Ibid. p.138.
4. *Out of the Shadows: UFOs, the Establishment and the Official Cover-Up* David Clarke and Andy Roberts. Piatkus. London. 2002. pp.98-99.
5. Ibid. pp.99-100.

occurrence. The Deputy Directorate of Intelligence (Technical) – charged with UFO investigations from 1952 to 1964, explained that after five years all such records were destroyed and that the practice had ended in 1967, meaning that the oldest surviving records would have been from 1962. However, Swiney did locate the 1952 report, and later recalled that "it was all there," as of the mid-seventies, but admitted that he didn't know what had happened to it since. As confirmation of his story, Swiney had kept a copy of the official log book in which he had himself written a brief account of the UFO encounter. When he sought the original, Swiney was again told that it had likely been destroyed, but once more he found it and saw that it included the notation that he had come across "three mysterious saucer-shaped objects," with the further notation that "the Air Ministry discounted any possibility of 'extra terrestrial [*sic*] objects.'" [6] (This makes me discount the Air Ministry.)

As authors Dr David Clarke and Andy Roberts point out, if there had been nothing strange about the incident, and certainly no possibility of alien spacecraft, then why go to the lengths of lying to an RAF officer posted to duty at the Ministry of Defence, and moreover, who had also been the very same pilot involved in the UFO encounter? Why the attempt to conceal the incident for a half century if there was nothing to hide?[7] Exactly, and, as stated previously, "Never believe in anything until it has been officially denied." (Otto von Bismarck.)

The Prime Minister Wanted to Know (And so Did a President)

Even before the Mainbrace sightings and the wave of UFO events in and near the UK, and just after the Washington, D.C. wave in the U.S.A. in 1952 – most of which, as we have seen, were military encounters with UFOs – Prime Minister Winston Churchill sent a memo to his Secretary of State for Air: "What does all this stuff about flying saucers amount to? What can it mean? What is the truth? Let me have a report at your convenience." The memo was dated 28 July 1952. The reply, dated 9 August, was that all UFO reports were the result of mistaken identity, delusions or hoaxes. However, the report carefully withheld such information as the testimony

6. Ibid. pp.100-102.
7. Ibid. p.102.

of RAF pilots, radar returns and other pertinent data. The note contained a reference to the United States reaching the same conclusion as a result of the Project Grudge report, but it cited U.S. press stories, not intelligence briefings.[8]

The assessment by the authors of *Out of the Shadows* – Dr David Clarke and Andy Roberts – is that in their opinion the Prime Minister was given the best information available at the time, and cite Sir Anthony Montague-Brown, Churchill's private secretary, who said the Prime Minister evidently had no great interest in the subject and merely wanted to be able to respond to Parliamentary inquiries.

Perhaps I am too much of a cynic, but I believe Churchill was being misled, but for "benevolent" reasons, primary among them the very same fact of the Prime Minister being subject to questions by elected officials in Parliament. It had been learned by intelligence agencies through the years, the hard way, that secrets leak out primarily from elected officials, be they in either the legislative or executive branches, often for political reasons. So, over time, in addition to a multi-level system of secrecy codes, compartmentalized Special Access Programs (SAP) were created for really critical secrecy. Only a very few people – those with a "need to know" – would be allowed to access information in an SAP.

By not giving it to the Prime Minister, most cabinet members (all who were not directly involved, such as ministers in areas outside of military affairs, etc.) would not have had access to the information at all. However, in addition to the lack of a need to know, keeping the secrets from the Prime Minister would have prevented Churchill from being caught in a lie should his denials to Parliament about knowing anything be disproven – giving him "plausible deniability." This possibility is reflected in accounts of former Central Intelligence Agency director George H.W. Bush withholding UFO information from his boss, President Jimmy Carter.

In an 18 December 2018 report in *The Scottish Sun*, journalist Emma Parry quoted from Steve Bassett, an American UFO lobbyist: "Bush knew the truth about extra terrestrial [*sic*] life and could have ended the UFO cover-up."[9] But, Bassett continued, "he kept all his UFO knowledge a secret right up until he died at his home in Houston."

---

8. Ibid. p.104.
9. *The Scottish Sun,* 18 December 2018.
https://www.thescottishsun.co.uk/news/3639818/george-bush-sr-took-ufo-secrets-to-the-grave-because-americans-couldnt-handle-the-truth-lobbyist-claims/

Parry further reported that on 19 November 1976, when asked about UFOs, Bush told Carter, while he was still President-Elect, that he, Carter, did not have a need to know about the reality of UFOs, adding that if Carter wanted to pursue the issue he could request the information from the Congressional Research Service. Carter had pledged to voters before his election that if President he would compel the United States government to disclose to the public what it knew about UFOs.

According to Parry's report, Bassett thought Bush deflected Carter's question because he knew some UFOs were extraterrestrial in origin. Carter fired Bush a short time later.

Bush went on to become the forty-first president. When asked while campaigning why UFO information was being withheld, Bush is reported to have replied, "Americans can't handle the truth." (This comment suggests to me that there was substantial and possibly alarming secret intelligence Bush regarded as "the truth.")

Parry continued her coverage by informing her readers that Bush was also questioned by UFO researcher Charles Huffer while going to a rally in Rogers, Arkansas in 1988. When asked if he would reveal to everyone the truth about UFOs, Bush replied, "Yeah, if we can find it – what it is," adding, "We are really interested." When asked about how much he knew then, Bush said, "I know some. I know a fair amount." (This, too, is a partial revelation that some people – evidently in governmental circles, wanted to know about the UFO phenomenon – "what it is," and they were "really interested," and, further, that he, Bush, knew "a fair amount." All of these remarks reveal that "a fair amount" of information of substance was known to at least some people.)

So, only a very select few insiders are privileged with UFO information; but they (usually) keep quiet about it. As is said within intelligence-gathering circles: those who know don't say; those who say, don't know.

First Encounter: Near Stonehenge, and a Royal Visit

In 1961, Lieutenant George Filer was assigned as a navigator to a KB-50J aerial tanker of the 420th Air Refueling Squadron. The 420th, along with the 4th Bombardment Wing and the 20th Fighter Wing was then based at RAF Sculthorpe, Norfolk, on England's east coast.[10] One night, their mission

10. *Strange Craft*, by Major George Filer III, USAF (Ret.) as told to John L. Guerra. Bayshore Publishing. Tampa, Fl. 2018. p.59.

refueling fighter planes over the North Sea complete, they headed back to base. Then London Control called to report a UFO somewhere between Oxford and Stonehenge. Asked if the KB-50J could go take a look, the pilot promptly complied. George said that when the KB-50J was 30 miles away he picked it up on his radar screen,[11] describing it as the largest blip he had ever seen for a target in the air, being more like the return of a ship or bridge, and that the image was sharp and clear, indicating the object was metallic. When the UFO was 10 miles away, George and the pilots saw it. At 5 miles distance the UFO appeared to have a row of lights, looking, George commented, "like a lighted cruise ship." He added that as the plane approached the UFO "seemed to come alive," its lights brightening tremendously, illuminating the KB-50J's cabin. Then it shot almost straight up, its lights even brighter as it soared past the tanker.[12]

After the pilot described the UFO to London Control, he was met with a pause of silence, and then came the reply, "Thank you for the intercept; you are now cleared to return to your mission."

Filer said the facts were entered into the flight log, and the crew discussed the incident the following day at operations; but there was no intelligence debriefing. (It seems that there was a remarkable lack of curiosity here, but perhaps both the RAF and USAF each thought the other would attend to at least a minimal inquiry.)

Two weeks later, at the Dining In, a place where RAF and USAF air crews dined and drank together, Prince Philip arrived, as was his habit, to mix with the military people and deliver a brief speech, after which he inquired of the crew who had seen the UFO.[13]

Their small group adjourned to an anteroom and spent an hour with the Prince discussing UFOs. George said the Prince told the crew two things: the same UFO had been seen by several RAF pilots and picked up on London Control radars over the past few months; and that he, the Prince, and his aides had been briefed on numerous occasions about UFOs that air and ground crews had detected on radar and seen with their own eyes.[14]

When George asked the Prince about his interest in the subject, Philip told them that his uncle, Lord Louis Mountbatten, had seen a UFO up close

---

11. On aerial tankers, the navigator also functions as an air controller, acquiring aircraft to be refueled on his or her twin radar screens, then directing the planes to a rendezvous.
12. *Strange Craft*, by Major George Filer III, USAF (Ret.) as told to John L. Guerra. Bayshore Publishing. Tampa, Fl. 2018 pp.74-75.
13. Ibid. p.75.
14. Ibid. p.76.

Anti-aircraft searchlights, gunfire explosions, smoke, clouds and mist. Early morning of 25 February 1942. (Photo courtesy of Associated Press)

F-18F Super Hornet Navy jet like the one that intercepted a "Tic-Tac" UFO off the California coast.

CH-47 "Chinook" heavy lift helicopter. More than twenty of these were reportedly seen tailing a UFO in the Cash-Landrum case in Texas. (Photo courtesy of United States Army)

Bristol Beaufighter Mark 1C – night-fighter version – like the one from which many "Foo-Fighters" were spotted during the Second world War.

Gloster Meteor jet fighter – many of these were involved in numerous intercepts over and near the United Kingdom.

KB-50J aerial tanker plane like the one from which George Filer saw a huge UFO on his radar scopes; he and the crew also observing the UFO above Stonehenge

P-51 Mustang fighter plane – later re-designated F-51 – like the one that Captain Mantell flew to his death while pursuing a UFO.

F-86 jet interceptor like the one flown by Lieutenant Milton Torres when he reported that he was ordered by RAF controllers to shoot down a UFO above East Anglia.

F-89 jet aircraft similar to one that disappeared above Lake Superior Ontario/ Michigan when its radar image merged with that of a UFO.

F-94 fighter like those that attempted to intercept UFOs over and near Washington, D.C.

F-4 Phantom fighter plane in Imperial Iranian Air Force livery – like the one that had its instruments and weapons disabled by a UFO during an attempted intercept above Tehran in 1976.

SU-22 of the Peruvian Air Force. Lieutenant Oscar Santa Maria Huerta flew this type of plane when he intercepted and shot into UFO above La Joya (Peruvian) Air Force Base.

De Havilland Venom jet fighter. Two of these were sent to intercept a UFO above RAF-USAF Lakenheath-Bentwaters, 13–14 August 1956.

Above: RB-47 Reconnaissance Plane like that stalked by UFO over the United States, 17 July 1957.

Right: Minuteman missile in blast-proof silo. This and different models of Minuteman and other missile types were disabled when UFOs hovered nearby.

Atlas Agena-D missile. This type of missile was used to hurl a test warhead into space that was attacked by UFO high-energy rays, which caused its destruction.

while serving as Viceroy of India some years before; and, after recounting the incident of the UFO on Lord Mountbatten's Broadlands Estate, which he mentioned was covered by Timothy Good, in *Above Top Secret*, George further reported that the Prince had said he thought "aliens were visiting our planet."[15]

Filer went on to explain that their tanker plane had been asked to make the intercept not only because it was as fast as contemporary fighter jets (at the fighters' nearly slowest speeds), but also due to the fact that the Air Force had lost too many fighter planes while pursuing UFOs. George then went on to quote General Benjamin Chidlaw, Commander of Continental Defense Command (U.S.) from 1951 to 1955: "We have stacks of reports about flying saucers. We take them seriously when you consider we have lost too many men and planes trying to intercept them."[16]

Shag Harbour, Nova Scotia

In an under-reported incident in Maritime, Canada, which is largely ignored by even many prominent ufologists, we find one of the earlier reports of a UFO that is also a USO – an unidentified submerged object. On 4 October 1967 at 7:19 p.m., Atlantic Time, aboard an Air Canada DC-8 en route on a short hop from Sherbrooke, Quebec, to St Jean, Quebec, Captain Pierre Guy Charbonneau observed a large, orange, rectangular object, followed by a string of lights. The objects flew parallel to the airliner's course when a large explosion detonated near the rectangle and it appeared to dissolve into a cloud – first white, turning red, shifting into violet, then blue. Two minutes later another apparent explosion faded into yet another orange but this time globular object. Like the rectangle, the sphere dimmed gradually to a blue color. The smaller lights shifted from near where the rectangle had been and darted around the sphere like insects.[17]

After discussing whether to file a report on the incident, in view of the fact that the objects and explosions had seemed to be close by, the flight crew decided to file a report. Their hesitancy stemmed not only from fear of ridicule by others in the industry; they were reluctant because Canada had an agreement with the United States that all airline and military pilots and crews were restrained from making UFO reports known to anyone outside

15. Ibid. pp.76-77.
16. Ibid. pp.78-79.
17. *Dark Object* By Don Ledger and Chris Styles. Dell. New York. 2001. p.11.

of official channels, on pain of an up to $10,000 fine and ten years in prison. This policy was set forth in the United States regulation JANAP 146d, which had been agreed to in 1962.[18] They later did file a detailed report.[19] The objects they had seen were proceeding eastward, toward Nova Scotia.

Half an hour later, William Thibeault and his brother were out stargazing at Eastern Passage, Nova Scotia, near Royal Canadian Air Force Station Shearwater when they saw two faint white lights, followed by a brighter one, all heading from the northeast to the southwest, in the direction of Shag Harbour.[20]

"Ralph Loewinger, one of the pilots aboard Pan Am Flight 160, a Boeing 707 cargo aircraft … at 33,000ft that same night … saw the same row of flashing lights over the Gulf of Maine as they approached the coast of Nova Scotia."[21]

About one hour later, Captain Leo Mersey ordered the men of the fishing boat *MV Nickerson* below because they were leaning over the side-rails, excitedly talking as all watched a spectacle in the sky. Captain Mersey and the first mate then consulted the radar screen, upon which were displayed four blips. Their vessel was 32 nautical miles south of Sambro, Nova Scotia, and the unidentified objects were about 16 nautical miles northeast. [22]

Looking skyward, they could see the four blips as bright red lights in a box pattern, about six miles on a side. The captain said he had checked with the Rescue Coordination Center (RCC) and harbormaster, and there were no planned naval exercises or tests scheduled in the area that night. One of the crewmen came topside to tell them that the radio was abuzz with UFO reports from Halifax. Then, one of the UFOs detached from the others and, arcing about 5,000ft above, flew over and beyond the *Nickerson* and proceeded toward the horizon. After that, a radio call came in: the Royal Canadian Mounted Police wanted to talk to Captain Mersey when the boat returned to port.[23]

About an hour after that, a woman (who remains anonymous) called the local radio station to report a glowing, orange object about 40 to 50ft in diameter hovering just above the water in Halifax Harbour, while, across

---

18. https://www.nsa.gov/portals/75/documents/news-features/declassified-documents/ufo/janap_146.pdf
19. *Dark Object* By Don Ledger and Chris Styles. Dell. New York. 2001. pp.12-13.
20. Ibid. pp.13-14.
21. *The Canadian Press* https://nationalpost.com/news/canada/we-saw-something-something-came-down-the-shag-harbour-ufo-sighting-50-years-later
22. *Dark Object* By Don Ledger and Chris Styles. Dell. New York. 2001. pp.14-15.
23. Ibid. pp.16-17.

the water, 10-year-old Chris Styles – later to become co-author of *Dark Object* – watched the same glowing orb.[24]

Near Lunenberg, Nova Scotia, about 50 nautical miles southwest from Halifax, Will C. Eisnor, Raymond Hiltz, and Saint Clair Croft were on the beach when they saw three bright lights hanging in the sky inland – one blue, one amber, the third not described as to color.[25]

A fleet of some fifteen herring seiners in the Bay of Fundy about 120 miles due west of Halifax were strung out in a line, floodlights on while they fished. Walter Titus, master of the *Quadra Isle* noticed that his crew had stopped working and were staring at the sky. Looking up, he saw an orb about the size of the moon to the southeast; then three smaller lights seemed to emerge from it, forming a triangle around it as all three began to flit around at high speed. Altogether, about 150 fishermen and people on shore were watching the light show. After roughly five minutes, the lights streaked away to the southeast.[26]

Near 11 p.m., a Royal Canadian Mounted Police constable and three game wardens on stakeout to catch deer poachers near Weymouth, a few miles east of the fishing fleet, saw an orange, glowing orb drifting above the trees.[27]

At approximately 11:20 p.m., five teenagers out driving around were on the road alongside Shag Harbour when they saw a dark object with a row of four lights descending toward the water at a 45° angle:

> 'There was four [lights] in a row, and they were going on and off,' said [Laurie] Wickens, at the time a 17-year-old driving home to Shag Harbour with a friend and three young women. 'One would come on, then two, three and four — and they'd all be off for a second and come back on again.'[28]

The object hit the water some 300 yards offshore. The young people stopped to look. For a couple of minutes the dark object, showing a single yellow light, bobbed on the surface. They thought an airliner may have crashed, so one of the boys decided to go for help; he got back into the car and sped

24. Ibid. pp.17-18.
25. Ibid. pp.19-21.
26. Ibid. pp.21-23.
27. Ibid. pp.24-26.
28. *The Canadian Press*. https://nationalpost.com/news/canada/we-saw-something-something-came-down-the-shag-harbour-ufo-sighting-50-years-later

off, stopping at a pay phone to call the RCMP detachment at Barrington Passage, and at first was not believed. The desk officer said he would call him back at the pay phone.[29]

Within moments the RCMP officer received several more calls about a dark object down in the harbor. The RCMP corporal called the pay phone, inquired for more information, then contacted RCMP headquarters in Halifax, expressing concern about a possible plane crash. It would later be determined that "Neither the Rescue Co-ordination Center in Halifax nor the nearby NORAD [North American Air Defense] radar facility at Baccaro, Nova Scotia had any knowledge of missing aircraft, either civilian or military."[30] The RCMP man then radioed for assistance, got into his patrol car and headed for the scene of the "accident."[31]

The harbor-side road was seldom traveled, and arriving RCMP officers were surprised to find more than a dozen people at the scene, watching the dark object in the water. One of the RCMP men, Constable Ron Pond, said, "The object had 'changed' during its descent to the water's surface, i.e., it changed shape, and that it appeared to be 'no known object.'"[32]

The RCMP corporal called the Rescue Coordination Center and asked them to check for missing aircraft. However, for unknown reasons, the RCC did not immediately alert the Royal Canadian Coast Guard; but, still, Coast Guard Cutter 101, sailing from 6 miles away, arrived on scene just after midnight.[33]

Even before midnight, the RCMP men who knew the local people had already begun contacting boat owners to conduct an impromptu and makeshift search and rescue effort. The Coast Guard ship and boats found nothing but strange yellow foam floating on the surface, and everyone detected a distinct sulfur odor. A couple of the fishermen stuck their hands into the foam, which transformed into a coating of an oily substance. A few bubbles rising from the depths suggested that something had recently sunk there.[34]

The Rescue Coordination Center people were puzzled because there were no indications of missing planes, so they began thinking in terms of an unknown aircraft, and by 10:20 a.m., the mystery object was being

29. *Dark Object.* By Don Ledger and Chris Styles. Dell. New York. 2001. pp.29-31.
30. https://mysteriesofcanada.com/nova-scotia/shag-harbor-ufo/
31. *Dark Object.* By Don Ledger and Chris Styles. Dell. New York. 2001. pp.31-35.
32. https://mysteriesofcanada.com/nova-scotia/shag-harbor-ufo/
33. *Dark Object* By Don Ledger and Chris Styles. Dell. New York. 2001. pp.39-41.
34. Ibid. pp.41-45.

referred to by authorities as a "UFO." The RCC alerted Canadian Forces headquarters with an outline of what the RCMP had reported, referring to the "UFO" as such, and also as a "dark object."[35]

Divers were called in and had been observed recovering aluminum-colored debris.[36] When a curious late-arrival asked the RCMP officers what the divers were looking for, he was told, "Flying saucers."[37] The number of divers was increased to seven, and they dove until Sunday, 8 October – four days after the crash of whatever fell into the harbor, then the search was officially called off the following day.[38, 39] That should have been the end of the incident; but it wasn't.

Twenty-five years later, Chris Styles saw the Roswell UFO crash being covered on the television documentary series *Unsolved Mysteries*.[40] Having been a witness to the Shag Harbour incident, Chris decided to actively investigate what had evidently been largely forgotten, or covered up. Over time, Chris investigated old press reports and records, and was eventually joined by his friend Bob MacDonald. They tracked down one of the divers, who told them over the phone that he had not been to Shag Harbour but had been assigned to dive and look for a UFO (USO – Unidentified Submerged Object?) at Shelburne Harbour,[41] about 25 straight-line miles to the northeast, but approximately twice that to sail around headlands to get there.

The two investigators set-up a meeting with the former diver, and he revealed that the Shelburne Harbour operation lasted about a week and had brought up debris and a strange, foam-like material that was decomposing as they moved it. He also reported that several ships were taking part in the recovery effort, not just a single Canadian Coast Guard cutter. Then, suddenly, their witness declared that he couldn't talk about it.[42] When

35. Ibid. p.47.
36. Ibid. pp.46-47.
37. Ibid. p.48.
38. Ibid. p.49. Also: "Seven navy divers from the HMCS *Granby* searched throughout the daylight hours until sundown of 08 October 1967. On Monday, 09 October 1967 …" https://mysteriesofcanada.com/nova-scotia/shag-harbor-ufo/
39. Chris Styles revealed on the Coast-to-Coast radio program of 11 May, 2024, that there is much more to the story regarding the Shelburne Harbour incident. The facts he discovered are in his new book, *Sweep Clear 5: NATO's UFO Encounter, a quest for the truth about the Shelburne USO story.*
40. *Dark Object* By Don Ledger and Chris Styles. Dell. New York. 2001. p.54.
41. Ibid. p.67.
42. Ibid. pp.68-70.

pressed, the man said he couldn't go any further, but did say, twice, that "it wasn't anything from here."[43]

A subsequent telephone conversation did not generally go well because as the investigators prodded the witness for more information he grew increasingly irritated until he became angry and blurted out, "… it didn't come from this planet … Don't call back." He then broke the phone connection. [44]

"'What sets this story apart is that the impact … was witnessed by several independent and very credible witnesses,' says Brock Zinck, a Nova Scotia seafood buyer and vice-president of the Shag Harbour UFO Society.[45] 'Nobody reported a UFO. Everybody reported a plane crash. That gives a boost of credibility to the story.'"

"'A preliminary investigation has been carried out by the Rescue Co-ordination Centre in Halifax,' a (Canadian Defence Department) memo says. 'It has been determined that this UFO sighting was not caused by a flare, float, aircraft or in fact any known object.'"

During the course of writing their book – *Dark Object*, which is the most thorough, original and in many particulars the sole credible source known to me for information on the Shag Harbour incident – Don Ledger and Chris Styles added many pertinent observations (and I will include some of my own in what follows), among them:

The Canadian Maritime Provinces occupied a key strategic position, as far as Cold War military considerations were concerned. Missile trajectories and military aircraft routes, and attempted incursions by submarines from the Soviet Union to the United States would pass over or near the eastern coasts of Canada. Therefore, the United States had placed hydrophones and underwater magnetic sensors nearby to be able to detect Russian submarines by hearing their propeller noise and picking up the magnetic "signatures" of their metal hulls. At first, the information would have been stored in a database for future comparisons so that individual sound and magnetic identifiers could be assigned to specific submarines and ships – friendly and potentially hostile.

In order to defend against attempts by Soviet submarines to infiltrate American waters – on both sides of the U.S.-Canadian border – a complex of American and Canadian military bases was concentrated in the Maritime

43. Ibid. pp.70-71.

44. Ibid. p.72.

45. *The Canadian Press.* https://nationalpost.com/news/canada/we-saw-something-something-came-down-the-shag-harbour-ufo-sighting-50-years-later

Provinces and America's New England. So, when a UFO – or several – appeared on radars and was seen by witnesses, whether approaching from any direction, this would have generated at least a regional military alert. Such an alarm could have triggered an anti-aircraft defense reaction, resulting in Canadian and/or United States aircraft or anti-aircraft weapons being vectored toward the UFO. Whether a shooting down of the object had been intentional or not, accidents happen. The most probable site of origin for an air-defense effort would have been Loring Air Force Base, in northeastern Maine. Such an event would explain the aerial explosions seen by the Canadian airliner crew, who filed an official report. Or, in that no technology is perfect, the UFO – in the context of being an alien spacecraft, which I suspect is the case – could have suffered one or more internal problems, resulting in explosions bringing the "dark object" down in Canadian waters.

Subsequently, the UFO-become-USO could have had enough in the way of residual capacity, or benefited from repairs, to travel underwater in an attempt to escape possible capture, until it had moved from Shag Harbour to Shelburne Harbour, about 50 miles away by a water (or underwater) route.

I know this speculation is, necessarily, tenuous, given the reluctance of both the Canadian and American governments to divulge any information, which is understandable for many reasons, some of which will be given later. (Also to be discussed are this author's theories regarding some of the more bizarre aspects of observations of the appearance and antics of UFOs when seen and detected by Earthlings' instruments.)

Meanwhile, based primarily on the large number of specifically named, credible eyewitnesses and the good detective work of Don Ledger and Chris Styles, I am strongly inclined to accept the theory that a spacecraft of extraterrestrial origin crashed into Shag Harbour, Nova Scotia, 4 October 1967.

Chapter 12

UFOs Over USAF Nuclear Sites

Several Specific U.S. Air Force Bases Visited by UFOs

Researcher, writer and director Robert L. Hastings has devoted decades to uncovering the connection between UFOs and nuclear facilities. In a 2006 article at the NICAP website, Hastings summarized many UFO sightings and even reported touchdowns at various strategic military bases where nuclear weapons were stored and/or loaded aboard USAF bombers and missiles. The number of sites and bases is extensive – too many to go over each in detail herein, due to numerous witnesses being reluctant to provide many specifics, or because the occurrences were fleeting and not that involved or complicated, as were the Roswell and Shag Harbour incidents. In other instances, there were too many details to cover in a book such as this, with its wider focus.

The reports of UFO encounters at military sites were given mostly to Mr Hastings directly in personal interviews; some were provided by other UFO researchers and teams. A brief breakdown here cites the ranks and titles and duty assignments of twenty-nine named (by Hastings, Lawrence Fawcett and Barry Greenwood – see note) witnesses – who will not be specifically renamed here. All military personnel are listed by rank (when given) and specialty or assignment, including: 1st Lieutenant, Minuteman ICBM targeting officer (Deputy Missile Combat Crew Commander); Staff Sergeant, former Minuteman ICBM maintenance clerk; Airman 1st Class, former Air Policeman; Staff Sergeant, former Minuteman ICBM maintenance technician; Staff Sergeant, former Security Policeman; three Staff Sergeants and two Sergeants, all former Security Police; Technical Sergeant, former Team Chief of Missile Handling; Base Commander of Francis E. Warren Air Force Base; Colonel, Commanding Officer of the Sioux Army Depot at Sydney, Nebraska; Airman 2nd Class, former Air Policeman; Airman 2nd Class, former Air Policeman; 1st Lieutenant, former Minuteman ICBM launch officer (Deputy Missile Combat Crew Commander); Airman 1st Class, former Air Policeman; 1st Lieutenant, former Atlas ICBM launch officer (Deputy Missile Combat Crew Commander); 1st Lieutenant, former Atlas ICBM launch officer (Deputy Missile Combat Crew Commander); Airman 1st Class, former Atlas ICBM Launch Facilities Specialist; Airman 2nd Class, former Atlas ICBM Missile Facilities Specialist; Staff Sergeant, (USAF Retired) former Electro-Mechanical technician; Major – aircraft commander, four Captains, Sergeant, KC-135 tanker crew approaching Wurtsmith AFB.[1,2] These are not duplicates.

In addition to the twenty-nine people who were courageous enough to make known the events and to give their names and other information, there were forty-four other witnesses mentioned in the article at the NICAP site, and many others in Fawcett and Greenwood's book. The forty-four referred to herein remain anonymous for a variety of reasons, not necessarily stemming from a wish to not be identified, but because they were part of a group, did not give their names to the witnesses who revealed the incident, or whose names were forgotten by the time an unofficial report was made. (Many military personnel felt compelled to stick to their oaths of silence for years until they learned of others stepping forward, and then decided that exposing the facts was too important to dissuade them, or realized they had never been properly sworn to secrecy to begin with.) The forty-four anonymous witnesses include an Airman assigned to refuel helicopters; a Commander and Deputy for Operations – who did not necessarily witness the incident but passed on a report; an anonymous officer who relayed news of the incident to Project Blue Book; a Base Commander who also informed PBB of a UFO incident; two members of the 44th Missile Maintenance Squadron; an Airman 1st Class who was a vehicle controller; and an Airman 1st Class who was a Minuteman (missile) Electro-Mechanical Team technician.[3]

1. UFO sightings at ICBM sites and nuclear Weapons Storage Areas. By Robert L. Hastings http://www.nicap.org/babylon/missile_incidents.htm
2. *Clear Intent: The Government Coverup of the UFO Experience* By Lawrence Fawcett and Barry J. Greenwood. Prentiss-Hall. Englewood Cliffs, NJ. 1984. pp.16, 17; 41,42.
3. UFO sightings at ICBM sites and nuclear Weapons Storage Areas. By Robert L. Hastings http://www.nicap.org/babylon/missile_incidents.htm

These witnesses and many more[4] who were entrusted with the maintenance, protection and even possible deployment (use) of nuclear weapons systems can hardly be regarded as "cranks and weirdos."

The events included observations of more than forty-four UFOs. ("More than" because I strove to avoid duplication, so, when in doubt, suspected duplicates were omitted.) They included: more than twenty-five "lights." (Definitely "more than," because I counted "several," as just one – as in a single incident with conflicting or confusing minor details.) At least ten of these lights engaged in erratic zig-zagging and other extreme maneuvers. One light spit-out a black object; one was described as a "disc." There was one fuzzy triangle;[5] and there were five triangles. The lights cruised, hovered, then raced away at high speed. One lingered above a base command center; two floated above missile silos. A white oval with red lights is said to have landed 10 miles east of a missile silo site; one tarried over a missile silo; and a UFO remained above while a maintenance crew worked on a missile.[6]

At least nine of these UFOs were tracked on local radar; and eight more were detected on North American Aerospace Defense Command (NORAD) radars remotely monitored from Cheyenne Mountain, Colorado, and NORAD then notified local commanders.[7]

These sightings occurred at the following sites on the dates indicated – some of which are necessarily vague due to faded memories and a lack of the release of official records. At Malmstrom Air Force Base: probably on the night of 24/25 March 1967, and again about two weeks later; late fall 1973; fall 1975; 7–9 November 1975; spring 1992; 7 and 18 January 1995; 20 January 1995. West of Malmstrom: 2 February 1996, at Missile Roll Transfer Building.

---

4. Some were only mentioned as part of a group, as "several," etc. However, to avoid exaggeration, I only included the one, two or three who were specifically cited. I made every effort to expunge those I thought were parts of duplicated descriptions or misidentified (repeats of) events. The lack of a more detailed breakdown, due to many factors beyond Hastings, Fawcett and Greenwood's control, caused some vagueness and confusion because while people can recall a narrative of events, some specifics such as dates, the names of people, even of particular missile parts, site names or commands tend to fade from memory. Some have expressed regrets for not keeping a diary or other written documentation; but few of us do so, especially when we are younger.
5. This could conceivably be due to effects described in the article cited earlier by Joel Carpenter, "Time reversed optical waves by arbitrary vector spatiotemporal field generation." This is not to suggest actual time reversal but instead in this case manipulation of electromagnetic waves to generate such an effect. *https://www.nature.com/articles/s41467-020-19601-3*
6. "UFO sightings at ICBM sites and nuclear Weapons Storage Areas". By Robert L. Hastings http://www.nicap.org/babylon/missile_incidents.htm
7. Ibid

F.E. Warren AFB, Wyoming: 1 August 1965; fall 1973; spring 1974; 1980–81. Minot AFB, North Dakota in 1968. Walker AFB (formerly Roswell Army Air Field), New Mexico 1963–65. Ellsworth AFB, South Dakota 1966; 27 October 1992. Also: "Declassified documents" obtained from the Air Force Office of Special Investigations (AFOSI) confirmed reports of UFOs hovering near the Manzano Weapons Storage Area, outside Kirtland AFB, New Mexico, in 1980.

> The Air Force and NORAD data provided detailed accounts of sightings of unexplained objects from Loring Air Force Base in Maine, Wurtsmith AFB in Michigan and Malmstrom AFB in Montana, all with(in) a two-week period."[8] Also, there was "a rash of UFO incidents … in the last days of October and the first two weeks of November 1975.
>
> Since 28 Oct '75, numerous reports of suspicious objects have been received at the NORAD COC [North American Air Defense Combat Operations Center]. Reliable military personnel at Loring AFB, Maine; Wurtsmith AFB, Michigan; Malmstrom AFB, [Montana]; Minot AFB, [North Dakota]; and Canadian Forces Station, Falconbridge, Ontario, Canada, have visually sighted suspicious objects.[9]

The units involved in just some of these incidents include but are not limited to: 42nd Security Police Squadron; 2192nd Communications Squadron; 341st Missile Maintenance Squadron; 341st Combat Defense Squadron; 343rd Missile Security Squadron; 379th Bombardment Wing; 379th Bombardment Wing, Police Unit Seven; 379th Bombardment Wing, KC-135 aerial tanker crew; 809th Combat Defense Squadron; 90th Strategic Missile Wing; 90th Security Police Squadron; 579th Strategic Missile Squadron; 44th Missile Maintenance Squadron.[10,11]

---

8. "What Were Those Mysterious Craft?" By Ward Sinclair and Art Harris 19 January 1979 https://www.washingtonpost.com/archive/politics/1979/01/19/what-were-those-mysterious-craft/1b9d1f3d-dddb-4a92-87b3-0143aa5d7a3e/
9. https://www.nytimes.com/1979/10/14/archives/ufo-files-the-untold-story.html
10. UFO sightings at ICBM sites and nuclear Weapons Storage Areas. By Robert L. Hastings http://www.nicap.org/babylon/missile_incidents.htm
11. *Clear Intent: The Government Coverup of the UFO Experience* By Lawrence Fawcett and Barry J. Greenwood. Prentiss-Hall. Englewood Cliffs, NJ. 1984. pp.16, 17; 41, 42.

Some of the circumstances and results of these UFO incursions include: missile targeting information was erased from missile memory. All three power sources – from the local utility, the emergency generators, the back-up batteries, were drained of power without evidence of tampering or damage. A reported landing occurred near a launch control center. Security units were mustered, issued arms, deployed in response to overflying "satellites." UFOs hovered above missile silos on many occasions. When a UFO landed, a security team refused to approach it, even after being ordered to do so – twice. The team leader asked for permission to open fire; the request was denied. The object was described as round and metallic, resting on a tripod of landing legs. The UFO departed rapidly when a helicopter approached. A UFO described as a boomerang or kidney-bean shape with row of lights, two or three times larger than full moon, drifted above a hangar.[12]

There were many more witnesses to these and other events who would not make a report due to fear of retaliation by being declared unfit and medically discharged, as was provided for in the Personnel Reliability Program, which regulated the performance of those trusted with executing duties in sensitive areas such as at nuclear weapons sites.

However, before these sightings – long before them, going back to the beginnings of the Nuclear Age, UFOs had been seen in the skies above nuclear development and production sites at Oak Ridge, Tennessee and Hanford, Washington.

At Oak Ridge, at about 11 p.m. on 21 June 1951, a Ground Observer Corps spotter sighted a slow-moving object near the edge of the Oak Ridge Laboratory reservation. Before the report was confirmed, the image on the radar that had also picked it up faded, but then an F-47 on combat air patrol nearby was visually vectored to the area. The pilot saw a light and pursued it. The fighter plane and UFO engaged in a dangerous game of tag, at altitudes between 10,000 and 27,000ft. At times, the object seemed intent on ramming the F-47. The pilot reported that it looked to be about 6 to 8in in diameter and white in color.[13]

On 10 December 1952 at the Hanford Nuclear plant in Washington state, the pilot and radar observer in an F-94 saw a light while cruising at 26,000ft. Ground control told them no planes were known to be in the area. The crew gave chase and spotted a white object with two red lights in "windows."

12. "UFO sightings at ICBM sites and nuclear Weapons Storage Areas". By Robert L. Hastings http://www.nicap.org/babylon/missile_incidents.htm

13. *The Report On Unidentified Flying Objects* Edward J. Ruppelt. E-artnow. No city listed. 2020. p.38.

They could not obtain a radar lock-on; and attempts to intercept the orb resulted in it reversing course and diving away. The pilot at times had to make emergency turns to avoid a possible collision.

Twice more we find trained professional pilots, and an equally capable radar operator, reporting on incredible sights that mystified them.

Did a Soldier Shoot and Kill an Alien in New Jersey?

Re-enter George Filer, who, through a series of unusual circumstances and random, chance events had become an intelligence officer charged with briefing more senior officers on the latest information of interest to the Air Force. Having been reassigned to McGuire Air Force Base at its complex of combined armed forces at the Army's Fort Dix, New Jersey, he was there when several UFOs showed up and displayed continuing extraterrestrial interest in the weapons storage area at the base.[14]

The incident began about 2 a.m. on 18 January 1978. George, then a Major, arrived at McGuire AFB shortly after 3 a.m. Near the fence between McGuire and Fort Dix, George could see the flashing of blue emergency lights in the distance, making him wonder if there had been a plane crash or other disaster. Being charged with delivering the 8 a.m. briefing, he went to the McGuire command center to find out what was going on. There were two other Majors and two Lieutenant Colonels there. The senior Master Sergeant in charge of the command post, who looked pale and upset, told George, "An alien has been shot at Fort Dix and they found it on the end of our runway."[15]

George could only ask if by "alien" the man meant someone from another country, but the Sergeant said it was a being from "outer space," adding that UFOs had been "buzzing around the pattern like mad." The Sergeant in charge also told Major Filer that a C-141 had been sent from Wright-Patterson AFB in Ohio to retrieve the body. Major Filer was informed that he had to investigate and brief the General at 8 a.m.[16]

Major Filer quickly discovered that tower operators had not only picked up some discs on radar but could see one from their own windows; and incoming pilots had seen several on their approach to McGuire. Being charged with conducting the initial investigation, Filer asked around, and

---

14. *Strange Craft*, Major (Retired) George Filer III, USAF and John L. Guerra. Bayshore Publishing. Tampa, Fl. 2018. p.165.
15. Ibid. pp.166-167.
16. Ibid. pp.167-168.

each person he interviewed told the same story: when the UFOs hovered above Fort Dix, near the fence separating the base from McGuire AFB, Army Military Police officers hopped into pickup trucks and went to the location. One MP noticed that a UFO was hanging above his truck, so he got out to investigate, and as he did so a short, humanoid figure stepped into the beams of his headlights. Following his training, the MP drew his sidearm and ordered the intruder to freeze, and when his order was ignored, the MP opened fire, and the intruder ran toward the fence.[17]

In their book *Strange Craft*, Filer and co-writer Joel Guerra quote from a news item in *The Trentonian* of 10 June 2007, stating that the being was "about four feet tall, grayish-brown, fat head, long arms, and slender body." The UFO was described as a glowing bluish-green oval.[18]

Not being an Army investigator, George says he remained on the McGuire AFB side of the fence, and had no chance to interview the MP, whose name "has been lost to history."

The New Jersey State Police had been called, and an airman from McGuire had been assigned to let in a state trooper at a back gate near the abandoned runway and hangar that had formerly been used by the New Jersey Air National Guard. The two men found the body. The airman was called by his commanding officer and asked to put the trooper on the radio link. The New Jersey State Police patched in and then informed the trooper that it was now an Air Force matter, and the police officer left. The airman stayed with the dead alien until a C-141 transport plane arrived. Debarking Air Force men in blue fatigues and wearing blue berets told the airman it was time for him to leave; but the airman said he lingered while the new arrivals sprayed the body with an aerosol substance, placed it into a body bag, then a crate, and after that put the crate and themselves onto the plane, which promptly left. The destination was said to be Wright-Patterson AFB, where foreign (and, presumably alien) artefacts and technology were investigated.[19]

During this time, George had been gathering information at the base tower and command complex while the alien had been quickly removed, so he had no chance to go to the site of the incident at the far end of the runway before that phase of the event had passed. He drew up the report based on what he knew for submission to General Thomas M. Sadler, Commander of the 21st Air Force. When Major Filer discovered that photographs had been taken of the dead alien, he went to the photo

17. Ibid. pp.169-170.
18. Ibid. p.170.
19. Ibid. pp.171-172.

lab to acquire copies to present to the General, but was denied access, so he went to the General's office, only to encounter the commander of the 418th Security Police Squadron, who told him that the General had already been briefed and then dismissed George.[20]

After he retired from the Air Force, Major Filer became involved in UFO investigations, and met UFO researcher Leonard Stringfield. When Stringfield learned of George's involvement, he connected him with the airman who had discovered the body that night. The airman said Air Force personnel had threatened him with death if he ever told anyone about the events of the Fort Dix-McGuire AFB incident, so he has remained anonymous, but confirmed his knowledge of that night's goings on.[21]

Re-enter Timothy Good, who reported that he, too, had interviewed the airman who had partially confirmed Major Filer's story, and he went further to reveal that another, unnamed UFO investigator had been told that all records of the Fort Dix-McGuire AFB incident had been destroyed. The anonymous researcher also said he had been warned away from the case. (So, the records were "destroyed" – or sealed and locked away – as if nothing had happened; but, if nothing had happened, why warn a researcher away from that "nothing"?) Good also revealed that his inquiry of the New Jersey State Police resulted in him being told that such information was privileged, not public. Good also learned of a possible additional witness who might have been willing to talk, but when re-contacted the man seemed very nervous and distant, and never renewed any interaction. Finally in this regard, when it became known in the ufology community that Timothy Good was investigating the case, none other than George Filer contacted him about the events of 18 January 1978.[22]

What to make of this case? The reliance almost exclusively on a single source, with corroboration by yet another single source who has remained anonymous, is concerning. But George Filer's account is overall very convincing and evidently based solidly on facts, which makes me inclined to accept his version of events at Fort Dix-McGuire AFB; and all the more so because he freely admits to being a peripheral observer of the incident, and not at the center of attention. Of great weight to me is the involvement of Timothy Good, a thorough and careful investigator and reporter of all things UFO. (Even though he – like many other ufologists, researchers,

20. Ibid. pp.173-175.
21. Ibid. 182.
22. *The UFO Report*, Timothy Good. Avon. New York. 1989. pp.188-189.

investigators and so on, has been deceived by a very sophisticated hoax perpetrated by veteran UFO experts.)

The puzzling aspect of this occurrence comes in trying to fathom why an alien being would have been on the ground by itself that night, and there exists speculation in UFO literature that perhaps an alien spacecraft had experienced a temporary crash landing, with the pilot inadvertently taking off again without one of the crew members; or that a UFO had landed and, when base security troops arrived, some mix-up had occurred and the being's fellows had mistakenly become airborne while it was still outside. (Accidents do happen, even to technologically very advanced entities.) The assertion that a UFO was hovering above the MP's vehicle before the alien ran out of the darkness indicates the extraterrestrials could have been searching for their misplaced colleague. Moreover, the unfortunate ET may have run out into the headlight beams in an effort to reveal itself not to the MP but to the other aliens looking for it.

So, overall I am strongly inclined to accept this incident as fact. I do not believe that Major Filer was hoaxing us, and I certainly do not think he was hallucinating or mistaken. This seems to be an instance where a life was lost during an alien encounter with one of Earth's military organizations.

Minot, Malmstrom, Warren – What Happened at America's Strategic Missile Bases?

Minot AFB

On 6 May 2013, an event was organized at the National Press Club – the "Citizens Hearing on Disclosure" – by UFO advocates through Paradigm Research. Former Senator Mike Gravel and former congressional Representatives Roscoe Bartlett, Merrill Cook, Lynn Woolsey, Carolyn Kilpatrick and Darlene Hooley were in attendance at the five-day event. The faux hearing was modeled after congressional proceedings to focus on evidence that UFO sightings could be linked to intelligent extraterrestrial beings. The aim was to pressure the United States government to disclose information known to the military and intelligence branches regarding the subject.[23, 24]

---

23. https://abcnews.go.com/Politics/truth-lawmakers-piqued-skeptical-ets/story?id=19086646
24. There was some negative publicity when it became known that the former members of congress were paid to attend. https://www.theguardian.com/world/2013/apr/29/ufo-conspiracy-hearing-congressmen-senators

At the event, Captain (Retired) David D. Schindele of the U.S. Air Force, delivered a statement regarding a UFO incident in which he was involved while performing his duties. He was "a Minuteman ICBM Launch Control Officer, a First Lieutenant, and a Deputy Missile Combat Crew Commander in a two-man Launch Crew with my crew commander who held the rank of Major."[25] Schindele further testified that despite the fact that he was ordered to remain silent, and was told of the event: "It never happened," which is the title of a book he later wrote about the experience, he had been going public anyway.[26]

Schindele specified that he was assigned to the Strategic Air Command as a member of the 742nd Strategic Missile Squadron – one of three such squadrons in the 455th Strategic Missile Wing, centered at Minot Air Force Base, North Dakota. His term of service there was from July 1965 to May 1968. Schindele testified that on 5 March 1967, as he arose for work he saw a television report about a UFO sighting at Mohall, North Dakota, which is about 3 miles west of the launch control complex where he performed his duties. Both are about 37 miles north of the main facilities at Minot AFB. During the morning briefing of all missile crews it was mentioned that some missiles had gone off-line at another complex, known as "November Flight." He added that after the briefing there was some speculation among the crews, including the Major who was his immediate superior, about the UFO news on television and any possible connection with the missiles going off-line.[27]

Upon arriving at the launch complex, the Site Manager – a Technical Sergeant, took him aside and explained that the night before a UFO had hovered just beyond the fence at their location. Based on what he was told, Schindele estimated that the object had been about 100ft in diameter. The Sergeant added that the UFO had been about the same distance – 100ft, from the above-ground building where they then stood.

When Schindele asked if it could have been a helicopter, the Sergeant told him it had been silent, with "flashing" lights that were like no others he had ever seen, and that they seemed to "pulsate," adding that it had then moved to hover directly above the below-ground launch control bunker and crew quarters. Schindele added that the Technical Sergeant's account was confirmed by the security team.

25. https://ufologie.patrickgross.org/rec/schindele.htm
26. *It Never Happened, Volume 1: U.S. Air Force UFO Cover-up* David D. Schindele. EdgarRock Publishing. No city listed, 2017.
27. https://ufologie.patrickgross.org/rec/schindele.htm

When Schindele and the Major in charge of his team alighted from the elevator at Launch Control, 60ft below ground, to relieve the other team there they immediately noticed that the Launch Control Console showed that all ten missiles supposedly under their command were "off alert and unlaunchable."[28] The crew they were relieving informed Schindele's team that the missiles had gone off-line at the same time that the UFO had hovered above the site.[29]

The next morning, following his duty assignment, Schindele checked with his Flight Security Controller to inquire about the missile shut-down, and was told he had been instructed not to discuss it, adding that the Air Force Office of Special Investigations (AFOSI) had ordered them all to remain silent about the situation. Thus, Schindele and his fellow missileers received no guidance from the Air Force regarding what to do in similar predicaments in the future.

Schindele prefaced his remarks with the background information that, "About 35 years after my experience at Minot and the study of an identical incident that occurred on Malmstrom AFB in Montana, I considered telling the truth." He also explained that the occurrence had not been discussed with his fellows, saying, "I never spoke a word about my incident for almost forty years, and my wife never knew."

Malmstrom AFB

Captain Schindele had been referring to an event that was just as consequential and kept hidden as well as possible by the Air Force at the Malmstrom AFB strategic missile fields. This situation was revealed to the world by Lieutenant Colonel (Retired) Robert Salas, who likewise wrote a book about his experiences.[30]

Also a former launch-control officer, Salas – then a First Lieutenant, was the on-duty Deputy Commander of a Launch Control Facility at Malmstrom Air Force Base, Montana, on 24 March 1967. (Like Schindele, Salas delayed for many years before writing of the incident, later recalling that it could have occurred eight days earlier, on 16 March.)

Salas said the facility's Flight Security Controller called from above ground and was in a panicky state as he shouted that there was "a large,

28. Ibid. Also: https://www.minotdailynews.com/news/local-news/2017/06/book-tells-about-air-force-ufo-incidents/

29. https://ufologie.patrickgross.org/rec/schindele.htm

30. *Faded Giant* Robert Salas and James Klotz. Booksurge. No city given. 2005.

glowing, pulsating, red oval-shaped object hovering over the front gate."[31] In a sworn affidavit, Salas declared that while awakening his commanding officer, alarms went off in the control room, indicating that all ten missiles in their flight had been disabled. The retired Lieutenant Colonel also reported that eight days prior to that incident, on 16 (or possibly 8) March 1967, there had been a similar occurrence at another Launch Control Facility at Malmstrom.[32]

Of course, Salas said that after the event, which is described in detail in *Faded Giant*, "Major Florenze J. Mansmann ordered him never to speak of what he had seen ever again." I find it coincidental – too coincidental – that the same officer was involved in the investigations and attempts to cover-up widely separated UFO incidents at Air Force bases – at Vandenberg in 1964 and Malmstrom in 1967. It seems that the information-suppression campaign, often denied by the Air Force, was in full operation then, as before and after.

Warren AFB

In an article at *The Atlantic* by Marc Ambinder, titled "Failure Shuts Down Squadron of Nuclear Missiles," dated 26 October 2010, the journalist reveals that "an engineering ~~power~~ [*sic*] failure at F.E. Warren Air Force Base in (Cheyenne) Wyoming … took fifty nuclear intercontinental ballistic missiles (ICBMs), one-ninth of the U.S. (ground-based) missile force, temporarily offline on Saturday."[33] The "Saturday" referred to would have been 23 October. The article goes on to explain that the problem was described by an Air Force official as originating in a launch control center computer; that the computer started to "'ping' out of sequence," causing a "surge" of "noise" within the system. This sequential mistake then caused receivers on the missiles to send out error codes.

Ambinder's article explains that this problem happens from time to time, so missileers attempted some quick fixes; however, in a cascading effect, more and more missiles went off-line, so the decision was made to shut down five Launch Control Centers, then restart them, which restored normal operation in three, leaving the "suspect LCC" still off-line. (This only accounts for four, not five.)

---

31. https://www.military.com/daily-news/2021/10/19/air-force-veterans-who-are-ufo-true-believers-return-newly-attentive-washington.html
32. https://nypost.com/2021/10/21/former-air-force-chief-claims-he-once-saw-ufo-firing-at-nuke-missiles-launched-from-secret-base/
33. https://www.theatlantic.com/politics/archive/2010/10/failure-shuts-down-squadron-of-nuclear-missiles/65207/

Other missile sites and higher commands were alerted to the problem. The Air Force, while offering the "pinging out of sequence" explanation, also declared that "engineers discovered that similar hardware failures had triggered a similar cascading failure twelve years ago at Minot AFB in North Dakota and Malmstrom AFB in Montana. That piece of hardware is the prime suspect." This is an interesting addition because twelve years before 2010 would have been in 1998, which means missiles had been shut down at two bases in that year as well – in addition to 1967. (As far as can be determined, the 1998 occurrences were never reported elsewhere.) Also, the story (alibi) had almost instantly become a "hardware" problem. I am far from being a computer expert, but an intermittent and periodic operating out of sequence suggests a software problem, not a hardware issue. Moreover, Lieutenant Colonel Salas reports in his book that after the missile control failures at Malmstrom in 1967, both the Air Force and Boeing Aerospace Company conducted an extensive and thorough investigation of the incident, including hardware and software trouble-shooting, and testing components for the effects of electromagnetic pulse, which is generated by nuclear blasts, and against which the missiles are shielded. The teams of technicians and engineers discovered no problems. They were mystified.[34]

"However, Lieutenant Colonel John Thomas, director of public affairs for Air Force Global Strike Command headquarters at Barksdale Air Force Base in Louisiana, denies there is a policy to silence eyewitnesses to unexplained phenomena at Air Force bases."[35]

Regarding the last two statements: on the one side we have an earnest and honest man who admitted to his human weakness of not always having a precise memory and who has gone out of his way, while also leading a very productive life, to bring the truth to the public. On the other side we have a spokesperson for an entrenched military bureaucracy that cannot admit to the fact that not only can it not protect the air space above its home country but also that it cannot prevent the neutralization of its weaponry by possible hostile entities. It is not difficult to see why I totally discount, once more, what Air Force representatives say. I am not about to accept the extraordinary claims of military and government representatives without at least a minimum amount of extraordinary proof. Show us; don't just talk about it.

---

34. *Faded Giant* Robert Salas and James Klotz. BookSurge. No city listed. 2005. pp.20-25.
35. https://www.dailymail.co.uk/news/article-2012406/UFO-cause-power-failure-Wyoming-nuclear-missile-base-say-technicians.html

Further, according to the report in *The Atlantic*, "The defense official said that there had not been a power failure, though the official acknowledged that that explanation had made its way through public affairs channels. Engineers working on the system presented a draft of their initial findings late this afternoon, the official said."[36] This seems to be a backhanded admission that the power failure story, which "had made its way through public affairs channels" was not true. The overstated cover story was, again according to journalist Ambinder, "'We've never had something as big as this happen,' a military officer who was briefed on the incident said. 'Occasionally, one or two might blink out,' the officer said." The unnamed officer went over the top again, because, according to both Captain David Schindele and Lieutenant Colonel Robert Salas, ten missiles went off-line in each of the two incidents we were aware of prior to this mass shut-down.

The Atlantic report continued by stating that the exact cause of the failure was still unknown but that it was suspected of being "a breach of underground cables deep beneath the base." That would be a power problem – remembering the strikeout – not a hardware defect. This excuse was offered by "a senior military official." We are now supposing a breach of one of the underground cables, which are armored and shielded from both excavation and electromagnetic pulses.

The story then stretches even further, with the assertion that "It is next to impossible for these systems to be hacked," adding that the Air Force does not suspect the activities of "malicious actors." (Not even extraterrestrial ones?) The story concludes by stating that about six missile silos had been affected by the shut-down. However, a "half dozen silos" do not contain fifty missiles (they are situated one missile per silo.) It seems at least one Air Force spokesperson or reporter needs to brush up on math skills. And, yet again: but, wait, there's more…

Our final quote from *The Atlantic* story tells us, "An administration official said that 'to make too much out of this would be to sensationalize it. It's not that big of a deal. Everything worked as planned.'" Now the political bureaucracy – in the form of "the administration" – got involved with yet another attempt to pat us on our little heads and advise us not to worry, because, "Everything worked as planned." If everything "worked as planned," then fifty ICBMs would not have gone off-line.

---

36. https://www.theatlantic.com/politics/archive/2010/10/failure-shuts-down-squadron-of-nuclear-missiles/65207/

The Air Force isn't very good at concocting excuses: it was a power failure – no, it was a hardware (or was it software?) issue; but, no, perhaps an underground cable breach. While the problem had been investigated up to that point to a level of exhaustion for a period of over forty-two years (1967–2010), a short analysis by engineers had found the complication was out-of-sequence pinging, which to this not-a-computer-wiz means software, but, no, it was hardware; but, wait, no, it was an underground cable breach. It is impossible for the system to be hacked. (Just as – in my recollections, it was impossible for the missiles to go off-line to begin with.) Because 50 of America's 450 to nearly 1,000 land-based intercontinental ballistic missiles[37] were beyond our control, "to make too much of this would be to sensationalize it. It's not that big of a deal" – no, just 50 missiles, with from 50 and up to 150[38] warheads. And, of course, "Everything worked as planned." (If the plan was to have them fail to be ready for launch if needed.)

Had enough yet? Yeah, me too; but, as you can guess, there's even more to this saga…

By the time the *Daily Mail* covered the item, 8 July 2011, the story went like this: "Did UFO cause power failure at nuclear missile base? Missile technicians claim sightings coincided with October outage. Fifty nuclear weapons lost touch with control centre. Blackout lasted almost an hour says Air Force. President Obama told of power supply interruption."[39]

UFOs return to the story, which, without doubt for me, the Air Force had hoped would not appear in this incident. The rather weak attempt to "explain" (away) the earlier problems in North Dakota and Montana with the ill-conceived software/hardware/cable-breach "solution" backfired and resulted in strange objects being a part of events, this time in Wyoming.

The *Daily Mail* reporting also relies on a figure who by now is familiar to the readers of this book: "UFO researcher Robert Hastings says eyewitnesses claim the interruption to the power supply also lasted much longer than the Air Force admits." The story continues with the revelation that "three missile maintenance technicians have agreed to speak to him

37. http://npshistory.com/publications/mimi/srs/intro.htm
38. The United States, in compliance with an agreement with Russia, was reducing the number of warheads on each missile from 3 to 1. The process was not complete until late 2014, so it is difficult – impossible, really – to accurately estimate the number of warheads as of October 2010, only the number of missiles. Also, the number of missiles themselves was also reduced. https://www.af.mil/News/Article-Display/Article/485611/malmstrom-completes-final-minuteman-iii-configuration/
39. https://www.dailymail.co.uk/news/article-2012406/UFO-cause-power-failure-Wyoming-nuclear-missile-base-say-technicians.html

[Hastings] on the condition of anonymity, revealing the military has kept UFO sightings that occurred during the power outage under wraps." (But we had already been assured: "Lieutenant Colonel John Thomas, director of public affairs for Air Force Global Strike Command headquarters at Barksdale Air Force Base in Louisiana, denies there is a policy to silence eyewitnesses to unexplained phenomena at Air Force bases.")

Hastings told the *Daily Mail* that the witnesses said a large cigar-shaped object had hovered high above the missile field on the day of the outage – 23 October 2010 – and that it was seen "throughout the weekend, both during the (missile) disruption and the following day." The witnesses also said it was not a commercial blimp because it was more torpedo-shaped, and that it lacked any sort of passenger gondola slung underneath, and there was no advertising on its hull.

Moreover, Hastings' witnesses said the outages were intermittent and lasted not just for fifty minutes, as the Air Force is reported to have told President Obama, but instead went on for twenty-six hours.

Lieutenant Colonel John Thomas, after promising us that no one had been silenced, went on to say, "'This incident is separate from all of that.' [The events at Minot and Malmstrom, in 1967.] 'We took it very seriously and we're very confident that we understand fully what happened.'"

Colonel Thomas and the *Daily Mail* concluded with his remarks: "'If people see things that are unusual, they are encouraged to report them,' … adding: 'When people join the military, they don't give up their First Amendment rights.'" If only the Air Force, and especially its Office of Special Investigations truly believed that, perhaps more Americans, among others, might put more faith in the words of not only the Air Force but also the United States government.

Did a UFO Almost Trigger a Nuclear Attack?

If we can accept, as an American administration official said, that having fifty of the USAF's 450 land-based strategic missiles rendered inactive was "not that big of a deal," then what about a UFO nearly causing a nuclear strike on numerous targets in the United States?

On 22 June 1997, *The Herald* of Scotland headlined the story: "Alien encounter sparked Soviet missile crisis."[40] The subheading read: "Aliens

40. https://www.heraldscotland.com/news/12318039.alien-encounter-sparked-soviet-missile-crisis/

nearly brought the world to the brink of nuclear war, it was claimed at a UFO conference yesterday."

The story explained that at a UFO conference at Imperial College in London, American UFO investigator George Knapp presented his "interviews with Russian military and scientific chiefs, shown in the UK for the first time." Among those interviewed was "Colonel Boris Solokov, an expert in radio waves and radio astronomy at the Russian Ministry of Defence."

Solokov told Knapp that "on the night of 4 October 1984 [all other sources, including NICAP,[41] set the date as 4 October 1982 – mistakes happen] dozens of soldiers working at a nuclear base in Usovo in Ukraine saw up to five UFOs."[42]

Solokov also explained that he was in the Kremlin in Moscow when all of the displays on the control panels for the Usovo base's nuclear-armed missiles spontaneously became illuminated. More upsetting, the highly secret missile access codes had also automatically displayed on the screens at the base.

The Herald story then goes on to change the date for the following day but got the year right as it continued, stating that Colonel Solokov was ordered to go immediately ("immediately" or the next day?) to Ukraine (on 5 October 1982). It was an urgent mission because the base commander reported to the chief of the general staff that:

> The previous day, the base observed a UFO for four hours. At the same time on the control panel they received an order to prepare the launch of the missiles. The lights lit up and the appearance of the launch codes meant the missiles were enabled. Dozens of officers witnessed this.

Knapp then reported that the incident, during which the command to initiate a launch was just as mysteriously terminated, instigated a ten-year investigation of UFOs and aliens by Soviet authorities.

> George Knapp, who has himself dismissed many UFO reports as hoaxes, believes the Russian were sincere. 'It was a question mark for me at the very beginning, but now I am convinced,'

41. http://www.nicap.org/821004sovietukraine_dir.htm)
42. https://www.heraldscotland.com/news/12318039.alien-encounter-sparked-soviet-missile-crisis/

> he said. 'These were not wide-eyed Ufologists. These were hardline, hardboiled Russian military figures secretly studying a potentially dangerous phenomenon.'

Further confirmation of this disturbing event was brought to light at NICAP's website, quoting from "*ABC News Prime Time Live* dated 5 October 1995." Citing the correct date of 4 October 1982, in then Soviet-controlled Ukraine, "numerous eyewitnesses" confirmed to ABC correspondent David Ensor that a huge, disc-shaped UFO – some 900m, or 2,950ft in diameter – hovered above the aforementioned missile silo. Quoting Lieutenant Colonel Vladimir Plantonev, who was a missileer in the bunker at the time, the story confirmed George Knapp's earlier report. As additional support for the truth of the account, the NICAP/ABC news item says that a member of the special commission sent from Moscow to investigate the incident, Colonel Igor Chenovshev also told Ensor the episode had in fact taken place.[43]

The missile in question was likely able to deploy ten warheads; "the Mod 2 missiles were all replaced by the Mod 4 variant by 1983 ... SS-18 Mod 4 - R-36UT. The SS-18 Mod 4 carries at least ten MIRVs and was probably designed to attack and destroy ICBMs and other hardened targets in the US."[44] Solokov said "the missiles," not just a single missile, were activated. But the ABC report said a UFO hovered above a single silo. The ABC report may have intended to indicate the missile-control bunker because a silo holds a single missile, not many "missiles." Had the launch order not spontaneously canceled then at least ten and possibly many more nuclear warheads would have been sent toward the United States that day.

In this case, with multiple and credible witnesses, and more than one very reliable reporting source, it seems this bit of malicious mischief – at the very least – by extraterrestrials is an established fact.

43. http://www.ufoevidence.org/documents/doc459.htm
44. https://nuke.fas.org/guide/russia/icbm/r-36m.htm

Chapter 13

A UFO on the Ground in Suffolk

UFO Lands at RAF-USAF Air Base in Suffolk

Nick Pope, who wrote a book on the subject,[1] also delivered an article that appeared in the *Daily Mail* that gives us an overview of the events in Rendlesham Forest, just outside RAF Bentwaters, leased in part to the United States during the Cold War.

In the article, which also goes into the Roswell UFO crash, Pope informs us about the general circumstances of the happenings in Suffolk. Pope describes the Rendlesham/Bentwaters incident as being the best-known in the United Kingdom.

In the very early hours of the morning of 26 December 1980, United States Air Force security personnel reported seeing odd-looking lights in the forest just outside a back gate. Believing that perhaps a plane had crashed, they went out to investigate.[2]

They discovered a brightly lit, pyramidal object, about 9ft across and 6ft high, propped up on three legs among the trees, and saw that branches overhead had been broken off.

The security soldiers took photographs. (They were informed by the Air Force later that the photos had not developed properly.) Stunned, the men briefed their superiors, who included the Deputy Base Commander, Lieutenant Colonel Charles Halt, who ordered them to file official reports, including sketches of what they had seen.

I must pause here to relate that a long-time attempted debunker of the Rendlesham Forest UFO reports has written an initially convincing

1. *Encounter in Rendlesham Forest: The Inside Story of the World's Best-Documented UFO Incident* Nick Pope, John Burroughs, Jim Penniston. Thomas Dunne Books. New York. 2014.
2. https://www.dailymail.co.uk/news/article-465276/Roswell-officers-amazing-deathbed-admission-raises-possibility-aliens-DID-visit.html (Updated 30 June 2007.)

effort to discredit the key witness to the opening phase of the events of December 1980. However, the excellent reporting by Mr Pope, and the written testimony of the witness whom the professional naysayer sought to besmirch, set me on the proper path. I made the error of reading the character-assassin's version first; but, when reading what actually happened, according to a long-time military man with an excellent record and who served in many sensitive duties, I quickly learned that, as usual, the "scientific investigation" was neither scientific nor an actual investigation as much as a nonsensical bit of propaganda. The principal witness at first did not divulge all of the facts for fear of ridicule, then, after interrogation by AFOSI agents, he was injected with drugs to distort and/or suppress his memories.[3] These memories only resurfaced later. The supposed debunker ignored these facts and other material evidence.

The actual facts as presented by numerous witnesses confound refutation and are verified by recent government and non-government sources. I urge readers to beware and to always read the original accounts by actual eyewitnesses – even though in many cases, including that of the events in Rendlesham Forest, the official and semi-official source materials were confiscated and kept hidden by government agencies.

The aspiring debunker in question sought the route of character assassination in his weak presentation of "facts" of a "scientific" nature that was anti-scientific in its ignorance of what actually happened according to numerous military professionals. This was done to try to disqualify the key witness, and to then try to shift the "lack of credibility" onto all other witnesses and evidence, which merely proved to me that the events at Rendlesham Forest as described by Mr Pope and his co-authors is a substantial and true representation of the complete story.

It is unfortunate that an individual with a long-time reputation for scientific accuracy and expertise in his field of astronomy should self-destruct his own credibility with a spurious attempt to jump onto the anti-UFO bandwagon, which has proven over the years to have become dilapidated and out of tune due to its own lack of thorough scientific analysis of the actual facts as presented by credible eyewitnesses. Some people, no matter how "learned," just never learn.

---

3. *Codes and Conspiracies: The UFO Cover-Up* Original air date: 23 March 2014. Flight 33 Productions. https://www.channel5.com/show/conspiracy/season-1/alien-cover-up Also: https://www.imdb.com/title/tt3695214/releaseinfo?ref_=tt_dt_rdat

I generally give little credit to debunkers because, as with this case, even a relatively short perusal, by consulting actual eyewitnesses and other such evidence as may still exist (not having been stolen and hidden), quickly reveals the sloppy and one-sided "investigations" foisted onto unsuspecting members of the public by the closed-minded. Let us continue with our own look at the Rendlesham Forest UFO encounter with the militaries of both the United States and the United Kingdom.

The foregoing disclaimer was to clear the "fog of war" generated by opportunistic and closed-minded people who may use the one over-enthusiastic, vague, mistaken, or even just reluctant witness to try to invalidate the corroborated testimony of many others, as well as physical evidence. Some efforts to "debunk" the Rendlesham/Bentwaters incident are based on fallacious and even maliciously invented "facts" that are in actuality baseless. I invite readers to consult Nick Pope's book, *Encounter in Rendlesham Forest* for a clearer picture of what actually happened there as described so far,[4] and as we continue.

The next night, while attending a get-together on base, Lieutenant Colonel Halt received an anxious call from an obviously distressed airman who said, "Sir, it's back."[5]

Halt recalls asking, "What's back?" The airman told him, "The UFO, Sir. The UFO is back."

The Deputy Base Commander mustered another security team, gathered up a tape recorder, and went to the woods to, in his mind, "Debunk this nonsense."

When the team went into the woods, their radios started failing, and the portable work lights they had brought in shut down. When Halt and the security team saw the UFO, apparently hovering at that point, it rose directly overhead, and shot a powerful beam of light at their feet. Weak efforts to claim the many witnesses saw a lighthouse beacon do not account for the light in question soaring overhead and sending a light shaft down onto the forest floor, which a lighthouse could not do.

Also ignored by skeptics who say the lighthouse was visible from one small area of Rendlesham Forest was the fact that the UFOs were seen by

4. *Encounter in Rendlesham Forest: The Inside Story of the World's Best-Documented UFO Incident* Nick Pope, John Burroughs, Jim Penniston. Thomas Dunne Books. New York. 2014. pp.5-13.
5. https://www.dailymail.co.uk/news/article-465276/Roswell-officers-amazing-deathbed-admission-raises-possibility-aliens-DID-visit.html (Updated 30 June 2007.)

dozens of witnesses from various angles. Moreover, the UFOs were reported on these two nights alone, not night after night, as would have been the case if the lighthouse were being seen on a nightly basis. Additionally, RAF radar operators tracked the UFO.[6] Yet again, people intent on debunking "surveyed" the situation just long enough to concoct an "explanation" that ignored material evidence, then declared their unfounded assertions to be "the truth." (Readers may have noticed that because would-be debunkers seek publicity, I avoid revealing their names.)

During all of these events, Lieutenant Colonel Halt was updating the goings-on by speaking into his recorder, making side comments such as "This is weird."[7]

After the UFO departed, Lieutenant Colonel Halt ordered an examination of the area. The Air Force men found three indentations in the ground where the object had been standing when the first security team had arrived the night before. Radiation measurements showed higher levels at the depressions apparently made by the craft's landing legs.[8]

After Lieutenant Colonel Halt made his report, the British Ministry of Defence launched an investigation and, despite agreement on the heightened radiation readings, and the testimony of several of the most reliable witnesses – men assigned to the security and administration of a military base where nuclear weapons were stored for possible use – as can be expected in a government report, the MoD decided the findings in the case were "inconclusive." However, for those deeply interested, the case file was later released for public scrutiny.[9]

Again, there is much more to this story, and government attempts to suppress it; but, due to space limitations, it is time to move on as I am convinced of the authenticity of the Rendlesham Forest incident as a genuine close encounter – a very close encounter with at least one United States Air Force security man – with not just a UFO in the sky but a landed and not positively identified object.

---

6. https://interestingengineering.com/21-facts-about-the-unresolved-ufo-incident-at-rendlesham-forest
7. *Encounter in Rendlesham Forest: The Inside Story of the World's Best-Documented UFO Incident* Nick Pope, John Burroughs, Jim Penniston. Thomas Dunne Books. New York. 2014. pp.275-296.
8. https://www.dailymail.co.uk/news/article-465276/Roswell-officers-amazing-deathbed-admission-raises-possibility-aliens-DID-visit.html
9. Ibid.

Dozens Report UFOs Over England, Including at RAF Bases

In the same *Daily Mail* column, Nick Pope cites a mass sightings over different areas of England, noting that observers included police officers. The UFOs were spotted above RAF Cosford, and RAF Shawbury.

Pope reveals to us that the Meteorological Officer at RAF Shawbury told of a UFO described as a huge, triangular object that would hover, then speed away faster than an RAF jet. He was only one person among some sixty observing UFOs during this, the wave of 1993. The same RAF man said the object was larger than a C-130 transport plane and a Boeing 747. He also reported that the object had dropped as low as 400ft and shot a narrow light beam at the ground while it emitted a low-frequency humming sound.

The Ministry of Defence investigated for several weeks, compiling a case file of over 100 pages. The report to the Assistant Chief of the Air Staff concluded: "there would seem to be some evidence on this occasion that an unidentified object (or objects) of unknown origin was operating over the UK."

Pope commented that this admission was probably the most forthright the MoD had ever made with regard to UFOs.

Peruvian Air Force Pilot Intercepts, Shoots UFO

It was early morning on 11 April 1980 at the La Joya Peruvian Air Force Base. One thousand eight hundred cadets, other military personnel and civilians were preparing for their daily exercises when a light-bulb-shaped UFO was spotted hovering over the end of the runway. At 23 years old, Lieutenant Oscar Santa Maria Huerta was already an expert fighter pilot; he was ordered to take his plane to the air and investigate.[10]

In an article for News.com.au, correspondent Frank Chung quoted from Leslie Kean's *New York Times*-rated bestselling book: *UFOs: Generals, Pilots, and Government Officials Go on the Record.*[11] As reported by Kean and Chung, Huerta quickly engaged the UFO, which his superiors and he at first believed to be a foreign surveillance balloon, and he opened fire with

10. https://www.news.com.au/finance/work/leaders/the-only-man-to-ever-shoot-at-a-ufo/news-story/8fdf6eddbe5363fb5823f1625a7713f5
11. *UFOs: Generals, Pilots, and Government Officials Go on the Record* Leslie Kean. Three Rivers Press, New York, 2010. pp.93-98.

his on-board guns in a burst of sixty-four 30mm rounds, which he said the UFO "absorbed" without any apparent damage.[12]

Huerta was a Colonel when he delivered his report at a press briefing by UFO researchers, former military people and other witnesses at the major journalistic event at the National Press Club in Washington, D.C. on 6 May 2013, cited earlier. He said that after shooting the bullets into the UFO he flew past the object, then performed a looping, hairpin turn and closed with it again; but it darted away at high speed, forcing him to go to afterburners in a pursuit that went for more than 50 miles until the UFO suddenly stopped in front of his jet, compelling him to veer off.

Running low on fuel, Huerta said he suddenly became frightened, due in part to the fact that he realized this was no balloon but a mysterious craft with a cream-colored dome on top and a silvery, metallic-looking lower half. He reported that he returned to base, gliding at times to save fuel, and upon his landing, noted that the UFO was hovering above the runway again, where it remained for two more hours.

Huerta also said that everyone at the base had seen the UFO, and that many of the witnesses had been required to make written reports on the incident. He described the object as having no jets, exhausts, wings, windows, antennae, and no visible source of propulsion.

Others may scoff, but I find myself compelled to accept this man's word, including his assertion that some 1,800 people, mostly military personnel, witnessed this incident, the significance of which I will briefly address later.

Iranian Jets Attempt to Intercept UFO Above Tehran, 1976

Also covered in Kean's *UFOs: Generals, Pilots, and Government Officials Go on the Record* is the 1976 UFO interception by then squadron commander in the Imperial Iranian Air Force, Major Parviz Jafari, who would later retire as a General.[13] The incident is also described at a U.S. government National Security Agency website[14] quoting an official but later declassified

12. https://www.news.com.au/finance/work/leaders/the-only-man-to-ever-shoot-at-a-ufo/news-story/8fdf6eddbe5363fb5823f1625a7713f5 And: *UFOs: Generals, Pilots, and Government Officials Go on the Record* Leslie Kean. Three Rivers Press, New York, 2010. pp.93-98.
13. *UFOs: Generals, Pilots, and Government Officials Go on the Record.* By Leslie Kean. Three Rivers Press, New York, 2010. pp.86-92.
14. https://www.nsa.gov/portals/75/documents/news-features/declassified-documents/ufo/us_gov_iran_case.pdf

report to the Joint Chiefs of Staff (U.S.).[15] These and other sources concur as to the reality of the events of that night. (Kean identifies the date as 18 September 1976; the *International UFO Reporter* (IUR) account gives the date as 19 September; and the official report to the JCS states that it was 20 September. These could result from time-zone and International Date Line complications.)

After receiving phone calls about mysterious objects in the sky above Tehran, air defense officials scrambled an American-made F-4 Phantom jet fighter. When the plane approached the UFO and attempted to engage it with air-to-air missiles, the crew reported that their instruments, armaments and communications systems shut down. So the pilot turned the jet away. As the aircraft moved farther from the UFO, the on-board instrumentation became workable again.

After the aircraft discontinued the pursuit, a second fighter plane was sent aloft; this one piloted by Major Jafari. As he attempted an intercept, a second UFO, which he estimated to appear as about half the size of a full moon, split-off from the first UFO and headed straight toward his aircraft. He attempted to shoot at this UFO with AIM-9 missiles, but his instrumentation also failed. He turned away and as he did so the second UFO arced inside his course, then darted back to and re-entered the first UFO. After that, incredibly, yet a third object was emitted by the primary UFO, which Jafari assumed would crash as it plunged straight down toward the Earth; but instead it made a soft landing, illuminating the area where it alighted on a dry lakebed.

With some difficulty, the second F-4 returned to base, and as it did so an approaching airliner also encountered instrument failures and communications interference in the area where the third UFO had landed. A subsequent, daylight investigation of the landing site turned up no evidence, although a few eyewitnesses reported loud sounds and bright lights there overnight.

The official report on the events of the night was circulated to:

> [The] Secretary of State, the Central Intelligence Agency, the White House, the Air Force and Army Chiefs of Staff, the Chief of Naval Operations, the Defense Intelligence Agency, the Commander in Chief of U.S. Naval Forces in the Middle

15. https://www.nsa.gov/portals/75/documents/news-features/declassified-documents/ufo/joint_chiefs_staff_report.pdf

> East, the Commander in Chief of the U.S. Air Force in Europe, the European Defense Air Command, and the Commander in Chief of Forces in Europe.[16]

While the circulation list is impressive, the *IUR*[17] report also states that *all* significant events in the Middle East/Near East area at the time were also routinely sent to these recipients, but it is not known if other UFO events in the region or elsewhere received the same attention. However, despite the oft-denied interest in all things UFO/UAP, I suspect that such reports regarding UFOs are distributed far and wide to the levels of top leadership, just as they are equally withheld from those without a "need to know." However, I believe the general public also has a need to know if some more alarming indications to be introduced later are a true representation of the current situation.

Reports and Rumors of Soviet and American Planes Vanishing in Pursuit of UFOs

As mentioned earlier, reports of UFO events in Russia and the former Soviet Union are necessarily fragmentary and sketchy.

According to ufologist Paul Stonehill, whose specialty is UFO events within the old Soviet Bloc, and now Russia, there have been numerous instances of Russian and Soviet planes not just being shot down by the objects they are attacking, but, instead, the aircraft and their pilots simply vanishing when closing on UFOs with the intent of destroying them. This situation extends from a Russian policy, according to Stonehill – quoting a former KGB officer – regarding UFOs as alien spacecraft with hostile intentions.[18] Stonehill's immediate source was Yuri Stroganov, who in turn cites former KGB officer Ivan Vasilyevich, who informed him that he – Vasilyevich – had been on a special commission that evaluated the UFO phenomenon and reported the findings to the Soviet Politburo.

---

16. https://www.nsa.gov/portals/75/documents/news-features/declassified-documents/ufo/us_gov_iran_case.pdf
17. *International UFO Reporter* (Magazine) (*IUR*) is the quarterly journal of the J. Allen Hynek Center for UFO Studies (CUFOS).
18. *The Soviet UFO Files*. By Paul Stonehill. Bramley Books. Godalming, Surrey, UK. 1998. pp.40, 41.

Vasilyevich said the commission decided that it would be unlikely for aliens to come to Earth to exploit a natural resource because any such substance would be readily available throughout the universe. They further reasoned that if an alien race were far in advance of ours, we would simply be ignored. The final conclusion was that if the aliens are reasonably close to our level of development, they would likely opt to invade and conquer the human race. It seemed likely to them at the time – as it does to me now – that, despite their overhead spectacular light shows and aerial acrobatics, the aliens are actually not that far ahead of our species in all areas of development. Therefore, in view of UFO activities, they – the Soviets – would not communicate or negotiate with the aliens, except to attempt to gain access to their technology. Otherwise, any alien landings would be forcibly opposed and if such opposition failed, then an immediate nuclear strike would be ordered. The account, according to Stonehill, did not reveal if the proposed policy was adopted; however, if the subsequent reports of UFO encounters resulting in the loss of Soviet aircraft and pilots are true, it would seem that such a course of action was implemented, at least for a time.

While I have no reason to doubt Mr Stonehill's assertion that he has confirming documentation from secret Soviet/Russian sources, they are not directly quoted in his book, *The Soviet UFO Files*. This is likely to protect the safety of his sources. However, without any confirmation other than second-, third-, fourth-hand vague and obscure accounts, I believe it would not be worthwhile devoting too much attention to the reports – rumors, really – about the disappearances of Soviet-era military planes and pilots other than to state that they are said to be more than a handful in number, with a few such occurrences possibly involving multiple witnesses – and several aircraft lost in single encounters, but none of the people are specifically named, with a few exceptions. The supposed anti-UFO attacks and their negative results, as we shall learn, are not entirely unbelievable. UFO encounters with military forces in Russia – some involving ground-based forces, too – are part of at least the unofficial "record." It has also been asserted by several sources that the policy of hostile action was quickly abandoned due to Soviet fears of severe alien retaliatory counterstrikes.

Stonehill's reports through his sources are indirectly confirmed by Tom Rogan's *Washington Examiner* commentary of 17 December 2019:

> This isn't to say that these UFOs are hostile (although it must be noted that the diverging shapes, behaviors, and capability patterns of UFOs suggest more than one originating source).

> On the contrary, UFOs appear to be quite friendly, except when rather ill-advised Russian aircrews attempt to engage them.[19]

According to Stonehill, again through Vasilyevich, there was an alleged meeting by the intelligence services of the major powers in Geneva, Switzerland, in 1958, wherein it was reportedly decided by all countries involved to keep the UFO phenomenon as secret as possible, using methods that included ridicule and even threats of violence against eyewitnesses; and using mass media to ignore, suppress, misinterpret, and mock UFO incidents, witnesses and evidence, and journalists reporting on them.[20] As we have seen, such policies were evidently in place in the United States as far back as July 1947.

There have also been assertions by various ufologists of unconfirmed reports by anonymous or at least unknown witnesses who have insisted on remaining unidentified of more than a few aircraft of the United States Air Force and Navy being destroyed or having disappeared when in the vicinity of UFOs. I wish I could report otherwise; however, except for recent revelations through the UFO footage released by the United States Navy, and the testimony of Navy pilots, even sightings of UFOs have routinely and generally not been acknowledged or have been denied by all branches of the United States military and government; so it is hardly reasonable to expect any such admission by these organizations because they have as yet apparently been powerless to meaningfully challenge UFOs without the anticipation of suffering disastrous losses. However, there have been some hints, if not acknowledgements, by a few people who can be presumed to have been "in the know" when they made certain remarks.

Tom Rogan, London-educated foreign policy and national security writer for the *Washington Examiner*, in an opinion piece for that publication on 17 December 2019, offers his view: "I believe … the few individuals in the U.S. government who know about this issue believe the phenomena might be a threat. And that they don't know how to deal with it."[21] Unfortunately, after performing research for this book, I am forced to agree. Rogan goes

---

19. https://www.washingtonexaminer.com/opinion/the-real-reasons-the-us-government-is-so-secretive-about-ufos
20. *The Soviet UFO Files* Paul Stonehill. Bramley Books. Godalming, Surrey, UK. 1998. p.41.
21. https://www.washingtonexaminer.com/opinion/the-real-reasons-the-us-government-is-so-secretive-about-ufos

on to cite columnist Kristen Soltis Anderson's item in the *Washington Examiner Magazine*:

> UFOs are popping up near the aircraft carriers due to those carriers being nuclear-powered … UFOs also like to pop up near nuclear submarines and Air Force nuclear weapons bases … this paradigm has been occurring since the Manhattan Project operations at Los Alamos, New Mexico, and also at nuclear sites in the Soviet Union and Russia.

These remarks are not originating with cranks and weirdos but people who have contact with those who are "in the know," as we are indirectly now after reviewing the testimony of very reliable military people reported herein.

What follows is a sampling of but a few events around the globe; most involving military forces directly, a few only peripherally, as examples of UFOs/UAP as worldwide phenomena.

Chapter 14

More Military UFO Encounters from Around the World

Russia

Renowned Soviet test pilot Marina Popovich, also known as "Madame MiG," test-flew more than 40 planes, set 102 aviation world endurance records, including the world record for the longest flight for a woman pilot, and became the first female pilot to break the sound barrier in a MiG-21 fighter jet.[1] After the Soviet Union collapsed, Popovich published *UFO Glasnost* (2003), wherein she wrote that Soviet pilots – civilian and military, had confirmed 3,000 UFO sightings. She also reported that the KGB and Soviet Air Force had recovered fragments from five UFO crash sites within the Soviet Union.

In post-Soviet 1991, Popovich addressed a UFO conference at the University of California, Berkeley, relaying the news that "Soviet scientists had placed a blood sample inside a purported flying saucer landing site, which had subsequently undergone chemical changes." She also displayed what she identified as the final photograph of the Russian space probe Phobos 2, showing an unidentified cylindrical object nearby before the Earth-manufactured spacecraft disappeared in 1989, just as it was arriving at Mars.[2]

In an interview in 1997, Popovich reported that while flying a MiG 21 she saw:

> a brightly lit object, which she could only describe as a flying saucer: 'We thought it could be an enemy intruder. But it was so large that this was impossible. A collision looked unavoidable

1. https://www.smh.com.au/national/marina-popovich-madame-mig-soviet-test-pilot-and-ufo-expert-20171208-h0125e.html
2. https://www.ufosightingsfootage.uk/2019/03/did-aliens-in-20-mile-long-ufo-destroy-phobos-probe-above-mars.html

> but then the object tipped sideways and disappeared in a flash. It was a really scary experience.'

The "tipping sideways" maneuver agrees with the testimony of Bob Lazar, who first said in a 15 May 1989 media interview that he had worked on alien spacecraft at a remote site at the infamous Area-51 secret U.S. Air Force research base in the Nevada desert.[3] This maneuver is also clearly seen on the "Gimbal" video of a UFO taken by a U.S. Navy plane in January 2015.[4]

While on the subject of the UFOs on camera, there is a clip that predates the "Tic-Tac" video as far as its release is concerned, showing a Russian military plane chasing yet another UFO of the same description. It was posted by Military.com[5] on 27 June 2011. While it is possible this video was hoaxed, if so then the hoaxer was psychic in anticipating the shape and color of the "Tic-Tac" UFO to be seen by the public six years later.

Near Pereslavl-Zalessky, 83 straight-line miles northeast of Moscow, on 21 March 1990, a report was made by Aviation General Igor Maltsev, Air Defense Forces commander, that combat planes were sent to intercept a UFO.[6] General Maltsev summarized more than a hundred visual UFO sightings compiled by unit commanders:

> I am not a specialist in UFOs, and therefore I can only link the data together and express my own hypothesis. Based on the data collected by these witnesses, the UFO was a disk 100 to 200[7] meters in diameter. Two lights were flashing on its sides … the object turned around its axis and performed an S-shaped maneuver in both the vertical and the horizontal planes. Next the UFO continued to hover above the ground, then flew at a speed two to three times greater than that of modern combat aircraft … The objects flew at altitudes ranging from 100 to 7,000 meters. The movement of the UFOs [*sic*] was not

---

3. https://www.nevadacurrent.com/2021/06/01/ufos-the-pentagon-and-the-enigma-of-bob-lazar/
4. https://www.history.com/videos/uss-roosevelt-gimbal-ufo-declassified-video
5. https://www.military.com/video/aircraft/unidentified-flying-objects/russian-mig-21-intercepts-ufo/1027445744001
6. *Unidentified Flying Objects Briefing Document - The Best Available Evidence*. By Don Berliner and Whitley Streiber. Dell. New York 2000. Chapter 9.1. Citing the newspaper *Rabochaya Tribuna* (*Workers' Tribune*), 19 April 1990, "UFOs on Air Defense Radars."
7. 328.084 to 656.168 feet for our American readers. As a quick rule of thumb, I approximate 1m per yard, less about 9 per cent.

> accompanied by any type of noise and was characterized by an astounding maneuverability. The UFOs appeared to completely lack inertia. In other words, in one fashion or another they had overcome gravity. At present, terrestrial machines can scarcely exhibit such characteristics.[8]

At the Kapustin Yar Cosmodrome, air base, and nuclear facilities site, multiple witnesses observed UFOs. The report was filed by an unknown KGB officer but named a "Lieutenant Klimenko" and listed two corporals and two soldiers as the observers.

Between 10:15 and 11:55 p.m. on 28 July 1989 – one hour and forty minutes, up to three UFOs were spotted. One displayed jerky movements with abrupt accelerations and decelerations between hovering episodes. When intercepting jets approached one UFO, it zipped away at high speed. The UFOs were silent.

Continuing that night, from 11:55 p.m. until 1:30 a.m. on 29 July a "Second Lieutenant Volochine" observed a UFO in the same area that varied at a distance from 300m to "a few kilometers." It was described as a disc 4 to 5m in diameter with a brightly lit dome atop.

The Lieutenant's sighting was corroborated by a soldier named "Tichaev." Lieutenant Volochine saw the UFO emit a phosphorescent green light as it hovered 300m away and 20m above a missile depot. It shot a shaft of light toward the depot for several seconds. Tichaev told superior officers it could not have been a helicopter as it made no sound. After some time, a guard team joined them and also observed the UFO for about two hours.

China

On 4 June 2021, *South China Morning Post* correspondent Stephen Chen in Beijing reported that the People's Liberation Army was using artificial intelligence to track "unidentified air conditions" – their euphemism for

---

8. As cited at the COMETA Report. "UFOs and Defense: What Should We Prepare For?" An independent report on UFOs written by the French association COMETA. This report details the results of a study by the Institute of Higher Studies for National Defence - This paper originally appeared in a special issue of the magazine *VSD* published in France in July 1999. https://www.narcap.de/dokumente/COMETA-Report-englisch.pdf

UFOs/UAP.[9] Although the newspaper poses as an independent journalistic enterprise, it is controlled by Beijing, but – as my late mother-in-law (from mainland Asia) characterized it – "on a longer leash."

In the item, Chen says "Chinese researchers confirm that sighting reports from across the country are on the rise but aliens are unlikely to be responsible." Chen continues: "Chinese military researchers have turned to artificial intelligence to track and analyze the increasing number of unknown objects in China's airspace." The report quotes from Wuhan-based "researcher" from the PLA Air Force Early Warning Academy Chen Li, who said, "The frequent occurrence of unidentified air conditions in recent years … brings severe challenges to air defense security of our country," in a 2019 report to a conference of senior information technology scientists in Beijing.

Chen cites Li in detailing that "human analysts have been overwhelmed in recent years by the rapidly mounting sighting reports from a wide range of military and civilian sources across the country."

The SCMP story continues:

> UFOs are a sensitive issue for any defense force, not only because they could be related to intelligent lifeforms from space, but also, and perhaps more likely, they may be incursions by another country's military.
>
> An intruding enemy drone or aircraft equipped with advanced interference technology, for example, could fool radar or other sensors by creating ghost images that jump around in an inexplicable manner on screen. Such incidents are usually classified for defense reasons, or to avoid embarrassment.

According to Li, AI can "think out of the box" to check crumbs of information gleaned from many different data sets originating at widespread locations and from other times to draw connections not noticed by humans. Possible causes could be hostile foreign craft, devices belonging to amateur aviation buffs, nature, or "other reasons."

Li notes that UFOs as possible alien spacecraft capture the popular imagination, and cites the U.S. Navy videos "in which flying objects appear to move in a manner that cannot be explained by current technology or physical laws."

---

9. https://www.scmp.com/news/china/science/article/3136078/china-military-uses-ai-track-rapidly-increasing-ufos

The SCMP report notes that "China's only officially confirmed UFO sighting occurred over a military airbase in Cangzhou, Hebei province, on 19 October 1998.

The SCMP cites the official provincial newspaper the *Hebei Daily*: two military jets were vectored to intercept an object that appeared suddenly at low altitude above the local airbase. (The Cangxian Airbase.)[10]

The UFO was described as "like a 'short-legged mushroom,' with two beams of light shooting down from its belly."[11]

The *Hebei Daily*/SCMP account says that as the jets came close, the UFO climbed with "ghostlike" speed to 20,000m before disappearing from view and radar screens.

Li elaborated that the PLA has a three-level system of dealing with "unknown aerial objects": The base level includes air force pilots, and military radar installations. The reporting is unclear but it seems the second level includes UFO observations from police posts, and at the third level weather stations. The Chinese Academy of Sciences observatories are "responsible for gathering as much raw data as possible."

He went on to explain that the data was assembled at the mid-tier of the PLA military administration for preliminary analysis prior to forwarding it to a central database. After that, AI assists human analysts in placing each event on a "threat index" according to the UFO's behavior, "frequency of occurrence, aerodynamic design, radioactivity, possible make and materials" and other unspecified details. The AI then draws in data from many sources to try to understand the UFO's purpose. If, for example, a UFO shows up at a political or military event, then it is considered to be human-made and sent by a foreign power to gather intelligence. The AI also cross-checks with sources such as weather satellites to rule-out atmospheric phenomena as the cause of the sighting.

A radar expert who asked to remain anonymous said that the increased volume of UFOs in Xian was likely due to relaxed rules over the use of low-altitude airspace and the recent availability of inexpensive drones for civilian use.

The report concludes with the observation that in view of increased international tensions in the South China Sea, it is likely the larger number of UFOs in the area was due to intrusions by aircraft and devices belonging to the United States.

10. https://centreforaviation.com/data/profiles/airports/cangzhou-airport

11. https://www.scmp.com/news/china/science/article/3136078/china-military-uses-ai-track-rapidly-increasing-ufos

India

As we have learned, China is very closed-mouthed about UFO interactions with its military. India is just as uncommunicative. While the CIA documented three sightings above Ladakh, India, and over Sikkim, Bhutan, and Nepal – all of which border India – in 1968, they were all civilian observations. Of the thousands of CIA documents, just one I have seen mentions a UFO sighting – above the Indian city of Mumbai.[12]

Indian Army soldiers at an outpost in Ladakh spotted UFOs above the Ladan Kher area in Demchock on 4 August 2013. During the preceding seven months there had been other observations of UFOs over border regions in Arunachal Pradesh, the Indian armed forces later conceded.[13]

While not a military sighting, there was a mass witnessing of a shape-changing UFO at Kolkata, West Bengal, in October 2007. It was captured on film, videotape and in photographs. "Because of the large number of witnesses this can be regarded as a genuine sighting."[14]

In October 2015, in the Ratnagiri district of Maharashtra, approximately 800 witnesses from "three villages near the TRP petrol pump" observed a UFO described by eyewitness Ijapada Chatterjee, the manager of a local mica mine, as having a diameter of around 12ft and was of a grey color. It descended to about 500ft before ascending quickly and disappearing.[15]

Also above India, a video shot by a German tourist from an airliner window captured a glowing white UFO that changed shape as it flew at a higher altitude.[16]

These cases are cited due to the lack of information from the Indian military; and the two lattermost are included to present a mass sighting, and a UFO on film – demonstrating the shape-shifting capabilities of these mysterious objects.

---

12. https://www.deccanchronicle.com/nation/current-affairs/280117/ufos-in-india-cia-report-lists-not-1-but-3-sightings.html
13. https://www.hindustantimes.com/trending/aliens-in-india-a-brief-history-of-ufo-sightings-from-around-the-country-101625192813527.html
14. https://www.cleartrip.com/collections/10-times-extra-terrestrials-paid-india-a-visit/ Also: https://timesofindia.indiatimes.com/city/kolkata/ufo-puzzle-has-city-in-a-tizzy/articleshow/2500882.cms And: https://www.dnaindia.com/india/report-did-a-ufo-come-over-kolkata-1130823
15. Ibid – https://www.cleartrip.com/collections/10-times-extra-terrestrials-paid-india-a-visit/
16. https://www.india.com/viral/viral-video-ufo-spotted-man-posts-video-of-shiny-shape-shifting-object-shot-from-plane-watch-4850510/

Pakistan

Not to be left out, India's arch-rival Pakistan suffered the indignity of having a "bulging triangle" UFO hover above its capital city of Islamabad for two hours.[17]

The Sun reported that Arslan Warraich, formerly from Birmingham, UK, filmed the UFO for thirteen minutes. The object apparently lingered above the city's posh DHA 1 District. The 33-year-old businessman said, "I filmed it for over 12 minutes at different times, took dozens of pictures and observed it for the best part of two hours. I still don't know what it was."

The following item was included because another UFO incident resulted in Earthbound repercussions with military implications. The *South China Morning Post*, quoting from Reuters, reported on 11 March 2022: "Pakistan warns India after crash of mystery flying object. Islamabad summoned New Delhi's *charge d'affaires* to lodge a protest after the high-altitude supersonic object crashed near Pakistan's Mian Channu. Pakistan also called for an investigation of the incident, which it said could have endangered passenger flights."[18] The two nuclear-equipped neighbors have fought three wars, and there have been numerous other armed clashes between their militaries. This incident illustrates another problem regarding UFOs, whether they originate on our planet or not: the possibility that their appearance could trigger a war. "Pakistan warned India in the statement 'to be mindful of the unpleasant consequences of such negligence and take effective measures to avoid the recurrence of such violations in future.'"

While it seems unlikely this UFO was of extraterrestrial origin, we cannot rule it out. However, if so, Pakistan would likely have turned it over to its benefactor, Communist China, for study and efforts at reverse engineering.

France

Two French military pilots testified before the COMETA (translated) "Committee for in-depth studies.") Committee. (Unless noted otherwise,

17. https://www.india.com/viral/viral-video-ufo-spotted-in-pakistan-mysterious-bulging-triangle-flies-over-islamabad-for-2-hours-5255430/
18. https://www.scmp.com/news/asia/south-asia/article/3170046/pakistan-seeks-answers-india-after-crash-mystery-flying-object?module=perpetual_scroll_0&pgtype=article&campaign=3170046

the following incident accounts are all derived from the COMETA Report, available at the NARCAP website.)[19]

The testimony of one pilot was corroborated by a record of radio communications between him and his ground controllers. On 7 March, 1977, "Pilot Herve Giraud and his navigator observed a very bright glow at 3 o'clock – their right wing – at their same altitude of 9,600m. The object was on an evident collision course and closing in rapidly. The French jet was a Mirage IV. It was 9 p.m., and they flew above Dijon at Mach .9 – 690.5mph. In an evident but unacknowledged routine response, the Contrexeville military radar station asked the plane's crew to check their oxygen supply – in an apparent effort to determine if the flyers were suffering from anoxia and having hallucinations.

The pilot turned the plane toward the object, which used its superior speed to outmaneuver Giraud, slipped behind the jet and began tailing it from about 1,500m distance.

Giraud reversed his bank to shake the object from his tail and to maintain visual contact. When he was able to place the UFO at his 11 o'clock position it moved away, so Giraud resumed his original course, toward Luxeuil.

Giraud testified that about forty-five seconds later he felt as if he were being "watched," in his words. He told his navigator, "You wait and see, it's going to come back." Then, "an identical glow" appeared, again at the plane's 3 o'clock position.

Giraud executed an even tighter bank, subjecting the Mirage's crew to a 6.5 g-force as he arced the plane toward the UFO in an effort to get behind it. But, again, the UFO out-turned and placed itself behind the jet once more, at a distance of about 2,000m. Giraud again reversed his turn, and in another repeat, the glow shot away.

The Mirage IV returned to base at Luxeuil. Ground control never detected either UFO on its radar.

The COMETA Report emphasizes two main points in this encounter: only a military aircraft could have out-matched the performance of the Mirage IV, in which case ground control would have had a radar echo, which it did not have. The second point is that to perform its maneuvers, the UFO should have generated loud sonic booms. "But no sound was heard in the region."

In the second French incident detailed in the COMETA Report, on 3 March 1976, Colonel Claude Bosc, then a student pilot at the Combat Flight School at Tours, was on a solo night flight in a T-33 training jet.

19. https://www.narcap.de/dokumente/COMETA-Report-englisch.pdf

He was at an altitude of 6,000m, on a course from Rennes to Poitiers, via Nantes. Several aircraft followed at five-minute intervals.

It was a cloudless night, with visibility greater than 100km. Bosc was flying at 460km/h when, straight ahead, he saw what he at first thought was the launch of a green signal flare. But within two seconds the "flare" had climbed to at least 1,500m above his plane. The UFO leveled off, then dived toward the T-33 on an apparent collision course until it seemed to fill the entire windshield. In an instinctive reflex, Bosc let go of the control stick and crossed his arms before his chest.

While his plane was entirely enveloped in bright, phosphorescent green light, Bosc saw a sphere that avoided a collision at the last second, passing above his right wing, but grazing it. (It would be interesting to see the results of tests of any residue, if such tests were conducted, which is likely. Also, with this report we see the evident return of "Foo-Fighter"-type UFOs.)

Colonel Bosc testified that the sphere was not large – about 1 to 2m in diameter. It had a tail comparable to that of a comet, which was also fluorescent green. (This sphere with a tail, or teardrop-shape, mirrors Kenneth Arnold's actual description of the objects the press dubbed "flying saucers.") He said the central portion of the UFO "consisted of a very bright white light (magnesium-fire type)." The ground controller had seen no echo from the UFO on his radar screen. "Upon return, two other pilots who had followed the same itinerary … stated that they had seen the phenomenon, but from a distance."

United Kingdom

A famous RAF case was reported on extensively elsewhere, but is covered herein from the COMETA Report:

Joint-Base Bentwaters, RAF-USAF, 13–14 August 1956: unknown aerial objects on radar scopes were judged "unidentified" by the Condon Report in 1969. These unusual blips first appeared at 9 p.m. At 11:55 p.m., radar operators detected a UFO approaching the base from the east at between 2,000 and 4,000mph. No sonic booms were heard, but Bentwaters control tower personnel saw a bright light pass overhead "at an incredible speed" at about 1,200m.

> At the same time, the pilot of a military transport plane flying over Bentwaters at an altitude of 1,200 meters stated that a bright light passed under his plane, tearing east to west 'at

> an incredible speed.' The two visual sightings confirmed the radar detection. The Bentwaters radar operator reported these concurring radar and visual sightings to the shift supervisor at the Lakenheath [air] traffic radar control center.

"[A] (sic) American noncommissioned officer to whom we are indebted for a quite detailed report of these sightings and those that follow." (Sentence fragment as in the original.) The NCO's report was sent to the Condon Committee. His account is:

> coherent and does not contradict the documents in the USAF [Project] Blue Book file except in a few minor points: among these documents, the regulation telex sent by Lakenheath to the Blue Book team on the day of the incident and the report forwarded two weeks later to that same team by American Captain Holt, an intelligence officer at Bentwaters.

The Lakenheath shift supervisor alerted his team's radar operators, and one of them observed a stationary UFO about 40km south of the base. The shift supervisor confirmed the radar return to the Lakenheath approach radar center, where the sighting was reconfirmed. Then, radar operators at the air traffic control center observed the UFO speed away about 600 to 950km/h.

The UFO engaged in several changes of direction in straight-line segments from 13 to 30km, stopped abruptly for from three to six minutes, then went from a standing stop to speed away at 950km/h with no transitional gradual acceleration phase. "The regulation telex sent by Lakenheath concluded: 'The fact that rapid accelerations and abrupt stops of the object were detected by radar and by sight from the ground give the report definite credibility. One can only believe that these sightings may have some meteorological or astronomical origin.'" (I wonder if the "astronomical origin" could include ET spacecraft?)

About thirty to forty-five minutes later, two RAF Venom two-seater jets were dispatched on an intercept mission. One of the pilots located the UFO visually and on radar, then lost view and the return. After being redirected by ground control, the pilot reacquired the target. He then reported, "My machine guns are locked onto him." The target was lost to detection once more, reacquired, but was lost again. Ground control then informed the pilot that the UFO was behind his plane and following. He confirmed this visually. The pilot tried "every maneuver" for ten minutes to get behind the UFO, but without success, despite engaging in "steep climbs, dives, sustained turns." Then, low on fuel, the pilot returned to base, asking to be informed if the UFO followed him, which it did do for a short time before stopping to hover, make "several short moves," then sped away to the north at 950km/h. The second Venom had to return to base just after take off due to mechanical problems.

An article on the incident in the Journal of Astronautics and Aeronautics – cited in the Condon Committee Report – concluded with: "If one considers the strong credibility of the information and the coherence and continuity of the reports, as well as their high degree of 'strangeness,' this UFO case is certainly one of the more troubling cases known to date."

United States

Also as delivered to us from the COMETA Report is an accounting of the case of an RB-47 on 17 July 1957, which the Condon Report listed as "unidentified." After some controversy the facts eventually prevailed and the story was upheld as genuine after an in-depth investigation.

The RB-47 was a bomber with its bomb bays converted to cabins containing equipment able to detect emissions from ground radar signals' direction and azimuth; but in the 1950s was unable to determine the distance or precise nature of the signals. The electronic gear was monitored by three officers.

Here is the sequence of events:

The RB-47 was on a training mission in the south-central United States, where various radar stations were emitting signals.

Flying up from the Gulf of Mexico at Mach 0.75, the RB-47 approached the Mississippi River Delta when, about 09:30Z (3:30 a.m. local time), a "Captain MacClure" observed a blip on his radar, and there was a corresponding pulsed microwave source at the same location – at the 5 o'clock position relative to the RB-47. The object passed the plane, turned across its path, and departed on the far side – between 6 o'clock and 9 o'clock. This meant the source was airborne, and supersonic. MacClure analyzed the signals coming from the UFO, which were the same as ground radars, but with a slower pulse duration – of two microseconds, which is half that of the former by but one microsecond. Since at that time there was no radar unit with that pulse duration that could be carried aboard contemporary aircraft, thinking his equipment was malfunctioning, MacClure at first did not report the reading.

About forty minutes later, at 10:10Z, above Louisiana, Commander Chase – pilot, and copilot Captain MacCoyd saw "an intense bluish-white light" beam apparently aimed at them from 11 o'clock. The shaft of light jumped to the 2 o'clock position and disappeared, causing Chase and MacCoyd to wonder aloud about the nature of the UFO.

Hearing their comments, Captain MacClure recalled his earlier mysterious radar return, and began looking for the same type of signal. At 10:30Z he found one; it was identical to the prior emission which, perhaps coincidentally, originated at the 2 o'clock position where the UFO had disappeared from view.

A Captain Provenzano confirmed the signal, which, since it remained at 2 o'clock relative to the plane, could have been from ground-based radar.

When the plane entered Texas airspace, Dallas radar operators informed the RB-47 that both it and a UFO about 18km distant appeared on their displays.

At 10:39Z Commander Chase saw a large red light he estimated to be traveling 1,500m below his plane at about the 2 o'clock position while the RB-47 flew at 10,500m. Despite clear skies, Chase could not discern the exact shape of the UFO but thought the light was emanating from the top of the object.

At 10:40Z Chase received authorization to pursue the UFO. First he slowed his plane, then sped up again, and the radar center informed him that the object was mirroring his movements while remaining 18km distant.

At 10:42Z Chase accelerated and made visual observation of the UFO as it turned toward Dallas. This change of direction was confirmed by MacClure. At about 10:50Z, just west of Dallas, the UFO came to a stop, and disappeared from both on-board and ground-based radars as the RB-47 closed with it. This mimics recent developments and practices by pilots using stealth technology. The pilot banked the aircraft to the left, and MacClure observed the UFO radar return again.

Both visual and radar observations were continued aboard the aircraft and, at 10:52Z, Chase saw the UFO descend to about 4,500m. He dove his plane from 10,500 to 6,000m, and the UFO disappeared from view and from ground-based and on-board radars. Then, at 10:57Z, still close to Dallas, the object reappeared on the RB-47's radar, and ground control radioed that they had prepared a "CIRVIS" (Communications Instructions for Reporting Vital Intelligence Sightings) Report. Also, a secret and urgent communication was radioed "to the Air Defense Command, which is mandatory in the event of a sighting by the Air Force of an unidentified aerial object."

At 10:58Z Chase regained visual observation of the UFO, again at 2 o'clock. After a few minutes, seeing that he was low on fuel, he opted to resume his preplanned course and flew the plane north toward Oklahoma City. The UFO then repositioned itself 18km behind his aircraft, as reported to Chase by ground control, which attempted to dispatch fighter jets to intercept the UFO. It was still following low and behind the RB-47, so it could not be seen from the cockpit, but it was displayed on Captain MacClure's screen until they approached Oklahoma City – beyond Dallas's radar. Finally, at 11:40Z the UFO suddenly disappeared from the screen, not to be detected again.

The Cometa Committee membership included: General Bruno Lemoine, of the French Air Force; Admiral Marc Merlo; Michel Algrin, Political Sciences PhD, and attorney; General Pierre Bescond, engineer for armaments; General Alain Orszag, PhD in physics, armaments engineer; Denis Blancher, Chief National Police and Superintendent at the Ministry of the Interior; Christian Marchal, chief engineer of the national Corps des Mines, and Research Director at the National Office of Aeronautical Research. Their report concludes that UFOs are piloted by extraterrestrials, and that the UFO phenomenon has profound security implications. As readers are by now aware, I completely agree with these findings.

UFOs Flaunt Their Presence Above Belgium

From 1989 until 1991, waves of UFOs, mostly triangular, appeared above Belgium, prompting the Belgian air force to scramble F-16s on several occasions, despite the fact that the objects left no radar blips, although they did leave some blurry images on film.[20]

The complete story is related to us by Leslie Kean in her book, *UFOs: Generals, Pilots, and Government Officials Go on the Record*, as reported by Belgian Major General Wilfried De Brouwer.

The strange craft would cruise slowly above at night, lighting up the countryside with powerful searchlight beams. The 120ft-wide objects would suddenly streak away, only to return to the same places on other occasions to resume their hovering while shining bright shafts of light Earthward.

20. *UFOs: Generals, Pilots, and Government Officials Go on the Record* Leslie Kean. Three Rivers Press, New York, 2010. p.17.

Thousands of witnesses observed the UFOs, and some people sent flashing light signals at them, which the objects "answered," with matching bursts of light of their own[21] (anticipating what unintentionally happened to me at my remote ranch in October 2004).

Belgian Congo (Now the Democratic Republic of the Congo)

In March 1952 it was reported that "two fiery discs" appeared above the uranium mines in the Elizabethville (now Lubumbashi) district, east of the Luapula River, which connects the Mweru and Banweolo lakes.[22]

In the CIA summary, it is stated that a "Commander Pierre" set off in pursuit of the UFOs in a fighter plane. He said he flew to within 120m of one of the objects, which he described as an aluminum-colored disc with a knob atop and flames coming off the rim. He said its diameter was about 12 to 15m.

Commander Pierre gave chase, with the UFOs engaging in maneuvers he could not imitate before they sped off at a velocity he estimated at 1,500km/h.

As we have seen, and will continue to discover later, UFOs have an extreme interest in all of the nuclear materials and assets of human beings.

Madagascar

In an item labeled "3.1 Phenomenon Observed by Numerous Witnesses at Antananarivo (16 August 1954) COMETA presents 'Testimony before the committee [by] Edmond Campagnac, a former artillery officer and chief of technical services for Air France in Madagascar … ' [It] … was observed … by several hundred witnesses at 17:00 hours."

Air France employees also spotted the UFO from their office. They described it as a large green ball moving at high speed. Everyone thought the object was a meteorite and expected it to fall to Earth, but it disappeared behind a hill only to reappear after a minute and pass directly overhead, being observed in more detail as "a sort of metal rugby ball preceded by

---

21. Ibid. p.33.
22. https://www.cia.gov/readingroom/docs/DOC_0000015463.pdf

a clearly detached green lens-shaped portion with sparks issuing from the rear." It was estimated to be about as large as a then-current DC-4 propeller-driven airliner – about 40m.[23]

Witnesses then reported that the green lens-shaped portion separated itself and proceeded to lead the orb by about another 40m out in front. It was described as also having sparks flaring behind it.

The UFO flew over Antananarivo at an estimated altitude of 50 to 100m – a calculation based on its course when it cruised past a nearby hill. As it passed, "shop lights went out, and animals exhibited a real anxiety."

As the UFO flew over the zebu (cattle from the Indian subcontinent who possess a fatty hump on their shoulders) park in town, it created a strong fright reaction among them. This was surprising to all who learned of it because the animals did not show any agitation when Air France planes passed at low altitude overhead.

Within three minutes, an identical UFO was observed 150km from Antananarivo, above a farm school. It was reported that again the UFO caused cattle herds there to be overcome with panic.

If the craft sighted above the farm school was the same one as the one in Antananarivo, its speed would have been about 3,000km/h. (1,864.114mph.)

These accounts of agitated animals recall the reports by rural residents of similar reactions to Dr Lincoln LaPaz with regard to his search for the location of the Roswell UFO crash just over seven years previous.

General Fleurquin, Commander-in-Chief in Madagascar, assembled a "scientific commission" to investigate. While no trace of this investigation could be found in the Air Force archives; however, "GEPAN[24] bulletin #6 of the 2nd half of 1964 described this sighting."

We see that at the time it was evident that even official investigations in French-controlled Madagascar received the same treatment – a document supporting the existence of UFOs mysteriously disappeared; but not always so, as we shall find later in the case of a heroic seeker of truth who made copies of official documents, proving that a commercial airline crew, ground controllers at a United States Air Force Base, and control-tower personnel at a major airport all were participants in a UFO sighting that defies "debunking."

---

23. https://www.narcap.de/dokumente/COMETA-Report-englisch.pdf
24. In 1977, the Groupe d'Etudesde Phenomenes Aerospatiaux Non Identifies – GEPAN [Aerospace Phenomena Study Group] was set up by the French government's Centre National d'Etudes Spatiales – CNES – France's version of NASA – to study UFOs/UAP.

Chile

Chilean Navy helicopters recorded a video of a UFO that looks like a submarine's torpedo, but traveling high in the sky. The Chilean naval aviators attempted to radio the craft but there was no reply.[25]

Even after two years of investigating, and interviewing the pilots, radar operators and ground controllers, Chilean military analysts admit they can't explain (or explain away?) the video footage. The object did not appear on any airborne or ground-based radar displays.

The videotape was recorded in November 2014, while the Chilean Navy helicopters were on a routine coastal patrol.[26]

The military pilots said the object at first seemed to be hovering in the clouds, then moved along while expelling some wisps of gas from its stern.[27]

Antarctica

Many scientists based in Antarctica have seen UFOs.[28] In 1965, military officials from Argentina, Great Britain and Chile observed red, blue and green lights flickering and darting through the remote Antarctic skyscape, according to the National Investigations Committee on Aerial Phenomena (NICAP).[29]

Military personnel have also recorded major magnetic measurement changes in their geomagnetic instruments when UFOs were present, causing them and their superiors to wonder what could possibly be creating these sightings and electromagnetic effects in such a remote part of our world.[30]

A CIA account also included sightings at Deception Island, near the Antarctic Peninsula, in the same year; and these may be duplicate observations. The CIA report adds "the flying saucers" were also seen cruising in formation over the South Orkney Islands in quick circles.[31]

25. https://www.thesun.co.uk/news/2569089/chilean-navy-cant-explain-footage-craft/
26. https://nypost.com/2017/01/09/chilean-navy-admits-it-cant-explain-ufo/
27. https://www.thesun.co.uk/news/2569089/chilean-navy-cant-explain-footage-craft/
28. https://bestlifeonline.com/ufo-facts/
29. http://www.nicap.org/docs/antarctica/650703rep.htm
30. https://bestlifeonline.com/ufo-facts/
31. https://www.cia.gov/readingroom/document/0005515662

Around Our Planet Earth – Literally; and Beyond

American Astronauts' UFO Reports not Disproven

In the early days of space exploration, virtually all of the astronauts and cosmonauts were test pilots and other military people, as are today's Chinese taikonauts. ("Taiko" is Chinese for "space".) Even later, when civilians crewed many flights, part of each space mission was devoted to military research and applications. Therefore, it is pertinent to our study to mention the following story from the *New Zealand Herald* published 8 April 2018.

Moon landing Apollo 11 astronaut Buzz Aldrin, who in 1969 was the second human to set foot on the moon, was given a lie-detector test to determine whether he actually believed he observed a UFO while he was on the moon. He said: "There was something out there that was close enough to be observed, sort of L-shaped." The test was administered at the Institute of BioAcoustic Biology in Albany, Ohio. He passed the test.[32] Later, however, after receiving volumes of blowback, Aldrin said his remark had been taken out of context, and that he agreed with NASA's explanation that he had seen a discarded spacecraft booster panel reflecting sunlight. While it would be amusing to entertain the UFO-as-an-alien-spacecraft theory, I believe that perhaps the latter story is the correct version. Yet, either way, whether Aldrin observed an alien spacecraft or part of an Earth-manufactured space vehicle, his story – if the lattermost – still does not discredit the reports of other astronauts. Of the 550 or so people who have been in space, a handful have asserted seeing objects that could be of alien origin; but, spacefarers are a very busy group of people.

Aldrin, then aged 88, took part in a test that also analyzed recorded interviews with astronauts Al Worden, Edgar Mitchell and Gordon Cooper. The voice recordings were analyzed using the latest technology, also at the same institute. Experts who performed the analyses said their findings proved the astronauts were "completely convinced" that their recollections and testimony regarding the existence of UFOs and/or aliens were genuine, according to the *Daily Star*.[33]

The institute analyzed the voice patterns of the astronauts as they spoke about their encounters. "BioAcoustics' Sharry Edwards told the *Daily Star* that their tests revealed Aldrin is sure he saw the UFO even though his logical mind 'cannot explain it.'"

---

32. https://www.nzherald.co.nz/world/there-was-something-out-there-apollo-11-astronaut-buzz-aldrin-recalls-encounter-with-alien-life/6J2OHHXIOBZDZ7JEN3AUUJKDIM/
33. https://www.dailystar.co.uk/news/weird-news/news-ufo-aliens-lie-detector-17126863

"Last year, Apollo 15 pilot Al Worden, 86, told *Good Morning Britain* that he saw extra-terrestrials during his mission."

The voice recordings of astronauts Edgar Mitchell and Gordon Cooper were also analyzed. Both had already passed away by then.

Test Pilot/Future Astronaut Gordon Cooper on UFO at Edwards AFB

Despite numerous efforts to discredit astronaut Gordon Cooper's report of witnessing a UFO – not in space but on the ground – as we saw above, his recorded testimony was validated as much as is possible today by acoustical and biometric experts.

Cooper, then a test pilot at Edwards AFB, was in charge of several advanced-technology projects, including a precision landing system. He said of the 1957 incident:

> I had a camera crew filming the installation when they spotted a saucer. They filmed it as it flew overhead, then hovered, extended three legs as landing gear, and slowly came down to land on a dry lake bed![34] These guys were all pro cameramen, so the picture quality was very good. The camera crew managed to get within 20 or 30 yards of it, filming all the time. It was a classic saucer, shiny silver and smooth, about 30ft across. It was pretty clear it was an alien craft. As they approached closer it took off.

The report states that the camera crew gave the film to Cooper, who followed standard procedures as he contacted Washington, D.C. to tell of the incident, commenting that "All hell broke loose."

He said, "A high-ranking officer ordered [him] to put the film in a pouch and send it to Washington as soon as it was developed." Cooper added that, "He didn't say anything about me not looking at the film. That's what I did when it came back from the lab and it was all there just like the camera crew reported."

Cooper said he mentioned the film evidence to the Air Force's Project Blue Book. "But the film was never found supposedly. Blue Book was strictly a cover-up anyway."

---

34. http://www.noufors.com/astronaut_Gordon_Cooper_witnesses_ufo_landing_at_Edwards_AFB.html Citing ufoevidence.org

Cooper also said that he had a friend who had been at Roswell Army Air Field who told him that the 1947-crash had happened, and that aliens were found in the wreckage. “He had to be careful about what he said. But it sure wasn’t a weather balloon, like the Air Force cover story. He made it clear to me what crashed was a craft of alien origin.”

When asked why the government kept UFO information secret, Cooper said:

> It started in World War II, when the government didn’t want people to know about UFO reports in case they panicked. They would have been fearful it was superior enemy technology that we had no defense against. Then it got worse in the Cold War for the same reason. So they told one untruth, they had to tell another to cover that one, then another, then another … it just snowballed. And right now I’m convinced a lot of very embarrassed government officials are sitting there in Washington trying to figure a way to bring the truth out. They know it’s got to come out one day, and I’m sure it will. America has a right to know!

Cosmonauts See Them, Too

Russian cosmonaut Ivan Vagner, while aboard the International Space Station stirred the pot after he recorded video footage of strange objects he christened “Space Guests.” He was reportedly filming auroras when he noticed something odd. He posted time-lapse footage on social media, noting that “In the video, you will see something else, not only the aurora,” Vagner said on Twitter. “Indeed, at the 9- to 12-second mark, a group of lights quickly shows in the video before disappearing. 5 objects appear flying alongside with the same distance,” the Expedition 63 crew member wrote. “What do you think those are? Meteors, satellites or ...?”[35]

“... There were five objects that suddenly appeared alongside the natural light phenomenon. Suggesting that authorities in … [Russia] were taking the sighting seriously, Vagner revealed that ‘information was brought to the

35. https://www.space.com/russian-cosmonaut-space-guests-video-from-station.html

notice of Roscosmos management, the materials were sent to … and the Space Research Institute of the Russian Academy of Sciences for further analysis.'"[36] The Russian space agency later speculated that the objects were "probably a group of SpaceX's Starlink satellites which had been launched the day before the cosmonaut's sighting."

Over the years there have been other reports of UFO sightings by Russian and Soviet cosmonauts, without, of course, video footage. Even if we dismiss this report as being too tenuous to be readily accepted; in their volume, I cannot in good conscious disbelieve the accounts of so many dedicated space explorers.

Soviet Cosmonaut Secrecy

In the official records, UFOs did not exist in the Soviet Union. So, despite the fact that they had much to share, Soviet cosmonauts did not publicly discuss the subject. But former Soviet cosmonaut Vladimir Kovalenok did have something to say at a recent press conference, announcing that he saw something unexplainable while aboard the Salyut Space Station. After observing the strange object, he instructed fellow crewman Viktor Savinykh to grab a camera. While Savinykh went for the camera, the object exploded as Kovalenok kept it in view. He stated that the UFO separated into two parts, with what seemed to be a sort of bridge linking them. Before his crewmate returned with the camera, the then dumbbell-shaped object disappeared. He concluded with the remark that Earth-based sensors detected a strong radioactive emission soon after the UFO exploded.[37]

Kovalenok said several fellow cosmonauts had observed unusual sights on many occasions, but they decided (wisely) not to bring the incidents to public attention. (This would change, briefly, with the fall of the Soviet government and a short period of "glasnost," or "openness.")

Pilot and cosmonaut Pavel Popovich flew from Washington to Moscow in 1978 at 10,000m when he saw a luminescent triangle on the same course. He said the triangle passed at an estimated speed of 1,700km/h while the jetliner flew at 1,100km/h.

---

36. https://www.coasttocoastam.com/article/watch-russian-cosmonaut-causes-stir-with-video-of-space-guests/
37. https://english.pravda.ru/society/106764-soviet_ufo/

Cosmonauts Gennady Strekalov and Gennady Manakov saw a brightly lit sphere appear in the cloudless sky over Newfoundland in 1990. Then, after ten seconds, the sphere disappeared without a trace.

In 1991, Musa Manarov was videotaping as a new crew was shuttling toward the Mir Space Station when "an antenna-like object" separated from the module. He radioed to the cosmonauts inside the relief ship that something had just undocked from their craft. It was never determined what the object had been, despite being on videotape.

Obviously, the cosmonauts informed their governing bodies of these and all other strange incidents; and, as in the United States and elsewhere, it seems evident the accounts were documented and subsequently classified as secret.

We will now turn to a triplet of events recorded by credible witnesses, one of which is supported by official records, of UFOs interacting with civilians, but with at least a peripheral involvement with the United States military.

Chapter 15

More Compelling Evidence from Reliable Witnesses

A UFO (Possibly) Killed Betty Cash

On the night of 29 December in the UFO-event-filled year of 1980, 51-year-old Betty Cash was driving 57-year-old Vickie Landrum and Vickie's 8-year-old grandson, Colby Landrum, on a country road north of Lake Houston, Texas, when they saw a low-flying diamond-shaped UFO. It briefly appeared in the distance, was lost from view then seen again hovering above the road just ahead. The UFO emitted light so bright it hurt the witnesses' eyes and lit-up the surrounding countryside. It also gave off bursts of flame from beneath, like a rocket.[1]

Betty stopped the car and all three got out to watch the object, but Colby became frightened and he and his grandmother re-entered the vehicle; then Vickie coaxed Betty back inside. When Betty grabbed the car's door handle she found that it was very hot to the touch.

The UFO bobbed up and down with each "rocket blast" and then moved away as numerous military-type helicopters approached. Almost as strange, when they drove out of the area they could see the UFO still being pursued by more than twenty black, distinctive twin-rotor "Chinook" large transport helicopters.[2]

Later, all three witnesses entered a local hospital for maladies resembling radiation sickness – hair and fingernail loss, burns, blisters, nausea, and rashes. They also had severe headaches and sore eyes. Eventually, Vickie Landrum fell victim to an extreme case of eye cataracts, and Betty Cash developed breast cancer.[3]

---

1. *Clear Intent: The Government Coverup of the UFO Experience* Lawrence Fawcett and Barry J. Greenwood. Prentiss-Hall. Englewood Cliffs, NJ. 1984. p.106.
2. Ibid. pp.106-107.
3. Close Encounters of the Lone Star Kind. https://www.texasmonthly.com/the-culture/close-encounters-of-the-lone-star-kind/ And: https://www.ufocasebook.com/Pineywoods.html Also: http://www.cufon.org/cufon/cashlani.htm

In an interview with reporters, Cash said that she had never believed in UFOs: "I was the first one to laugh." But, following the incident, she said, "I was terrified," adding, "Now, I'm afraid to look up."

Two competing theories that later developed were that the object was an experimental craft belonging to the United States government or that a captured alien device was being test-flown by human pilots. I would like to add a third possibility – that an alien craft being operated by extraterrestrials found itself in trouble, landed to make repairs, had been located and then pursued by the United States military when it attempted to escape, and was being closely followed by a military force large enough to effect a capture of the machine and its occupants if it went down; to secure the area from curious people; to prepare the device for transport to, for example, Wright-Patterson Air Force Base. Obviously, a military operation of such size and complexity as to require the loading of troops and equipment onto more than twenty large helicopters would take planning, and considerable time. Nevertheless, if given the opportunity, I have no doubt that the United States government, or any government, would exert any and all efforts to capture an alien spacecraft in order to exploit extraterrestrial beings and technologies.

Eventually, Cash sued the government over her illness, alleging some responsibility due to the presence of the evident United States military helicopters, but testimony by officials ranging from NASA to the Air Force, Army and Navy convinced the court that no government agency possessed or flew a craft answering Cash's description, and the case was dismissed in 1986. (Note that the government and military officials would have been truthful if my theory holds.)

Several other people were later located who had also observed CH-47 (Chinook) and/or other heavy helicopters in the vicinity that night.[4]

This case is one of many that cause me to caution family, friends, and others to keep a good distance from any suspected alien spacecraft, whether airborne or on the ground.

Moreover, despite Cash's inability to obtain a judicial victory over the government, a release of public documents in the spring of 2022 has confirmed the official reception of reports of UFOs having adverse physical effects on humans.

According to Luis Elizondo, who at one time was in charge of the low-profile Advanced Aerospace Threat Identification Program (AATIP), who indicated indirectly (so as not to violate his oath of confidentiality) that pilots who had flown near to UFOs reported symptoms akin to radiation burns,

---

4. https://www.ufocasebook.com/Pineywoods.html

microwave damage to their tissues – the latter requiring hospitalization – and also time-dilation – where it seemed as if only a few minutes had passed, due to timepiece readings and fuel consumption rates – when in fact events had taken half an hour.[5] With the Rendlesham incident for example, one witness thought several minutes had passed, while another, farther from the landed object, felt as if only a few moments had transpired, but when reunited with other security men who had been outside the immediate area, the two men's watches were out of synchronization with the other teams' by forty-five minutes.[6]

Also: "UFO sightings can leave witnesses injured, suffering radiation burns, brain problems and damaged nerves, according to newly released Pentagon files."[7] Note that neither I nor *The Sun* newspaper are asserting the truth of these accounts but only that witnesses have testified about the effects to government agencies. The documents from the Defense Intelligence Agency were provided to *The Sun* subsequent to the newspaper's Freedom of Information Act request.

"The report added it had possession of forty-two instances from medical files and 300 similar 'unpublished' cases where humans had been injured after 'anomalous' encounters."[8]

Multiple Eyewitnesses of a Crashed UFO That Was Spirited Away by Military People: Kecksburg, Pennsylvania, 1965

Late on the evening and early night of 9 December 1965 there were numerous reports coming in from Canada, Michigan, Indiana, Ohio and into Pennsylvania of an unidentified flying object. The descending UFO was described variously as like a flame. One witness later told UFO investigator Stan Gordon the fallen object was brownish and acorn-shaped. Evidently, according to many witnesses where the object fell near Kecksburg, Pennsylvania, a large contingent of state police and military people quickly

5. https://www.the-sun.com/news/4038088/fighter-pilots-intercepted-ufos-radiation-warped-time/
6. *Encounter in Rendlesham Forest: The Inside Story of the World's Best-Documented UFO Incident* By Nick Pope, John Burroughs, Jim Penniston. Thomas Dunne Books. New York. 2014. p.8.
7. https://www.the-sun.com/news/5053647/ufos-injuries-radiation-burns-pentagon-docs/
8. https://www.the-sun.com/news/5053632/us-government-releases-1500-pages-secret-documents-ufo-programme/

cordoned-off the area and removed whatever had come to Earth. A later Air Force explanation was that it had been the fall of a meteor or meteors.[9]

When I first learned of the incident, decades ago, I reasoned that an acorn-shaped object seemed to describe an Earth-launched space capsule – probably Soviet, and indeed a later attempt to debunk the supposed UFO crash tried to attach the event to the fall from orbit of a Soviet spacecraft – Cosmos 96; but, as that idea was floated it was shot down by the information that while Cosmos 96 had indeed fallen from the skies on that date, it had dropped from orbit over Canada at 03:18 a.m. – about eighteen hours earlier. A Freedom of Information Act request by journalist Leslie Kean elicited the response from NASA official Nicholas L. Johnson that "No part of Cosmos 96 could have landed in Pennsylvania" at that time. The Kecksburg UFO fall occurred about 5 p.m., local time. Cosmos 96 fell at 03:18 a.m. Universal Time, which would be 11:18 p.m. EST *the previous day*, 8 December, according to an early report by the United States Air Force Space Command.[10] However, later, the NASA Space Data Coordinated Archive conflicted with the Air Force with their assertion that the object fell at 21:43 Universal Time, which would have been 5:43 p.m. Eastern Standard time for Keckburg, which is in the EST, on that same day.[11, 12]

9. *Need To Know: UFOs, The Military and Intelligence* Timothy Good, Pan Books. London. 2007. p.255.
10. Ibid. p.257.
11. https://savvytime.com/converter/utc-to-est
12. "The Great Lakes Fireball and Kecksburg Incident. There is some speculation that the reentry of the Cosmos 96/Venera-type spacecraft was responsible for a fireball which was seen over southwestern Ontario, Canada and at least eight states from Michigan to New York at 4:43 p.m. EST (21:43 UT)(*) on 9 December 1965. Investigations of photographs and sightings of the fireball indicated its path through the atmosphere was probably too steep to be consistent with a spacecraft re-entering from Earth orbit and was more likely a meteor in a prograde orbit from the vicinity of the asteroid belt, and probably ended its flight over western Lake Erie. U.S. Air Force tracking data on Cosmos 96 also indicate the spacecraft orbit decayed earlier than 21:43 UT on 9 December. Other analyses of the spacecraft orbit definitively indicate it could not have been the Cosmos 96 spacecraft. Some unconfirmed reports state the fireball subsequently landed in Pennsylvania southeast of Pittsburgh near the town of Kecksburg (40.2 N, 79.5 W) at 4:46 p.m. EST (although it should be noted that estimating the impact point of fireballs from eyewitness accounts is notoriously inaccurate)." NASA Space Data Coordinated Archive.
(* Note that this time estimate at the NASA website is in error: EST is 4 hours behind UT, not 5 hours, which would make the time 5:43 p.m., EST.) https://nssdc.gsfc.nasa.gov/nmc/spacecraft/display.action?id=1965-094A

There have been belated attempts to blame yet another de-orbited space vehicle.

Almost exactly fifty years after the event, in a 5 December 2015 story, the *Pittsburgh Post-Gazette* reported that researchers had by then decided that the unidentified flying (or plunging) object was in fact "a General Electric Mark 2 Re-entry Vehicle that had been launched by the Air Force as a spy satellite."[13] However, *The Smithsonian* reports that the Mark 2 re-entry vehicle was crafted to carry a nuclear warhead – not a spy satellite.[14] The same source, at the same website, shows that the Mark 2 was not acorn-shaped but more of a flattened cone. The re-entry vehicle is not brownish but one side – the smaller portion, was copper-colored, with the larger part being of stainless steel.

In an unusual step for the U.S. Space Command, it decided to get involved with the renewed debunking attempts by identifying the falling UFO as "The classified Russian spacecraft … COSMOS 2551," which had been launched exactly three months before, on 9 September 1965.[15]

There was a counter-claim by the Russian Ministry of Defense that COSMOS 2551 had not fallen back to Earth; however, U.S. authorities stated that shortly after launch it gradually lost altitude, but that its re-entry angle had created "no cause for concern." (Even though, according to them, it had actually come down near the city of Pittsburgh, Pennsylvania.)

While I do not fault the sincerity of the researchers at the newspaper, it is evident we still have not received enough hard information about the launch of the alleged spy satellite, or the trajectory or timing of the re-entry vehicles' – both of them – flight. It seems to me that after so much time such information would not be too important to reveal, and all the more so in that Soviet-based space watchers at the time were already probably well-aware of those facts. Also, the witness cited above who reported on the object being "acorn-shaped" was far from the only person to so describe it, as cited in numerous press reports and books over the years since 1965. While this case may be described as inconclusive, I, for one, do agree with that determination of uncertainty, with the reservation being that something did indeed fall to Earth then and there, with the only question being if it was of an Earthly or un-Earthly origin; and I, like many people who are more expert on the subject, remain puzzled as to what, exactly, came down

13. https://www.post-gazette.com/news/science/2015/12/06/50-years-later-the-Kecksburg-Westmoreland-County-UFO-is-identified-probably/stories/201512060146
14. https://www.si.edu/object/missile-re-entry-vehicle-mark-2%3Anasm_A19751430000
15. https://www.nytimes.com/2021/10/21/science/russian-satellite-break-up.html

in 1965 at Kecksburg, Pennsylvania. For now, I lean heavily toward an alien spacecraft; otherwise, there would be no lingering need for secrecy. Attention Federal Government: more facts, please.

Japanese Cargo Plane Stalked by Huge UFO over Alaska: Truth-Seeker Foils Cover-Up

On the night of 17 November 1986, one of the best-documented – despite attempted government interference – UFO incidents took place in the skies above the interior of Alaska. A Japan Airlines Boeing 747 cargo plane, Flight 1628, with a crew of three was requested by the Anchorage Air Route Traffic Control Center to make a course correction on its flight from Paris to Tokyo via Reykjavik and Anchorage. This was at 5:09 p.m., and a few minutes later the flight crew reported UFOs in the area.[16]

The UFOs played their usual "games" of dogging, tag, disappearing then reappearing; but then an enormous UFO joined in the aerial activities. Captain Kenju Terauchi was an ex-fighter pilot, then senior airline captain, had logged more than 10,000 hours flight experience. He reported that the enormous UFO was about the size of two aircraft carriers. (Later, he drew a sketch of the gigantic UFO, which looked like a walnut held sideways,[17] so that it had a bulging rim or "equator.")

At first the UFOs displayed no image on ground-based radars, but the largest one did show up on the cargo plane's screen. Then, as the incident continued, the civilian radar for the air controller detected the UFO, as then also did nearby military radar.[18]

Captain Terauchi initially felt no apprehension, but as his plane flew above Eielson Air Force Base he became alarmed. Ground controllers directed him through some evasive maneuvers, but the UFO continued to dog his plane. Air Force dispatchers asked if Terauchi would like them to scramble interceptors but he declined, fearing violence if the UFO and military aircraft became involved in a confrontation.[19]

---

16. https://www.anchoragepress.com/news/unfriendly-skies-the-extraordinary-flight-of-jal-1628-alaska-s-best-known-ufo-encounter/article_8e2d3270-f9d5-11e9-b9db-7ba9229138ae.html
17. *UFOs: Generals, Pilots, and Government Officials Go on the Record* Leslie Kean. Three Rivers Press, New York, 2010. p.225.
18. Ibid. p.226.
19. Ibid. p.221.

(As of spring, 2024, the United States Air Force does scramble jets to intercept and escort, for example, Russian reconnaissance planes away from American territory, including Alaska,[20] as is traditional practice – that is until UFOs of a possible extraterrestrial origin are suspected. In many of those cases no planes are sent aloft and air controllers merely passively observe in order to be able to warn other aircraft away from the area. To me, this practice is yet another - at least partial - admission that the USAF is aware that it remains impotent in the face of aerial incursions into United States territorial airspace by likely alien spacecraft. The lack-of-intercept attempts methodology also suggests that American military aircraft have been lost while intercepting extraterrestrial aerial vehicles.)

After almost an hour the enormous UFO departed, and the cargo plane landed at Anchorage. Reports were made, including to James Callahan at the Federal Aviation Administration in Washington, D.C. Tapes, transcripts, recordings and charts of radar returns and other documentation were sent to him. He was then called to a meeting, and a man from the CIA in attendance told him the events regarding the huge UFO in Alaska had never happened; that the meeting had not occurred; and that he – the CIA man – had never been there. The CIA man demanded Callahan's evidence, which he promptly turned over to him. Later, Callahan revealed at the aforementioned National Press Club event that he had made copies of the evidence, which afterward he made available to the press.[21]

What we see in this instance is proof of clear evidence of a UFO event with supporting materials that are irrefutable by the government then being the subject of attempted suppression, hence the subsequent booming silence from official sources on this incident, as with so many others. We also have the testimony of the man with impeccable credentials who preserved and presented the evidence at the National Press Club event, and who also delivered his testimony as to the fact that the United States Central Intelligence Agency was involved in an effort to cover up a UFO incident.

So, where are we now? We have a few more aspects of the UFO phenomenon to briefly look at before we can reach any truly informed conclusions.

---

20. https://abcnews.go.com/US/us-intercepts-russian-bombers-off-alaska-2-straight/story?id=97260923#:~:text=The%20Alaskan%20Region%20of%20North,including%20two%20Tu%2D95%20bombers.

21. *UFOs: Generals, Pilots, and Government Officials Go on the Record* Leslie Kean. Three Rivers Press, New York, 2010. pp.218-221.

Chapter 16

Crop Circles, Cattle Mutilations, Alien Abductions

More Mysteries

Up until now we have been able to more or less rely on the testimony of individual eyewitnesses who were (or were not) part of a military or government organization, and even other evidence such as radar returns and government records of these, including the sworn statements of multiple witnesses, even active-duty military personnel who had a lot to lose by dishonesty, hallucinating, or even just being in error. However, henceforth we will be looking into phenomena that, despite also having tangible, physical evidence, strain the credulity of almost anyone not already made familiar with the topics, and also even for the readers of this book who have at least been introduced to the foregoing accounts and analyses. Moreover, in all truthfulness, I, too, was initially inclined to reject much of what is to follow, as with some of what has gone before, until taking another look with a more open-minded attitude. I have been reminded that we should at a minimum consider some possibilities – even if we do not outright accept their reality, whether at first or maybe later on – despite their seeming too fantastic to be accepted by anyone of rational mind. We may be looking into what initially might seem to be absurdities and nonsense straight out of what I refer to as "woo-woo-land." After at least learning of the topics herein – and, for those who are really interested, by consulting the many books by long-time genuine experts cited in this overview and appearing in the bibliography – maybe, just perhaps, what at first seems too outlandish to be believed enters even minimally into the realm of possibility, if not probability and actual, physical reality. So, again, as at the beginning of our mutual journey of discovery and exploration of the many phenomena involving a history of military encounters with UFOs, I urge readers – one and all, even habitual skeptics – to approach what follows with as accepting an attitude as can be mustered.

Crop Circles

While crop circles may seem to be extraneous to our investigation, in some respects they may have at least incidental relevance to this report. While I have seen the video of two small orbs supposedly crafting crop circles,[1] and despite claims that it is authentic, I can't help but be skeptical, given the ease with which experts can now synthesize virtual images. However, I do believe that neither "Doug and Dave" nor other hoaxers are capable of creating such precisely engineered and complex *objet d'art* in farm fields overnight.[2] Moreover, the evidence shows that hoaxed crop circles result in plants with broken and otherwise damaged stems, branches, leaves, flowers, and other components, while the large, complex designs of possible alien origin possess radiation and electromagnetic anomalies, and the plants are merely pressed or folded down without much evident kinetic tissue damage.[3] If crop circles are, as some believe, messages from extraterrestrials, then the intent of such "messages" is, at best, unclear.

While military organizations have not, to my knowledge, announced any curiosity regarding crop circles, in their book *Crop Circles: Signs of Contact*, Colin Andrews and Stephen Spignesi include a photograph of a military helicopter flying above three crop circles. The pilot, identified therein as being from 648 Squadron of the British Army Air Corps – Captain D.F. Borill – is quoted as saying he was assigned to photograph the formations.[4]

Before moving on: for those who mistakenly believe that crop circles only appear in England, or in England and the United States, again in their excellent book *Crop Circles: Signs of Contac*t, Messrs Andrews and Spignesi posted a list of where crop circles have appeared, which includes twenty-seven countries in which anything from a few up to more than several hundred occurred, and another twenty-two countries in which just one or two of these mystery crop formations have been reported. Some of these locations were also in other parts of the United Kingdom, but crop circles have indeed been discovered around the world.[5]

1. https://www.pinterest.com/pin/266416134177921311/
2. https://www.britannica.com/art/crop-circle Also: https://www.theguardian.com/travel/2011/aug/12/crop-circles-wiltshire-tour-dixe-wills And: https://www.bbc.com/news/uk-england-wiltshire-23545622
3. *Crop Circles: Signs of Contact*. By Colin Andrews, with Stephen J. Spignesi. New Page Books. Franklin Lakes, NJ. 2003. Note that his book contains an excellent chart of very many crop circle designs.
4. Ibid. 19th photo and caption between pages 144 and 145.
5. Ibid. pp.75-82.

Animal Mutilations

With regard to most UFO sightings, and/or reported interactions with alien beings – usually during abduction events, I make every effort to suspend disbelief – at least long enough to engage in some degree of investigation. I intend to give witnesses every possible benefit of credibility. I also now believe that the animal mutilations we will look at next are not the work of crazed cultists, animal-haters or other weird (human) criminals. Let us consult with some press outlets that originate with and/or cater to a rural readership – a category of people who cannot be mistaken for being other than generally conservative and literally down-to-earth (the earth they work upon and with), rock-solid folks.

In rural Crook County, Oregon, beginning 27 February 2021, six cattle with the same strange mutilations were found dead within seven days. In each case the animals' reproductive systems and udders had been removed with surgical precision. Not only were the carcasses seemingly not brought down by predators, scavenging creatures had "hardly touched" the dead cattle.[6] Crook County Sheriff's Office detectives were baffled by the "unnatural deaths."

Sheriff John Gautney reported that there had been similar cases through the years, coming in spurts before stopping. He added that there was "no reason to panic." Gautney also said his office was not engaging in any speculation about the strange incidents, explaining, "We try to keep an open mind and look at all possibilities." (I prefer that all government officials, media people, and professional cynics would do likewise.)

Similar incidents have occurred throughout the American West since the 1960s. Generally called "cattle mutilations," they have certain features in common such as genitalia, eyes and other body parts removed as if by advanced surgical techniques; the cattle seemed to be healthy prior to their deaths; there will be little to no blood present.[7]

The FBI was coaxed into conducting an investigation in the 1970s but found no motives or perpetrators; yet some people theorized the animals had been "dropped from a helicopter."

In the recent string of strange cattle deaths in Crook County, a rancher had reported a dead cow with an odd slash along its spine. The animal's left cheek, tongue and three teats had been removed. He said the cow's eyes –

6. https://www.bluemountaineagle.com/news/cattle-mutilations-perplex-investigators/article_2244ee16-a14c-11eb-8c07-5bcc149c99b9.html
7. https://modernfarmer.com/2021/03/lets-talk-about-cattle-mutilations/

usually the first to be consumed by scavengers – were intact. There was no blood, and no tracks were around the animal. There were no bullet holes, and a scan showed no metal inside the carcass. The cow was 200 yards from a road, with no vehicle tracks or footprints nearby.[8]

In yet another Crook County case, on 5 March 2021, Sheriff's Sergeant Timothy Durheim reported no animal or human tracks around the dead animal, and only a small amount of blood at the site, writing in his report that he knew from past experience that any animal killed or scavenged by predators would have a large and bloody, and messy, area surrounding its body.

Prineville veterinarian Taylor Karlin said, "I wish I had an answer. We're kind of at a loss."

Regarding the spate of strange cattle deaths, past and present, "As yet, no arrests have been made – not in 1975, and not now."

In yet another case, National Public Radio reporter Anna King, who visited the scene of a bull's mysterious death, said, "Weirdly, there are no signs of buzzards, coyotes or other scavengers … he's bloodless and his tongue and genitals have been surgically cut out."[9]

The 5,000-acre ranch's vice-president said that five prized breeding bulls had been found dead just that summer, all drained of blood and with some of their "body parts precisely removed." He added that cowboys had since been ordered to work in pairs, and to be armed.

Two years prior, near New Princeton, Oregon – 200 miles away – rancher Andie Davies found a cow that was discovered, "cut up and bloodless." She said she and her husband circled the carcass and that they found no tracks; and she reported that in such dusty country, "everything you do leaves tracks."

Rancher Terry Anderson's mother's cow was killed on his ranch at Pendleton, Oregon. He pointed to the exact spot where it was found, saying, "And not one drop of blood anywhere."

Okay, one of the sources was National Public Radio, but the other two were publications aimed at ranchers and farmers. (And rural people listen to NPR, too.) Nevertheless, these reports, and others I have read on line (including "'The UFO Phenomenon': Australia's cattle mutilation

8. https://www.bluemountaineagle.com/news/cattle-mutilations-perplex-investigators/article_2244ee16-a14c-11eb-8c07-5bcc149c99b9.html
9. https://www.npr.org/2019/10/08/767283820/not-one-drop-of-blood-cattle-mysteriously-mutilated-in-oregon

mystery"),[10] and heard other reports on the radio while researching this book have convinced me that cattle mutilations are likely the work of extraterrestrials operating from alien spacecraft, for whatever reason. I have found competing theories to be unconvincing, including an accusation that the United States government was using helicopters to hoist the animals up, take samples, then dump them; but the government has access to almost unlimited numbers of all types of animals through various legitimate means such as by purchase. I concede that others may disagree with my current belief, but, again, if the facts change, so shall my opinion.

Alien Abductions

Now we really stray into "high-strangeness" with the topic of humans reportedly being abducted, biologically tested, and medically molested and experimented with.[11] I know how this sounds, but, once more, please bear with me while, as briefly as possible, I summarize.

Several learned, credentialed people have devoted thousands of hours to researching, investigating and analyzing reports by hundreds of people they each have interviewed who say they had been abducted by aliens piloting UFOs. Unsurprisingly, investigators have come to widely divergent conclusions.

It was Budd Hopkins who trail-blazed investigating the alien-abduction phenomenon; this despite the fact that the widely publicized reported abductions of Barney and Betty Hill had occurred many years earlier, in 1961.[12] Hopkins remained firmly convinced that aliens are continually abducting human beings for their own purposes.[13]

Dr John Mack, PhD, at first thought that people reporting having been abducted by aliens needed psychiatric treatment, but after just over a few interviews he then switched to being convinced that the persons making what had initially seemed to be fantastic claims were actually telling the truth. He is one of those investigators who later believed Earth's alien

10. https://7news.com.au/spotlight/the-ufo-phenomenon-australias-cattle-mutilation-mystery-c-3035029
11. *UFOs, ETs and Alien Abductions: A Scientist Looks at the Evidence* Don Donderi, PhD Hampton Roads. Charlottesville, NC. 2013. pp.125-129.
12. Ibid. pp.87-102.
13. *Missing Time: A Documented Study of Alien Abductions* Budd Hopkins. August Night Press. No city given. 1981. Also: *Sight Unseen* Budd Hopkins and Carol Rainey. Pocket Books. New York. 2003.

visitors are not hostile but are instead here to deliver good advice and assistance to humankind.[14]

Dr David M. Jacobs has also written about the abduction phenomenon from the perspective of one who regards it as a reality – and a menacing one at that.[15, 16]

Our now familiar Nick Pope has also written about alien abductions.[17] Initially, his stance seemed to me to occupy somewhat of a "middle ground" between alien-abduction true believers and skeptics, but, as I read on in his book *The Uninvited* I found that, like me, he agrees with the extraterrestrial hypothesis regarding UFOs as alien spacecraft. He also gravitated toward accepting the alien-abduction phenomenon in a straightforward way – that it is occurring.[18] Pope further points out that the alien-abduction experience, while often traumatizing, has been reported by some experiencers to have resulted in expanding their mental, spiritual, even psychic – in the sense of acquiring enhanced psychic or ESP (extra-sensory-perception) abilities – horizons.[19]

Other ufologists and researchers agree on this, and point to the alien-abduction experience as therefore being essentially a positive inducement to human psychological, spiritual and psychic growth. But here I partly disagree and contend that many different types of traumatic experiences can literally shatter one's mental and spiritual and even parapsychological bounds.

When an individual's world, and therefore worldview, is heavily affected – as through the death of a loved one; a crime or war experience or injury; the beginning or ending of a romantic, professional, personal or other serious relationship; a move to a new location; ingesting psycho-active drugs, and many other developments, can (and often do) result in profound changes in one's psyche.[20] Renowned Israeli psychic Uri Geller has stated that when he was playing outside as a child a UFO appeared and

---

14. *Abduction: Human Encounters with Aliens.* John E. Mack, M.D. MacMillan. New York. 1994.
15. *Walking Among Us: The Alien Plan to Control Humanity* David M. Jacobs, PhD Disinformation Books. San Francisco, CA. 2015.
16. *Secret Life: Firsthand Documented Accounts of UFO Abductions* David M. Jacobs, PhD Fireside. New York. 1993.
17. *The Uninvited.* Nick Pope. The Overlook Press. Woodstock, New York. 1997.
18. Ibid. p.263.
19. Ibid. p.90.
20. Increase in Psychic Phenomena Following Near-Death Experiences. By Bruce Greyson. https://med.virginia.edu/perceptual-studies/wp-content/uploads/sites/360/2017/01/NDE10.pdf

directed an energy ray at his head. "I was around five when I saw a sphere of light floating over Rothschild Boulevard," he told *The Jerusalem Post*. "An [Israeli] Air Force officer actually corroborated the story years later."[21]

Nick Pope also added (in 1997) that while people may be the victims of kidnappings by extraterrestrials, the government of the United Kingdom and that of the United States did not (at that time) take alien abductions seriously.[22] (This finding has been superseded in 2022 by the release of new information to be covered shortly.)

At the other end of the spectrum of alien-abduction beliefs we once more find another infidel in the temple (in addition to this writer) Lieutenant Colonel Kevin D. Randle, who was joined by Russell Estes and Dr William P. Cone in concluding that reported abductees were not taken aboard alien spacecraft but were instead led – or, more accurately misled – by people who put them under hypnosis and were not careful enough in using the proper technique in their interrogations.[23] Subsequent reviews, and re-reviews, of the book by the above-cited authors, and other books of theirs, have reassured me that Messrs Randle, Estes and Cone are badly mistaken; the witnesses often recalled the events without undergoing hypnosis, and Dr Jacobs and Mr Hopkins described in great detail how they avoided leading (misleading) witnesses. Moreover, multiple abductions and abductions witnessed by others confound the notion that abductions, except for a very few, are imaginary or hoaxed. There will be much more about this subject in a forthcoming volume, which I am currently researching

While our investigation is intended to be a serious study of a history of military encounters with UFOs, by its very nature the coverage of the topic must at times stray into "woo-woo-territory" to *One Step Beyond* the *Outer Limits* of the *Twilight Zone*. Therefore here, yet again, I find myself caught in a middle-ground – a limbo – between what seems firmly grounded in physical reality and that which may be imaginary, or at least beyond the imagination of most practical-minded people. Let us assume briefly that almost all alien-abduction accounts are mistaken, or the products of hoaxes

21. https://www.jpost.com/omg/uri-geller-to-post-i-saw-aliens-with-nasa-helped-uk-win-in-euro-2020-672812
22. *The Uninvited: An Exposé of the Alien Abduction Phenomenon. Nick Pope.* Overlook. Woodstock, NY. 1997. p.282.
23. *The Alien Abduction Enigma* Kevin D. Randle, Russ Estes, William P. Cone, PhD Forge. New York. 1999.

and/or over-active imaginations; but still, there are at least two cases that at first seemed to defy debunking, or not, by being explained away.

The first case is that of Linda Cortile, whose actual identity was later revealed to be Linda Napolitano. In a 10 May 2013 story for *Vanity Fair*, Cortile/Napolitano told journalist Paul Blumenthal that at 3 a.m. on 30 November 1989 she had been abducted by three small aliens from her twelfth-floor New York City apartment near the Brooklyn Bridge. She said they had levitated her aboard their spacecraft.[24] Okay, some might react: so, what else is new? Well, there is something new – alleged witnesses. She commented that if she had been hallucinating, then the eyewitnesses who said – or, more properly, wrote – that they also saw her being abducted were hallucinating in unison, remarking, "That sounds crazier than the whole abduction phenomenon."

But three of the witnesses weren't just identified as average people – two were self-proclaimed to be police officers (who were later described as security guards) escorting a high-ranking United Nations diplomat. While the men chose to remain anonymous, and the diplomat also declined to become involved, he was eventually named by researchers as then U.N. Secretary-General Javier Pérez de Cuéllar, who, when questioned about the incident many years later pled a faulty memory due to his age of 92, when he was finally asked. After the abduction, the disc-shaped craft was reported to have dived into the East River.[25]

All of this testimony was delivered to Budd Hopkins. Additionally, a woman who also was at first only "identified" by a pseudonym wrote to Hopkins that she, too, had seen the abduction.[26] All of the witnesses stated that they had observed the incident when stuck in traffic after their cars' engines had quit – which is a widely reported side-effect of the presence of UFOs.

After this, there were supposed complications regarding the mental breakdown of one of the guards, the other's alleged later love affair with Cortile/Napolitano, and Pérez de Cuéllar also being abducted. There is much more to this story, but my credulousness had already passed far beyond exhaustion during my preliminary research; and, I must admit that it was incomplete when I made the determination that while Linda

24. https://www.vanityfair.com/culture/2013/05/americans-alien-abduction-science
25. https://listverse.com/2020/08/13/8-alien-abductions-that-suggest-underwater-alien-activity/
26. https://gregsandow.com/ufo/Contents/From_IUR_--_An_Analysis_of_the/from_iur_--_an_analysis_of_the.htm

Napolitano's account of what happened to her may be true (at least in her mind), the fact is that almost all of her story was relayed through a single source, and also that, except for her own testimony, it seemed as if the would-be corroborative materials were delivered anonymously, long-distance, in writing, and not through in-person interviews. I was not faulting Budd Hopkins because one or more hoaxers could have targeted him through indirect means; but it seemed to me that he was taken in by a fraudulent narrative with this case, which is always a possibility when corroborative testimony by clearly identified witnesses and/or other supporting evidence is lacking, or being withheld. All of this counts heavily toward my unwillingness to accept the complete accuracy of what has been told to us about this incident. Therefore, I could not at first enumerate the Cortile/Napolitano case as supporting and legitimizing the validity of the alien-abduction phenomenon at that time. However, I later discovered that my overreliance on sources of information other than Mr Hopkins was a grave error, and that by consulting his book[27] that focused specifically on the Cortile/Napolitano case, I now believe the story to be true; and I again caution the curious to be as thorough as possible and to not reach premature conclusions about any and all aspects of the UFO/UAP and extraterrestrial hypothesis (ETH) phenomena.

Then there is the strange case of Travis Walton. On 5 November 1975, Travis Walton, then aged 22, a logger working a job in the Apache-Sitgreaves National Forest in Arizona was allegedly struck by a light beam emitted from a UFO that knocked him unconscious and propelled him 20ft away.[28](*) Terrified, his six co-workers went for help. Meantime, Walton said he revived in a chamber in the company of alien beings.

(* Another example of extraterrestrials possessing energy rays with weapons potential; but the aliens suggest to humans who say they have been in contact with them that it is *we* who are the overly aggressive ones with too many weapons. It seems to me that ETs do not always practice what they preach.)

Walton recounted his interactions with the aliens, which included his lunging at them in an attempt to get away. He later was rendered unconscious, and when he regained awareness he found himself lying on the ground at

27. *Witnessed.* By Budd Hopkins. Pocket Books. New York. 1997.
28. Also: https://www.travis-walton.com/ordinary.html
https://www.phoenixnewtimes.com/news/wheres-walton-is-arizonas-best-known-ufo-abductee-bound-for-hollywood-stardon-6425907

the outskirts of Heber, Arizona. He reported that he had thought an hour had passed during the incident; but he had been missing for five days.[29]

All of the witnesses underwent law-enforcement interrogation (because the sheriff's office thought they had murdered Walton and concocted a fantastic cover story) and psychological testing, and were given lie-detector tests. One test results was determined to have been inconclusive (when the subject thought – incorrectly – that the test was not being administered properly, and did not complete it);[30] while all the others were declared positive – the subjects had passed successfully.

In a planned television appearance, Walton did not take the test due to the presence of large crowds and many members of the press, creating a circus atmosphere at the television studio. So, despite numerous attempts over the years to debunk this story, those who would have invalidated it have not only not produced extraordinary evidence to support their extraordinary claims of denial, they have instead come up with weak "explanations" that explain only their own closed-mindedness. A much later claim that the contractor had his crew invented the story to avoid a fine for being late in completing the forestry work has no corroborating evidence and is merely fantasizing on the part of a would-be debunker.

Moreover, partial corroboration of the alien-abduction phenomenon has surfaced as of April 2022, when none other than Emma Parry brings us more information via *The Sun* newspaper, which filed a Freedom of Information request that produced more than 1,500 pages of documents relating to various aspects of UFO phenomena.

Within the newly released stacks of information, Parry points to the featuring of a "useful database" (the government's description, not Parry's or *The Sun*'s) compiled by the United States-based civilian UFO research group "MUFON" (Mutual UFO Network). The report-within-the-report cited "the biological effects of UFO sightings on humans and their frequency." The MUFON sub-report within the government study "included bizarre occurrences such as 'apparent abduction,' 'unaccounted for pregnancy,' 'sexual encounters,' 'experience of telepathy' and 'perceived teleportation.'"[31]

Let us for a moment disbelieve almost all of the accounts of humans being kidnapped, biologically screened, subjected to invasive medical procedures and, as abduction experiencers often testify through various researchers,

29. https://www.buzzfeed.com/ryanbergara/are-alien-abductions-real-these-guys-figured-it-out
30. *Fire in the Sky*. By Travis Walton. Marlowe & Co. New York. 1996. Page 85.
31. https://www.the-sun.com/news/5053647/ufos-injuries-radiation-burns-pentagon-docs/

being also psychologically abused by aliens using mental telepathy to insert distressing images of a worldwide apocalypse into their minds.[32]

If we eliminate 90 per cent, or 95 per cent, or even 99 per cent of these reports as being untrue, that would still leave us with a significant number of alien-abduction accounts being factual. This extrapolation is based on the many calculations by numerous researchers that even mere simple UFO sightings are only reported at a rate not even closely approaching 100 per cent. In alien-abduction reports, many experiencers do not make the incident known for many years – and probably a like number never do tell anyone, except, perhaps a family member or close friend. Such reluctance to report an abduction, and much less so a UFO sighting, stems from fear of ridicule, or being misjudged as hallucinating, or of being a liar.

There is sufficient testimony – no matter how fantastic it all seems – for me not to just dismiss all of it entirely, even with regard to extraterrestrials spiriting humans away to be subjected to invasive medical practices – some of a sexual nature – as well as to be invaded mentally and having images inserted into the imaginations of victims; and, generally, to manipulate the memory process of humans in an effort to make them forget the entire ordeal.

I must, at the very least, not automatically disbelieve people who report alien-abduction experiences, despite the fact that I was strongly inclined to do just that prior to researching this book. There is much more in the way of the testimony of alien-abduction experiences in the books on the subject to be found in the bibliography, and I urge readers of this book to, if they are truly interested, obtain and read all of those works.

There is, of course, much more to the Travis Walton story, and the many others not even touched upon in this volume, but, even the bare essentials, presented above, make me strongly inclined to accept his account as fact; and, once more, if the facts change so will my opinion.

Did Aliens Cause Planes, Ships, People to Disappear?

The disappearance of Malaysia Airlines Flight MH-370 on 8 March 2014, led to speculation among some that the entire plane and its passengers had

---

32. "Mind-reading machines are coming — how can we keep them in check? Devices that can record and change brain activity will create privacy issues that challenge existing human-rights legislation, say researchers." By Liam Drew 24 July 2023 https://www.nature.com/articles/d41586-023-02405-y

been abducted by aliens. However, over time, various parts of the aircraft were found in widespread areas around the Indian Ocean. MH-370 was the eighty-fourth plane to vanish (for a while) since 1948.[33]

Aircraft losses such as the Navy training mission Flight 19, in the Bermuda Triangle, are often blamed on UFOs; and other missing flights over the years have the same attribution after they, too, disappeared. Yet recent technological developments and the curiosity of underwater explorers and land-based adventurers have located many of those once "lost" aircraft.[34]

On average, each year more than two dozen large ships either sink or disappear, taking their crews with them.[35] While it may entertain some to speculate that these vessels were also taken away by aliens, I am skeptical. Likewise, I also doubt – with the possible exception of the Frederick Valentich case, to be presented shortly – if any of the planes that disappeared were captured by UFOs. Yet there are exceptions, the subject of which are beyond the scope of this book. As for missing individuals: more than 600,000 people go missing in the United States every year.[36] Almost all of them are found, or return voluntarily. However, tens of thousands of individuals remain missing for more than one year – what many agencies consider "cold cases." There were 15,172 open missing person cases as of 24 May 2022.[37] When it comes to missing children, 99.8 per cent are recovered alive.[38] For adults the rate of location is lower, in part due to the fact that some are murdered and never found, others become lost in remote areas where they ventured alone, some are fugitives, and others *want* to "disappear."

The federal government does not track the number of missing persons in national parks, but experts believe about 1,600 individuals mysteriously vanish each year while visiting parks throughout the United States.[39]

33. https://www.fastcompany.com/3027794/infographic-84-planes-thatve-vanished-off-the-face-of-the-earth
34. https://www.cnn.com/2017/03/08/asia/mh370-debris-found/index.html#:~:text=Authorities%20say%20this%20piece%20of,of%20the%20missing%20Boeing%20777
35. https://actuarialeye.com/2014/03/30/how-many-ships-disappear-each-year/
36. https://www.google.com/search?q=FBI+missing+persons+database&sa=X&ved=2ahUKEwjJ_qen7PP3AhUrkWoFHfeXDbgQ1QJ6BAg6EAE&biw=1309&bih=688&dpr=1.1
37. https://worldpopulationreview.com/state-rankings/missing-persons-by-state
38. NamUs: Homehttps://namus.nij.ojp.gov
39. https://nypost.com/2020/07/04/why-hundreds-of-people-vanish-into-the-american-wilderness/

In Mexico, more than 100,000 have disappeared between 1964 and 2022[40] for, of course, the same reasons. The country with the most disappearances per capita is Sri Lanka, where between 60,000 and 80,000 people have vanished since the late 1980s.[41] This number is no doubt due in part to unacknowledged losses in a now ended civil war, and also due to the fact that people had fled the country to avoid the violence without contacting authorities.

To me, it is in this category where aliens intent on abducting human beings on a permanent basis (without returning them) could act to perform whatever mischief or crimes they may have in mind. It is much more convenient to abduct a single person alone in a remote location than to try to take away an entire plane or ship, but it could have happened – assuming the abduction crime by aliens occurs at all, which I am inclined to accept now due to the testimonies of scores of victims as related to us in the books cited herein.

Assuming the Travis Walton tale is true – and I do believe it – then I speculate that perhaps the intent was to make Mr Walton disappear permanently as he was taken from a remote area; but then it occurred to his kidnappers, or their supervisors, that there had been six witnesses, so the best course would be to return him to avoid too much bad publicity.

Why should aliens be concerned about bad publicity? I do not know, but, based on their usually secretive behavior it is evident that they are generally keeping as low a profile as possible. Maybe there really is an agreement between ETs and (some) human authorities about keeping abductions temporary and doing not too much mental and physical damage to their kidnapping victims. Perhaps there is some Prime Directive by a type of interstellar authority prohibiting certain activities. It could be, as some abductees assert, that there are multiple extraterrestrial races who have agreements about what to do with more primitive beings such as humans. It could be that humanity has been designated an endangered and protected species. Some abductees assert that several races of ETs are in competition yet are restrained by some sort of treaty, so that, while they vie for control of our planetary resources they do not overtly go to war with one another. In this regard, in that people in Europe, Latin America, Russia,

40. https://www.cnn.com/2022/05/17/americas/mexico-disappearances-data-intl/index.html#:~:text=From%201964%20to%20the%20present,of%20516%20people%20is%20unknown.
41. https://www.amnesty.org/en/what-we-do/enforced-disappearances/#:~:text=Sri%20Lanka,vanishing%20since%20the%20late%201980s

North America, elsewhere report aliens with distinct features appearing in each of those areas, it could be that the various extraterrestrial races have apportioned our planet into spheres of investigation, influence and exploitation, just as European nations once divided Africa and, with the inclusion of the Japanese, parts of Asia into separate economic and political zones and/or colonies.

In any case, I do believe part of the reason for the memory-suppression and other attempts at secrecy – no matter how awkward, or sabotaged by other ETs who encourage their craft and themselves to be seen – is to keep their hidden agenda largely from view, which to me has sinister implications. I do hope I am wrong about all of this negative speculation, but, in the meantime, we must do as much as possible in our quest to catch up to ETs technologically so we can end their activities, which, based on the evidence of numerous credible eyewitnesses, range from merely mischievous to grossly criminal.

As for myself, I am often at the edge of the wilderness where I remain on guard against all potential threats, be they rattlesnakes, bears, mountain lions, other humans, or even possible ETs; but I do not become fixated on any of these possible dangers, only prepared to take forceful defensive action should the need arise while I keep busy with maintenance chores and improvement projects. (Recalling the 5,000-acre ranch executive ordering all cowboys to be armed when working remotely.) I recommend the same caution on the part of Earth's political and military leadership for our national and planetary wellbeing.

The Disappearance of Australian Pilot Frederick Valentich

As 20-year-old pilot Frederick Valentich flew his small plane from Adelaide, Australia, to King Island, in Bass Strait between the mainland and Tasmania, he radioed air traffic control to inquire about other aircraft in the area, telling them that he was being pursued by a strange object. This was just after 7 p.m. on 21 October 1978.[42]

What follows is a reproduction (by me) of his dialogue with air traffic control. I have removed overly repetitive hailing and call letters, added

42. https://www.adelaidenow.com.au/news/truth-was-out-there-after-all/news-story/2973bd131c27da0a31f4a7b8eba643fe

punctuation, but not removed or added content. (Words in parentheses may have other interpretations.)

Valentich: Melbourne, this is Delta Sierra Juliet. Is there any known traffic below five thousand?

FSU: [Melbourne Flight Service Unit – air traffic control.] No known traffic.

Valentich: I am – seems (to) be a large aircraft below five thousand.

FSU: What type of aircraft is it?

Valentich: I cannot affirm – it is four bright – it seems to be like landing lights. [FSU starts to call him, but he interrupts.] The aircraft has just passed over me at least a thousand feet above.

FSU: Roger. And it is a large aircraft? Confirm.

Valentich: Err, unknown due to the speed it's travelling. Is there any air force aircraft in the vicinity?

FSU: No known aircraft in the vicinity.

Valentich: It's approaching now from due east toward me. [FSU calls him, followed by his open microphone for two seconds.]

Valentich: It seems to me that he's playing some sort of game. He's flying over me three times at a time at speeds I could not identify.

FSU: Roger. What is your actual level?

Valentich: My level is four and a half thousand – four-five zero, zero.

FSU: And confirm you cannot identify the aircraft?

Valentich: Affirmative.

FSU: Roger. Stand by.

Valentich: It's not an aircraft; it is ... [his microphone stays open 2 seconds].

FSU: Can you describe the, err, aircraft?

Valentich: As it's flying past it's a long shape. [His microphone stays open for 3 seconds] ... (cannot) identify more than (that it has such speed). [His microphone is open for 3 seconds] ... Before me right now, Melbourne.

FSU: Roger, and how large would the, err, object be?

Valentich: It seems like it's stationary. What I'm doing right now is orbiting, and the thing is just orbiting on top of me. Also, it's got a green light and sort of metallic (like) it's all shiny (on) the outside.

FSU calls him again; but Valentich continues after his microphone is open for 5 seconds:

Valentich: It's just vanished. [FSU addresses him again by his call letters, "Delta Sierra Juliet," but once more Valentich interrupts.]

Valentich: Would you know what kind of aircraft I've got? Is it (a type of) military aircraft?

FSU: Confirm the, err, aircraft just vanished?

Valentich: Say again?

FSU: Is the aircraft still with you?

Valentich: It's, ah, nor … [his microphone is open for 2 seconds] … now approaching from the southwest. [FSU calls again, but Valentich continues] The engine is rough-idling. I've got it set at twenty-three, twenty- four, and the thing is [coughing].

FSU: Roger. What are your intentions?

Valentich: My intentions are, ah, to go to King Island, ah, Melbourne, that strange aircraft is hovering on top of me again … [his microphone stays open for 2 seconds] It is hovering, and it's not an aircraft …

FSU: Delta Sierra Juliet …

Valentich: Delta Sierra Juliet, Melbourne … [his microphone remains open for 17 seconds] …

FSU: Delta Sierra Juliet, Melbourne … [Despite repeated calls from Melbourne FSU, Valentich was never heard from again.][43]

Just reading the radio log gives me a creepy feeling. It seems Valentich is concerned, alarmed, even fearful, and air traffic control was, too – as well as confused. Altogether, it does not seem to be a hoax, hallucination, mistaken identity. The description of the UFO and its reported behaviors are all-too-familiar to us by now. If I were on a jury, I would find that Frederick Valentich was the likely victim of an alien-abduction or a UFO-aircraft collision.

43. https://www.snopes.com/articles/383824/frederick-valentich-ufo-disappearance/

This incident does not involve the military, but is illustrative. I suspect that if similar events had occurred to missing military planes, such as the disappearance of a USAF C-54, flying from Alaska to Texas with a stop in Montana with forty-four persons aboard on 26 January 1950, any details relating to UFOs would have been withheld by the government. (This is not to suggest that is what actually happened in this case; it is cited as an example of a mysterious disappearance of a military plane.) The majority of missing aircraft mishaps occur over water or mountains, making it probable they were the result of accidents not related to UFOs.

Recently, researcher Keith Basterfield discovered by accident some records of the Valentich incident while conducting a quest for unrelated documents. The official papers revealed that aircraft wreckage with partial serial numbers were found in Bass Strait five years after the disappearance. The serial numbers of Valentich's plane fell within the range of those found on the wreckage, almost eliminating the theory that the pilot staged his disappearance.

There was later testimony given after the case became well-known where others said they also saw a UFO in the area, and one account of supposedly seeing a small plane adhering to the side of a strange object; I am skeptical. While Frederick Valentich could have been abducted in mid-air, I think it is much more likely that if an encounter with a UFO occurred, which does seem likely to me, there could have been an accidental, or even intentional, collision between Valentich's plane and an alien spacecraft. Or, again, he could have suffered some mishap, possibly due to pilot error while he was in distress regarding the UFO. In this regard it recalls the disappearance above Lake Superior of the F-94 jet in 1953. The uncovering of more facts will solve the mystery. Mr Basterfield concluded the news item with the remark, "The only thing we can say for sure is that the plane and pilot disappeared while he was describing a UFO – which is one of those things that just makes people wonder."

Alien-Human Hybrids

The researchers and therapists investigating alleged cases of alien-abduction were soon shocked to learn more from the unfortunate victims. Numerous abduction experiencers report even stranger events than just kidnapping, such as being subjected to biological procedures centered primarily on human reproductive organs.[44] This reported alien fixation on human

44. *Sight Unseen*, Budd Hopkins and Carol Rainey. Pocket Books. New York, 2003; *The Secret Life*, Dr David M. Jacobs. Simon & Schuster. New York. 1993 – Chapter 4,

reproduction began with not just the first widely reported abduction – of Barney and Betty Hill, in 1961.[45] Before then, in 1956 a Brazilian farmhand claimed he was sexually coupled with an alien female during his abduction experience. (It has later been conjectured that he was actually subjected to humiliating sperm-removal procedures and that his sexual fantasy was a psychological defense reaction.)

These victims of kidnapping, if their abduction accounts are true; and if the testimony of hundreds of people is to be taken as factual – then, as will be shown in the next chapter, such crimes would have serious implications of not only a humanitarian nature but would also call into question the potential of our race to deal with the problem with first political means, then, if those do not succeed, a military response.

Alien-abduction researchers, investigators and therapists report that their interviewees, and patients in the cases relayed by counselors, have told them that eggs and sperm have been involuntarily extracted. Many female abductees testified that they were impregnated – mostly by artificial means, but sometimes overtly raped by human-looking entities – and that their fetuses were subsequently removed during later abduction events.

In an article at *The Political Insider*, dated 18 April 2022, "The Truth is Out There," correspondent Kathleen J. Anderson quotes former AATIP Director Luis Elizondo, who in turn referred to a recent Defense Intelligence Reference Document (DIRD), which "focused on the biological consequences of encounters" with alien spacecraft and beings, together with "forty-two different cases that include 'unaccounted for pregnancies.'"[46]

Many abduction victims – both male and female – also state that over time in future abductions they were placed in the company of odd-looking infants and children, and urged to cuddle, play and bond with them, being informed that these youngsters were the victims' own offspring.[47] (If interested, see all of the works dealing with alien abductions cited above; and please consult the bibliography.

The Uninvited, Nick Pope. The Overlook Press. Woodstock, New York. 1997; *Abduction*, John E. Mack, M.D. MacMillan. New York. 1994 – Chapter 9; *The Abduction Enigma*, Kevin D. Randle, Russ Estes, William P. Cone, PhD Forge. New York. 1999 – Chapter 5; *UFOs, ETs and Alien Abductions: A Scientist Looks at the Evidence* Don Donderi, PhD Hampton Roads. Charlottesville, NC. 2013. p.128.

45. See: *Interrupted Journey* John G. Fuller. Dell. New York. 1987.
46. https://thepoliticalinsider.com/the-truth-may-very-well-be-out-there/?utm_source=home-headline-stories
47. *UFOs, ETs and Alien Abductions: A Scientist Looks at the Evidence* Don Donderi, PhD Hampton Roads. Chalottesville, NC. 2013. p.129.

More than a few alien-abduction experiencers also report being informed, through telepathic means, that the strange infants, children, even young adults, are extraterrestrial-human hybrids that are being produced "for the benefit of both races."[48] Yet again: but, wait, there is more…

Dr David M. Jacobs has learned through the testimony of abductees who have "cooperated" with the extraterrestrial of a program to integrate alien-human hybrids into Earth's societies in a grand scheme of "planetary acquisition."[49] This brings to mind the mysterious "Mr Janus," who met with Sir Peter Horsley and asked for a meeting with Prince Philip.

Finally in this regard, more than a few of the abductees advise us that alien-human hybrids are also telepathic[50] – capable of reading human minds, communicating with us mentally, and even inserting externally generated thoughts – not of our own making; injecting emotions – such as fear, possibly false "memories" and visions of "future events" that may not be what they seem at all; and, finally, making abductees forget what happened to them, at least for a time – a few victims were sometimes "triggered" to remember later – often much later.'[51] (Again, the books on alien abductions cited above and to be found listed in the bibliography will substantiate that these occurrences were perceived by some abduction experiencers, and have been accepted as fact by researchers and counselors. I shall have more to reveal about this in a forthcoming book.)

I agree with the skeptical and doubtful that this is all too extreme to be readily accepted without a minimum of confirmatory evidence. However, some of that already exists in the form of a few alien-abduction witnesses informing researchers and therapists that until they had become victims, they had never even heard of alien abductions, and had not been previously acquainted with the recollections of other experiencers, thus (evidently) ruling out the possibility of their testimony being "contaminated" by the accounts of other people. These same witnesses also said they had no prior interest in or exposure to alien-abduction stories in the press or other media.[52]

Yet again, doubters are urged to not merely search the internet for a few negative articles by professional skeptics but to at least initially consult

---

48. *Walking Among Us* Dr Davie M. Jacobs. Disinformation Books. San Francisco. 2015. pp.39-40.
49. Ibid. pp.225–251; and 248–250.
50. Ibid. p.126.
51. Ibid. p.245.
52. Ibid. p.7.

the books I have referred to on the subject before making an informed judgment; then check the original information against the claims of those who try to discredit sincere witnesses by ignoring at least some of the evidence – even if that evidence stands alone in a particular case. For me, however, the multiple witnesses in the Travis Walton case, among others, defy being explained away.

The documents released by the United States Defense Intelligence Agency to *The Sun*, and covered by Emma Parry on 5 April 2022, and titled "Anomalous Acute And Subacute Field Effects on Human and Biological Tissues" investigated injuries to "human observers by anomalous advanced aerospace systems."[53] In other words, electromagnetic and/or gravitic/anti-gravitic drives have, according to the information gathered by government employees, resulted in damage to human tissues and bodies. As discussed earlier, the released text of the intelligence briefing includes the statement that people suffered injury by "exposures to anomalous vehicles, especially airborne and when in close proximity." So, once more: keep your distance.

Therefore, in the end – again accepting as little as the remotest possibility that even just a few crop circles, animal mutilations, alien abductions, interbreeding and mind-control accounts are true – what to do now?

All governments and militaries routinely plan for and "game out" different scenarios concerning possible social, economic, political and military courses of conduct in reaction to even very unlikely future events. Diplomats, politicians, economists and military commanders all have plans laid out in advance about how to deal with specific contingencies, no matter how unlikely they might seem ahead of time. Shouldn't all the nations of the Earth make at least some preliminary plans in the event that our extraterrestrial visitors prove to be hostile or merely indifferent to our wellbeing? I'll get back to these considerations shortly.

I believe I must emphasize yet again that if just the smallest percentage of the evidence discovered has even a kernel of truth, then we are evidently already in a state of war – even if at a very low level – with at least one alien species. Moreover, it is not a condition of surreptitious warfare we initiated but is instead one being imposed upon us. We did not travel to other worlds and commit the offenses cited herein. We now have no choice but to defend ourselves; and such a defense requires that we take the fight to our extraterrestrial opponents – our alien enemies.

53. https://www.the-sun.com/news/5053647/ufos-injuries-radiation-burns-pentagon-docs/

Chapter 17

More Videos, and Continued Secrecy

The Congressional Hearing of 17 May 2022

The United States House of Representatives Intelligence, Counterterrorism, Counterintelligence, and Counter-proliferation Subcommittee held an open hearing on Unidentified Aerial Phenomena on 17 May 2022. In his opening statement, Chairman André Carson, (Democrat) Indiana, stated:

> [UAPs represent] A national security threat to be monitored and investigated: in 2017, we learned for the first time that the Department of Defense had quietly restarted a similar organization tracking what we now call Unidentified Aerial Phenomena or UAPs. Last year, Congress rewrote the charter for that organization now called the Airborne Object Identification and Management Synchronization Group or AOIMSG for short. Today, we will bring that organization out of the shadows. This hearing and oversight work has a simple idea at its core: unidentified aerial phenomena are a potential national security threat, and they need to be treated that way. For too long the stigma associated with UAPs has gotten in the way of good intelligence analysis, pilots avoided reporting or were laughed at when they did. It's true, but they are real. They need to be investigated. And many threats they pose need to be mitigated.[1]

His statement is a great encapsulation of where UFOs/UAP stand today with relation to American, and world, circumstances – militarily and in general.

1. https://www.rev.com/blog/transcripts/congress-holds-historic-open-hearing-on-ufos-5-17-22-transcript

The two witnesses, Ronald S. Moultrie, Under Secretary of Defense for Intelligence and Security, and Scott W. Bray, Deputy Director of Naval Intelligence seemed to lack adequate intelligence (information) on the subject, and at times were even misleading, which is not surprising, but is illegal if they were intentionally lying to Congressional Representatives.

Specifically, Bray cited two videos recorded aboard Navy ships that were published by filmmaker Jeremy Corbell, who manages the website ExtraordinaryBeliefs.com. One of the videos, evidently a crew member's cell-phone footage of a night-vision screen, appears to show a triangular or pyramid-shaped aerial object with flashing lights above the San Diego-based guided-missile destroyer *Russell* in 2019.[2] Corbell commented to Fox News, "This is probably the best UFO military-filmed footage certainly that I've ever seen, but I think also that the world has ever seen."

But a would-be debunker came along to try to poison the well with his opinion, saying the footage was displaying a photographic effect that occurs when a camera captures images of out-of-focus light called "bokeh." He demonstrated with a video clip of his own making. (But by what exact process we were not informed, only indirectly told about.)

The aspiring debunker went on to try to deflate the "Tic-Tac" videos; but Commander David Fravor, who was the prime participant in the 2004 encounters off the California/Baja coasts, observed, "It's funny how people can extrapolate stuff who've never operated the system."

The *San Diego Union-Tribune* story cited here went to extremes in devoting column space to the supposed debunker, while avoiding substantiating information by UFO/UAP advocates, which has been a problem for decades with superficial press coverage. Moreover, despite attempts to disqualify the evidence, the fact remains that the Navy verified the authenticity of the aircraft videos, and, again, there were numerous eyewitnesses who have great credibility.

Corbell noted on the *Coast-to-Coast AM* radio program that Director Bray, at the congressional hearing, attempted to extrapolate the "green pyramid" footage, citing the "bokeh" effect, to then try to invalidate other footage of the "drones" the Navy contends were the actual nature of the UAP dogging our Navy ships in the Channel Islands area off California's coast. However, Corbell commented that if it were the case that the objects were not UAP of a possible extraterrestrial nature and were actually "drones"

2. https://www.sandiegouniontribune.com/news/military/story/2021-05-29/navy-ufo-videos-skeptics

being directed by Earthbound persons or powers unknown, then that would be just as serious a threat to our national security, if not more so.[3]

Moreover, it is evident from the congressional guests that they seem to know little about UFOs/UAP – much less than the readers of this book, or else they are concealing much even as the government is suddenly open about needing more information. This is the classical "one-way street" where they are willing to receive but not give. As pointed out before, a certain amount of secrecy may be required to keep adversaries – whether Earthly or extraterrestrial – in the dark, yet the public in the United States and the United Kingdom, and worldwide, must receive more openness and honesty.

Extraterrestrials: Who (or What) Are They?
Why Are They Here – What Do They Want?
What Should Be Our Strategy?
Concluding Remarks.

United States Navy Videos, Redux

Recently, to buttress my opinion that UFOs have a physical existence, likely as alien spacecraft (and/or alien-controlled probes or drones), there has been additional proof in the form of official, government-generated videos.

Images from videos provided by the United States Department of Defense show a UFO in 2015 as it flits about above the clouds over the North Atlantic – moving against the wind.[4] One Navy pilot involved in the interception that resulted in the video radioed his fellow fliers and ship-based controllers, "There's a whole fleet of them."[5] The video is named "Gimbal," after the appearance of the unidentified flying object. (I wonder who will label these pilots, the DoD, and those who see the video "cranks and weirdos.") As reported by Rich Hoffman, of the Scientific Coalition for UAP Studies, pilots involved in the East Coast UFO encounters said they were an almost daily occurrence for several months in 2015.[6]

3. *Coast-to-Coast AM*, 22–23 May 2022, with guest host George Knapp. https://www.coasttocoastam.com/
4. https://www.history.com/videos/uss-roosevelt-gimbal-ufo-declassified-video
5. https://www.nytimes.com/2020/07/23/us/politics/pentagon-ufo-harry-reid-navy.html
6. [*Coast-to-Coast AM*, with guest host George Knapp, 26–27 March 2022.] https://www.coasttocoastam.com

Moreover, a "swarm" of UFOs, referred to as "drones" in press accounts, stalked U.S. Navy ships on maneuvers in the Channel Islands area off the southern California coast in 2019,[7] adding to the mystification and alarm among government and military officials in the United States.[8] There was an attempt at the Congressional Hearing on 17 May 2022 to dismiss these as drones of Earth-origination, but in view of their superior performance, and their distance from any conceivable base of operations, it is my belief that these objects are of extraterrestrial origin. I have watched the videos. There are also numerous video clips of UFOs/UAP appearing along the U.S. southern border, as shown on monitoring cameras on the ground and aboard Customs and Border Protection and military aircraft.

> According to sources The Debrief has interviewed, these incidents include encounters with aerial objects that appear to perform maneuvers well beyond the capabilities of conventional aircraft. Some of these events, which were also captured on video, have left a number of veteran pilots and other personnel questioning the nature and origin of these objects.

The unclassified video footage from as recently as 9 February 2021 was available for viewing [as of 2 June 2022].[9] The release of the Navy aircraft videos, coupled with increased pressure from lawmakers and others within and without government to investigate the UFO phenomenon, and to make more findings public, prompted the release of the report of 25 June 2021 in which it was admitted that just 1 of 144 UFO incidents cited therein could be explained.[10] (The 143 others could not be explained away.)

Despite disclaimers that the UFOs could not be extraterrestrial visitors, I disagree. No nation on Earth possesses aircraft able to duplicate the maneuvers and speeds of these and other UFOs shown on official videos;

---

7. https://www.thedrive.com/the-war-zone/39913/multiple-destroyers-were-swarmed-by-mysterious-drones-off-california-over-numerous-nights
8. https://thehill.com/opinion/national-security/588223-ufos-the-channel-islands-and-the-navys-drone-swarm-mystery
9. https://thedebrief.org/incursions-at-the-border-homeland-security-agents-tell-of-encounters-with-uap/
10. https://missoulian.com/news/national/us-intel-report-on-ufos-unable-to-explain-more-than-140-cases-of-strange-aerial/article_c126e6f1-3d09-5e9a-8626-1631c44b8216.html

the only logical conclusion is that they are the products of technologies alien to our Earth at this time.

The 2021 report, the videos from 2004, 2015 and 2019, and other information made known to Congress and the public has resulted in the introduction of separate items of legislation sponsored and co-sponsored by Arizona Representative Ruben Gallego (D); and New York Senator Kirsten Gillibrand (D); Florida Senator Marco Rubio (R); Missouri Senator Roy Blunt (R); New Mexico Senator Martin Heinrich (D); and South Carolina Senator Lindsey Graham (R).

The intent of these laws is to order the collection and analysis of data regarding UFO incidents; and also to create a scientific theory and program to not just understand advanced UFO technology but also to "'replicate any such advanced characteristics and performance' [or reverse-engineer (my phrase here)] the UAPs."[11]

What we now see is that, at long last, the United States government is (at least temporarily) acknowledging the existence and challenges of UFOs as possible if not probable alien spacecraft; and is recognizing the necessity of attempting to "catch-up" to Earth's extraterrestrial "visitors" – in a technological way.

Under the influence of GEPAN, then COMETA, it was the French, as always being independent-minded, who first "broke the ice" regarding public disclosure by government agencies of what they knew about the UFO phenomenon. In the United States, people like defense-industry magnate Robert Bigelow influenced some in government such as the late Senate Majority Leader Harry Reid, and former Secretary of Defense, CIA Director, and White House Chief of Staff Leon Panetta to get the government to at least acknowledge publicly that the U.S. military was still investigating UFOs, despite denials of such investigations since the shut-down of Project Blue Book in 1969.

However, in a story dated 2 December 2021, it is reported that the Department of Defense still seeks to automatically classify as "Secret" videos and photographs of UFOs/UAP, preventing their release for viewing by the general public, now and in the future.[12]

11. https://www.military.com/daily-news/2021/12/07/pentagon-ufo-rapid-response-teams-ordered-congress.html
12. "New Pentagon Office Criticized as Effort to Control UFO Investigations, End Transparency. A Defense Department group will now oversee U.S. government-wide investigations into UFOs – with little hope for transparency or oversight." https://www.usnews.com/news/national-news/articles/2021-12-02/new-pentagon-office-criticized-as-effort-to-control-ufo-investigations-end-transparency

As a curious person, and as a taxpaying citizen and voter who requires adequate information to make educated judgments about government policy and spending before casting my ballot, I am reluctant to endorse such secrecy. Also, it has been pointed out that releasing the UFO videos has enhanced public awareness regarding national (and planetary?) security, which is necessary in order to participate in decisions to improve our national (and planetary) defense. As one who has chosen to write on the subject of a history of military encounters with UFOs, I am also inclined to seek access to more information. Yet there are other considerations, which may or may not remain valid as we look further into this subject.

An Alien Presence as an Established Fact

As readers of this book are by now aware, this investigation of UFOs and their encounters with military organizations on our planet has almost by necessity strayed into territory that is not just odd but strange, bizarre, esoteric, and – dare I state without unintended humor – otherworldly. It was never my intention to drift into realms of inquiry, observation, and investigation that seem to take us away from a serious, historical, scientific study (in the sense of relying on the best evidence available), which is often if not usually limited to eyewitness testimony and impressions left on electronic sensors such as digital media and radar sets – and yet is also as thorough and complete as is possible, based on the limited (by governments) information available to us today.

Despite more or less believing at times during my life in the existence of UFOs as likely alien spacecraft generally being much less of a belief than I had thought at those times, looking back I realize that the mysterious "answer" to my (unintended) "signal" into the night sky with a powerful hand-held lantern had created in me an instant fear reaction and an unconscious acknowledgement that whatever had returned three flashes of light was something alien and possibly menacing; hence my immediate suggestion that my sons promptly accompany me inside our rural residence.

I now understand that it was this instinctive fear reaction that caused me to instantly craft a spurious attempt to explain away, rather than explain, the possibility that we had been observed – and remotely "contacted" – by some device or beings of an otherworldly nature. I reasoned that since our family retreat is within an aerial military operations zone, probably some (human) pilot of a conventional, likely military, aircraft was teasing us with flashing lights. As a result, both my wife and I, and our sons, were put more at ease – especially when outside, alone, at the edge of the wilderness.

Therefore, regarding at least some of the people who refuse to open their minds to the probability of UFOs as vehicles containing alien beings, it has occurred to me that they resort to automatic attempts to dismissively explain away UFOs/UAP because of their own instantaneous fear reactions. While this may be suitable for average people, in the case of media personalities, scientists, engineers, and government officials – especially those in our military charged with our protection – such an instinctive cowering behind denial is not only inappropriate but a dereliction of professional duty.

Moreover, in view of eyewitness accounts – at least one of which was substantiated by multiple witnesses – I have revised my attitude regarding possible alien abductions. The information disclosed by abductees and some of the people who observed the incidents has convinced me that alien abductions – no matter how many or few in number – are a very uncomfortable truth. This is despite my initial reaction that abductees had grave mental problems requiring equally serious psychological counseling and treatment.

I acknowledge my misinterpretation regarding alien abductions, based on my ignorance of the facts presented to us by abductees and dedicated researchers and therapists. I also acknowledge my unconscious fear that the alien-abduction phenomenon actually is a terrifying fact of life on our planet today. The facts have been updated and consequently my opinion has belatedly changed. Moreover, the reality that the Defense Intelligence Agency has received, retained, and released information about alleged alien abductions, as reported by Emma Parry at *The Sun*,[13] adds even more weight to the case in favor of the phenomenon as a distressing truth.

Yet, even if we dismiss all evidence of animal mutilations, and accounts of alien abductions as being untrue, and if we also reject the idea that crop circles are some sort of messaging or artwork created by extraterrestrials, there has been too much evidence – some of it physical, in addition to numerous eyewitness accounts by very credible witnesses in different military organizations, foreign and domestic – to allow us to simply dismiss it or try to explain it all away. Therefore, please allow me to build on the speculations of others and to add more conjecture of my own as we conclude our investigation of a history of military encounters with UFOs.

---

13. https://www.the-sun.com/news/4038088/fighter-pilots-intercepted-ufos-radiation-warped-time/

Who (or What) Are They?

Competing theories about the strange entities encountered by humans include beings from other dimensions, time travelers, and, of course, extraterrestrials – these lattermost existing as biological entities, robots, biological-artificial hybrids, or even some type of synthetic life forms.

For the reasons described herein, I believe that the capacities attributed to UFOs and alien entities are not the result of interdimensional capabilities but, rather, advanced technologies that merely make what they do seem impossible, magical or beyond our natural, physical realm. Neither do I think they are spiritual entities, or the products of human imagination. As for time travelers: while not impossible for me to imagine, if they are able to travel through time, what is their origin – the future or the past? Why do they concern themselves with our activities at this point in time? If from the past, then they are curious about the future; but why now if they can just skip ahead into our own future and learn what lies later than today? If they are from the future, they may be taking enormous risks to their subsequent existence if they do something now that could change happenings in the "course of history" enough to eliminate themselves in an altered progression of events. Time travel may be impossible, or at the very least much more difficult than we can imagine, for any civilization – no matter how far advanced; it is an extremely remote possibility.[14] However, I cannot in good conscience declare time travel to be absolutely impossible. If such a feat were a possibility, then it seems to me that it would necessarily be accomplished while one is in deep space, to prevent materializing in another time within, for example, a mountain, etc. It is my belief that observed interdimensional and time-warping effects of UFOs/UAP are the result of extraterrestrial manipulation of electromagnetic and gravitic forces, not the other way around.

UFO expert Jacques Vallée has gravitated to the belief that our visitors and their "craft" are manifestations of interdimensional and/or psycho-spiritual – in the sense of reflecting higher and therefore altered – not distorted – states of consciousness.[15] While this belief could, in part, be true, I still adhere to the extraterrestrial hypothesis – ETH – because, even if we assume interdimensional and/or time-travel visitations, those visitors would yet be "extraterrestrial," meaning outside of our Earthly existence.

14. What Is Time? https://nautil.us/what-is-time-17483/

15. *Confrontations* Jacques Vallée. Ballantine Books. New York. 1990.

It is inconceivable to me that even if ETs originated in an altered dimensional realm that in their continuum they would exist on anything other than the equivalent of a planetary body, given their evident appearance with, for example, a pair of legs to allow them mobility on a planetary surface. In the possibility of time travel, the aliens' world, even if it was planet Earth at some distant past or future time, would be vastly different from ours. Therefore, in either case, whether interdimensional or time-travel, or even existing on Earth within a different continuum at present, UFOs/UAP and their crews would be from outside of our current planet Earth – or would still be "extraterrestrials."

There is also the possibility that the "aliens" are not fully biological beings but are instead synthetic or robotic lifeforms. For various reasons, such as an effort to dispel distrust by humans, they may be posing as biological entities. Some of the traits observed by people who report being taken captive aboard alien spacecraft tell us that extraterrestrials do not seem to eat, drink, or eliminate waste products, indicating a non-biological existence. Also, some of the abilities aliens are reported to possess may be not ingrained as far as biology is concerned, or even the result of utilizing helpful devices; the extraterrestrials could themselves be devices – instruments with built-in capacities for, as an example, extrasensory perception. These traits indicate that, particularly with regard to the "Greys," they may be a hybrid – part synthetic – lifeform.

There is also the possibility that the extraterrestrials are a combination of one or more alien species with subordinate synthetic or robotic entities performing routine tasks; just as, likewise, the smaller orbs seen being emitted from, accompanying, re-entering larger UFOs are likely similar to our own probes or remotely piloted vehicles – RPVs, or drones. It is also postulated that the "standard-sized" UFOs – of about 100 to 200ft in diameter – are alien equivalents of "scout ships," while the huge ones – such as those seen above Alaska and Stonehenge described earlier, would likely be the "mother ships," akin to our aircraft carriers, which dispatch the other craft on routine assignments while they generally remain in orbit "above and beyond" the fray here down below.

All of these possibilities having been put forth for consideration, I remain inclined toward the alien visitors being extraterrestrial biological entities – EBEs. It is also possible that the variously reported "races" of aliens are of the same species, but at different stages of development, as in our infants, toddlers, children, pre-teen adolescents, teenagers, full-grown but youthful adults, the middle-aged, and the elderly.

Some abductees report that the more-exotic aliens they have encountered are of three distinct main types, arranged in a hierarchy. They are: humanoid but also "insectoid"; that is, mostly human-looking but very tall and reminiscent of insects, sometimes attired in high-collared, white robes. They have angular, almost triangular heads, reminding witnesses of those of the Praying Mantis species. They seem to be in charge. Next come the "reptilians" – again humanoid but with necks and heads according to abductees as being similar to those of lizards or turtles. They seem to be at an intermediate level in the extraterrestrial hierarchy – and akin to technicians or specialists, and are fewest in number. The most numerous are the typical "Greys," which are the evident foot-soldiers who perform routine duties. There are also "humans" or near-humans who come in two main varieties: short, compact, auburn-haired, serious-minded and also of evident low-rank, but seeming to operate beyond the supervision of the insectoids in their own, independent spacecraft. Finally there are the "Nordics," who resemble humans the most: they are tall, blue-eyed and blond, and who are rare and seem to operate in small contingents also aboard spacecraft separate from the others, although they are occasionally seen with or near the insectoids, reptilians, other humanoids, and "Greys."[16]

In the UK, people who report close encounters with extraterrestrials describe them as being humans; in the United States, eyewitnesses state most often that they conform to the description of the "Greys" – about 4ft tall, with large heads, very large and black eyes, long arms – with hands featuring just four fingers, and short legs, with tiny mouths and flat noses and ears. Some speculation is that there are several species of aliens; that some of the "humans" are actually ET-human hybrids; or the extraterrestrials could be manipulating our perceptions to disguise their true appearance. There is also the likelihood that people perceive what they see with regard to UFOs and ETs according to their own worldview and cultural background. Generally, entities with the most bizarre appearances are reported from Russia. It is also possible that several alien races each have a territory on our planet as their exclusive or primary domain, just at European nations once divided-up Africa and, along with the Japanese, China and the Mongols, portioned-out among their own tribal entities their different provinces in East Asia, South Asia, the Near East, the Middle East and, briefly, parts of Eastern Europe and Western Asia.

It has been testified by abductees that the insectoids seem to have the greatest telepathic powers, along with the Nordics. The reptilians seem less adept at ESP, as do the compact humanoids, and, least of all perhaps, the "Greys."

16. *Walking Among Us: The Alien Plan to Control Humanity* Jacobs, David M., PhD Disinformation Books. San Francisco, CA. 2015. p.19.

Whether these beings are from another place or places in space or not (some people believe they inhabit Earth, but on a "different plane" or altered dimensional time-space continuum), we must thoroughly investigate their motives for coming to our planet. The United States government now recognizes this, as acknowledged by Ohio Congressman Carson at the hearing of 17 May 2022.

Why Come to Earth? What's in it For Them?

Evidently – obvious, really – alien expeditions to our planet are being conducted for a logical reason. There must be some resource here that attracts their continuing interest.[17] The Soviet analysis was that the same natural substances would exist throughout the universe and not be exclusively on Earth alone, but that presupposes that those resources are easily obtainable everywhere. Perhaps, for example, "rare earths" were once abundant but are so rare now because they have already been heavily harvested – by aliens.

Today, people are advised that when they use a "free" media resource, such as a website for example, and cannot identify what of value they are exchanging for the benefit of using that website, then the item of value is the user; or, more precisely, her or his information, to be sold to marketers. This takes us back to the possible implications of alien abductions: perhaps the "information" being (involuntarily) exchanged is our human genetic makeup.

We now enter deeper into the realm of "woo-woo-land" again because, as we have seen, most abductees report having had medical tests and procedures performed on them. They also tell of what can only be defined as the forcible harvesting of their eggs or sperm, and some females report outright, physical acts of rape. This biological program is further described as part of an overall project to temporarily impregnate female abductees, with the forcible removal of the fetus in a later abduction. The object of this activity, according to what some abductees have learned, is to produce

17. "Scientists Discover Unexplained Abundance of Rare Nuclear Fusion Fuel on Earth. Helium-3, a potential source of limitless clean energy, may be ten times more common on our planet than previously thought, reports a new study." By Becky Ferreira. 9 May 2022.
https://www.vice.com/en/article/7kbndq/scientists-discover-unexplained-abundance-of-rare-nuclear-fusion-fuel-on-earth

a hybrid human-alien species. Yes, I, too, at first rejected the notion of human-alien hybridization; however, as we stray further into science-fiction territory, there are ways to postulate through and around the problem.

Human genetic engineers have found ways to combine genes from extremely divergent species; so, in theory, widely separated DNA structures could be hybridized. Again though, why would creatures from different worlds, and all the more so from remote star systems, share *any* DNA or other molecular structures at all? The partial answer is that astronomers have detected substances essential to life as we know it – organic compounds with the capacity to be assembled into and from Earth-based RNA and DNA molecules – floating in deep space. Also, certain natural claylike and other substances self-organize in nature into similar repetitive arrangements – akin to soft-bodied crystals or some cellular sub-structures; and it is assumed that they, too, will assemble themselves in closely aligned patterns throughout the universe. It could be the case that the same elements would follow nearly identical patterns in molecules close to RNA and DNA in structure in widely separated locations such as on different worlds or in star systems far removed from one another.

Then there is the theory that we – humans and aliens – have closely related roots originating in the distant past. For this to be so there would necessarily have been an interplanetary and/or interstellar civilization in existence eons ago.[18] Subsequently, it may be reasoned, this grand culture collapsed, and the isolated remnants pursued independent evolutionary development, creating separate species, subspecies, or "races," which could yet interbreed, just as, for example, today's widely divergent breeds of dogs, all of whom have descended from wolves. These canine "mildly divergent subspecies" or "races" "hybridize." (There is no hard and fast "rule" regarding human "races." Our species originated in one area – Africa, then spread over the entire planet, becoming separated in relative isolation in Africa, Eastern and Western Eurasia, the Pacific, the Americas, leading to subspecies or "racial" divisions. But my extended family now includes people from these areas through interbreeding, not inter-marriage, except the Pacific Islands, thus proving that having been isolated into distinct groupings in the past, like canines and other species, we humans can in fact "hybridize." Perhaps this would be possible with one or more species external to our planet.) Getting back to expertise at genetic engineering: if

18. https://bigthink.com/the-past/dinosaur-civilization/

the aliens are so adept at creating human-alien hybrids, then they should be sufficiently advanced so as not to need human DNA at all, and would be capable of creating almost any sort of beings at will; we would be superfluous and not necessary to their gene-manipulation program. If they are not that advanced, then there is an indication that the extraterrestrials are not that far ahead of us in at least one area.

As for the ancient-origins theory: the biological record on Earth such as we understand it today clearly shows a constant, Earth-based progression without the evident interjection of alien genetic material or manipulation – a possible exception being two cephalopods – squids and octopuses, whose DNA was evidently "scrambled," giving them enhanced intelligence.[19] So, claims that extraterrestrials have in the past engineered human development to advance our species seems unlikely to me because, for example, humans and chimpanzees possess genetic structures that have 99.8 per cent of their DNA makeup in common.[20] Moreover, if ETs are in competition with us, as seems likely from their secrecy and evident attempted manipulation of human attitudes about them while they work from a hidden agenda, then any efforts to modify humans would be not to our benefit but to theirs. They would not seek to alter our species to improve us but to instead aim to degrade our DNA composition.[21]

Altogether, it stretches the credulity of most people, I believe, to at or beyond the saturation level to trust in human-alien hybridization as being potentially successful; and it is only brought up here to consider it as a distinct possibility as we analyze conceivable alien motivations in coming to our planet in the first place. However, if conquest of our planet is the goal, then doing so through a "vertical envelopment" by raising generations of alien-human hybrids to form an interplanetary Fifth Column to infiltrate and subvert our human race's independence would be preferable to out-

---

19. "Mind-boggling' scrambled genome found in octopus and squid. It could explain their smarts."

    By Stephanie Pappas. 10 May 2022. https://www.livescience.com/squid-octopus-genome-brains
20. https://www.amnh.org/exhibitions/permanent/human-origins/understanding-our-past/dna-comparing-humans-and-chimps#:~:text=Humans%20and%20chimps%20share%20a,%2D%2Dand%20yet%20so%20different%3F
21. "Why human brains were bigger 3,000 years ago. Although our modern civilisation is probably the most advanced to ever exist, our brains are smaller than our ancestors." By Chris Baraniuk. 8 May 2022. https://www.bbc.com/future/article/20220503-why-human-brains-were-bigger-3000-years-ago

and-out combat; all the more so in that humans now possess different types of weapons of mass destruction.

With regard to alien intentions, I refer to the late, great, Stephen Hawking, speaking in reference to the potentially habitable alien planet Gliese 832c: "One day, we might receive a signal from a planet like this, but we should be wary of answering back. Meeting an advanced civilization could be like Native Americans encountering Columbus. That didn't turn out so well."[22] Alberto Caballero, a PhD student in conflict resolution at the University of Vigo, Spain, estimates that there are likely four malicious civilizations in our galaxy – extrapolating from Italian SETI (Search for Extraterrestrial Intelligence) scientist Claudio Maccone's assessment that there could be as many as 15,785 civilizations in the Milky Way.[23]

Prior to the appearance of the Spaniards, the Aztecs and other residents of today's Mexico believed a myth that bearded men from the east would one day arrive to rule over the local inhabitants, thus setting up the notion that submission to the foreigners would be the result of fate, and not a bad idea. Many people are willing to throw all skepticism and reserve aside and to grant extraterrestrials – should they exist – a like status as our "space brothers" and potential saviors (from ourselves?); yet what if, as Hawking suggested, our would-be deliverers are not bringing something of benefit to humanity but are instead taking resources of value from us, to them? Moreover, even if at this late date ET visitors were to suddenly step forward and offer us a cure for cancer, to extend our lifespans to 200 years, to help us clean up our Earthly environment and clear all of the space junk we have cast upward, we should still be cautious, and "Beware of ETs bearing gifts." "Help" is the sunny side of control.

As noted before, abductees report that aliens possess psychic abilities – to read minds; manipulate perceptions and emotions; to communicate non-verbally; to exert control over human bodies; to erase memories – but only temporarily for many victims; or to insert thoughts, visions and concepts into their captives' minds.

Do humans have psychic capacities? The jury is still out for many people about our species having extrasensory perception (ESP).[24] I, however,

22. https://www.livescience.com/62015-stephen-hawking-quotes.html
23. https://www.vice.com/en/article/qjbgkm/there-are-4-malicious-extraterrestrial-civilizations-in-milky-way-researcher-estimates
24. "Claim that ESP Is Real Stirs Outrage in Scientists." https://www.livescience.com/32922-claim-that-esp-is-real-stirs-outrage-in-scientists-.html

do believe that most of us have had experiences – either ourselves or by acquaintances, friends, relatives – that seem to confirm that, yes, we can sense and act on information that could not possibly have been derived through our normal, day-to-day ways of perceiving the world.

Through the use of the latest technology, people are now able to detect signals from the human brain and harness those energies.[25] We know from the most recent research and development projects that brain signals can be manipulated to control devices such as artificial limbs, just as our brains also control our bodies, so it is not beyond the realm of possibility that a sufficiently advanced technological base could provide the tools to control the actions – even thoughts – of people, as so many abductees report was done to them. The situation may seem fantastic, but the witnesses are definitely not delusional as such capacities, while in an embryonic stage for us so far, seem just around the next bend in the long and twisting road of scientific progress.[26] Given enough of a head start, could a race of aliens not be granted the theoretical ability to control our perceptions, actions, thoughts, even our memories, noting what we humans have already discovered?[27]

Abductees who have managed to somehow "shake off" extraterrestrial mind control report that this development distresses the "Greys," who often then call in reptilians, Nordics (when they are present) and especially insectoids to "restore order," even if the abductee does not become "disruptive."

Human scientists who experiment with, and people who claim to be adept at, ESP report that skepticism, cynicism, sarcasm and hostile attitudes interfere with psychic phenomena. Those abductees who seem to "awaken" and energize during capture evidently possess those attitudes and outlooks, and often one or more insectoid, reptilian, Nordic or even a "Grey" "specialist" or "familiar" may move in to try to calm and interact with the captive in a back-and-forth wherein the human is able to briefly interrogate her or his kidnappers (with demands such as "Why are you doing this?") and to acquire some information about the extraterrestrials and their programs.

---

25. "The brain-reading devices helping paralysed people to move, talk and touch." https://www.nature.com/articles/d41586-022-01047-w
26. https://www.militaryaerospace.com/computers/article/14235600/mental-health-machine-learning-sensors
27. "How Stress Works With and Against Your Memory."
    By Elizabeth Scott, PhD. Updated on 7 October 2021. https://www.verywellmind.com/stress-and-your-memory-4158323#:~:text=Stress%20and%20Memory,memories%20we%20form%20as%20well.

These people are invaluable intelligence assets for our species and must be located and coaxed – actually coaxed, and not coerced – into cooperating with human intelligence and military personnel so we may get to know our opponents better in this apparent interstellar "game" or "struggle" (war?) with the highest of stakes. We know very little about ETs, while their intelligence-gathering efforts may have yielded so much information that they now know more about us than we understand about ourselves.

Allowing for a very advanced technology also concedes to alien beings a sophisticated level of intelligence – enough to permit them to adapt their devices and perhaps eventually themselves to use mental telepathy without the benefit of artificial tools. Research has also discovered that low-frequency electromagnetic waves affect the physical capacities of other Earth creatures,[28] so why not humans? Moreover, in that electromagnetic forces create stress proteins that affect our memories,[29] it is also possible that we can accept accounts by people who have had close encounters with extraterrestrials who tell of memory problems, including failure to recall events for up to many years later; memory distortions and discrepancies among witnesses in close proximity to one another during the presence of aliens and/or their spacecraft; and sudden reversals of these symptoms, also up to many years afterward. Some of these complications were present with regard to the military people involved in the Rendlesham Forest events.

The overall extraterrestrial objective is evidently, according to some analysts, to create a sub-race of hybrids to oversee and rule over humanity through a combination of mind control and physical coercion. This is the conclusion of Dr Donald C. Donderi, based on his experience and knowledge of the testimony of people who can best be described not only as eyewitnesses, but also as "mind-witnesses" because they assert that their extraterrestrial captors transmitted thoughts directly into their minds while preventing humans, and evidently other aliens of lower socio-political status, from reading their minds in turn.[30]

Understandably, just an alien encounter or even only seeing a UFO can be very traumatic, particularly for non-believers and those who are fearful

28. "Exposure to extremely low frequency electromagnetic fields alters the behaviour, physiology and stress protein levels of desert locusts." https://www.ncbi.nlm.nih.gov/pmc/articles/PMC5093409
29. "How Stress Works With and Against Your Memory." https://www.verywellmind.com/stress-and-your-memory-4158323#:~:text=Stress%20and%20Memory,memories%20we%20form%20as%20well
30. *UFOs, ETs and Alien Abductions: A Scientist Looks at the Evidence* – by Don Donderi, Ph.D

regarding the phenomena – as many of us are. But people who believe they have experienced ESP events with other humans also suffer from the psychological impact, and are successfully counseled – and not just by researchers working only with abductees.[31] The psychological shock of suddenly being introduced to mind-to-mind communication can be very disorienting.

If even a tiny part of what abductees and researchers report is true, then of course we humans have a very serious problem for it is obviously already too late to avoid detection and exploitation by aliens who are at best impartial to, and at worst hostile toward, our future welfare.

Further, abductees also inform their questioners that extraterrestrials exhibit few traits of individuality or independent thinking; that there is no evidence of artistic endeavors, decorations, music or entertaining activities aboard their spacecraft; that they have no real personal lives and see their only purpose in life is to work for and serve their system of operations.

We in the United States, United Kingdom, Europe and other parts of the world who are steeped in the traditions of Western Civilization are horrified by the prospects of living in what can only be termed a totalitarian, communistic society of human creation and, naturally, will abhor the evident regimentation and complete conformity demanded by the civilization of extraterrestrials. Again, this was the description given to us by abductees who have somehow managed to regain memories "lost," or, more properly, evidently suppressed by alien mental intervention – the ultimate memory hole. If we can accept an almost infinitesimal part of what is reported to us as the truth and, further, if our political and military leaders suspected for many years the implications of an indifferent or hostile alien presence, then we should hardly wonder at our establishments' shock, horror, paranoia, secrecy, denial, and desperate attempts to suppress the knowledge of such an alien presence while they seek to acquire the technological expertise to allow successful human resistance to the extraterrestrials' totalitarian and authoritarian way of doing things through thought-monitoring and control. If this is an accurate depiction, then George Orwell's thought police in his novel *Nineteen Eighty-Four*, would be childlike amateurs in comparison.

One more aspect of alien abductions and other potential threats posed by extraterrestrials and their spacecraft is that these beings also insert

31. "What is Extra Sensory Perception?" https://www.medindia.net/patients/patientinfo/extra-sensory-perception.htm

apocalyptic images into the minds of abductees and others who have encountered them, even at a long distance or indirectly. The images usually relate to nuclear warfare, but also include the sights of environmental catastrophes and even natural disasters such as massive volcanic eruptions. Sometimes, when questioned by abductees, the aliens allegedly respond to their victims with statements suggesting that we humans are destroying our planet, with the implication being that extraterrestrials will "help" us prevent a threatened cataclysm of extinction-level potential. (Again, "help" is the sunny side of control.)

At the start of this report we introduced the senior radar operator aboard the U.S. Navy cruiser *Princeton*, Kevin Day. He says that he, too, has been having terrifying visions of cataclysms since the incidents off the west coasts of Mexico and the United States in 2004 when he vectored F-18 jets to intercept the "Tic-Tac" UFO.[32] I believe him and, further, his testimony validates the accounts by many abduction victims who report similar visions inserted into their minds by their alien captors. If we believe Kevin Day's testimony (which I do), and that the large percentage of abductees have been sincere in what they have told researchers, then extraterrestrials are waging a not-so-subtle psychological propaganda war against our human spirit – our sense of self-worth, and morale.

If we assume that the reports of abductees, and other witnesses who were not abducted, such as Kevin Day, then the aliens coming to Earth are committing further acts of what can only be described as cruel, even criminal, intrusions into the emotional comfort and lives of Earthlings. This is so because the kidnapping crimes, or just the observations of UFO incidents, have intensely traumatized them – most for the remainder of their lives.

In their interactions with aliens, people report that their captors seek information but divulge little about themselves – keeping us "in the dark." To me, this also has sinister implications. As always, we must ask: If you are being fair with us, why all the secrecy? If there is some compelling reason for coming to our planet, why not be forthright with us? Why not initiate fair trade, open scientific discovery, and a free exchange of

---

32. *UFO Witness* television program. Season 1, Episode 1, first aired 14 January 2021. https://www.google.com/search?q=UFO+Witness+episode+guide&oq=USO+Witness+TV+show&aqs=chrome..69i57j33i22i29i30.8751j0j7&sourceid=chrome&ie=UTF-8&stick=H4sIAAAAAAAAAONgVuLVT9c3NMw1ykuvNE9Ke8RowS3w8sc9YSn9SWtOXmPU5OIKzsgvd80rySypFJLmYoOyBKX4uVB18uxi4gspcy3ILM5PSXUvzUxJXcQqGermrxCeWZKXWlyskAqRUkgHyQEA1_9n13kAAAA&ictx=1&ved=2ahUKEwiqxN3l9P32AhVQkWoFHUnCAlAQw_oBegQIOhAC

information and ideas on a mutually beneficial basis of equality and respect, and out in the open?

It does seem as if our "visitors" are operating from a hidden agenda. This probability alone should alert us to a potential threat that is itself a possible extinction-level event.

This Writer's "Estimate of the Situation." What is to be Our Strategy?

From the beginning of widespread government awareness of the potential threat posed by UFOs/ETs, it has been recognized that we must investigate and analyze all aspects of the problem – from alien technology to extraterrestrial intentions. In the batch of documents released by the Defense Intelligence Agency to *The Sun* was the admission: "And the report – prepared for the DIA – warns that such objects may be a 'threat to United States interests.'"[33] This is an indirect, partial official concession that, after decades of official denial, UFOs and ETs may be a threat to national and therefore planetary security. "Never believe anything until it has been officially denied." However, as we learned from Congressman Carson's opening statement on 17 May 2022, the threat potential is now officially acknowledged and no longer denied.

Physicist/astronomer Avi Loeb agrees regarding the need for a scientific approach in a column at *The Debrief*, 19 May 2022: "... the government is discussing UAP seriously and wishes to understand their nature. It is therefore the duty of scientists to assist the government in this quest."[34]

It is rumored that President Dwight D. Eisenhower entered into an agreement in the 1950s with extraterrestrials to allow human abductions, with the proviso that the abductees be returned in reasonably good mental and physical health. In exchange, it has been suggested that Earthlings – as represented by the government of the United States – benefited from the aliens awarding humanity some advanced technology. (Again, beware of ETs bearing gifts.) Why make an agreement with President Eisenhower? Extraterrestrials monitoring our radio communications and viewing our activities from above would have been aware that in the 1950s the United States was the sole superpower – in possession of a massive arsenal of

33. https://www.the-sun.com/news/5053647/ufos-injuries-radiation-burns-pentagon-docs/
34. https://thedebrief.org/reflections-on-the-first-congressional-hearing-on-unidentified-aerial-objects-in-half-a-century/

nuclear weapons, and was also the only major combatant country in the Second World War to emerge with almost no physical damage. It would be logical for ETs to bargain with the leader of the paramount power on the planet. If false, then the tale can be ignored; if true, then we must say to one and all – especially the government of the United States – that such a concession of the rights of all humans is unacceptable, and that any such "deal" or "treaty" is now null and void; but in order to assert our rights and independence, we must be able to make a stand from a position of relative strength – not our current evident powerlessness in relation to extraterrestrial advanced technology.

It is believed by many that, as had been reported by Major Philip Corso, alien technology – in the form of debris from the 1947 Roswell UFO crash – has been the basis of some of our later technological advances such as lasers, fiber-optics and composite materials.[35] It is also rumored that captured, reverse-engineered craft have been developed and duplicated as a result of what humans have learned from crashed and recovered extraterrestrial spacecraft.[36] However, relying on aliens directly need not be the only avenue to a more rapid progress, because just witnessing the high performance of alien space vehicles would give inspiration to human scientists and engineers armed with the knowledge that such feats are not just possible but are a reality.[37] Human beings, despite our faults, are truly brilliant in innovation and the creation of "the impossible." Case in point:

> Scientists (from Britain and Finland) have created the first 'time-crystal' two-body system in an experiment that seems to bend the laws of physics ... Time crystals were long believed to be impossible because they are made from atoms in never-ending motion. The discovery, published in *Nature Communications*, shows that not only can time crystals be created, but they have potential to be turned into useful devices ... time crystals exhibit the bizarre property of being in constant, repeating motion in time despite no external input.

35. *The Day After Roswell*. By Lieutenant Colonel Philp J. Corso, with William J. Birnes. Pocket Books. New York. 1997.
36. https://www.yourcentralvalley.com/news/local-news/i-team-a-look-at-how-bob-lazar-interviews-match-up-with-pentagons-admission-of-studying-ufos/
37. https://www.thedrive.com/the-war-zone/31798/the-secretive-inventor-of-the-navys-bizarre-ufo-patents-finally-talks

> Their atoms are constantly oscillating, spinning, or moving first in one direction, and then the other.[38]

(Time itself is in practice if not reality, "crystallized," allowing for the isolation of the atoms within to remain in a suspended yet simultaneously active and endlessly repeating state – a "perpetual-motion machine.")

There may have been an unintentional disclosure as to the certainty of the retrieval of crashed UFOs in recent legislation, quoted in part in a news report as stating: "The bill says the information could be used to justify requests for funding in the future to 'replicate any such advanced characteristics and performance' – or reverse-engineer the UAPs."[39] The word "replicate" hints at utilizing captured equipment to so "replicate" and reverse-engineer. Sounds far-fetched? The United State Navy does not think so, as shown by an article from 13 December 2021, at the online magazine "Sandboxx": "The Navy's Fusion Plans Could Produce a World-Shattering Weapon," by Alex Hollings. Hollings reports that the Naval Air Warfare Center Aircraft Division had filed patents in 2019 for, among other advances, a High Energy Electromagnetic Field Generator. Such a system, as noted previously, is theorized by UFO researchers (including established thinkers in physics, astronomy, etc. – who are not "cranks and weirdos") as the means of propulsion evidently utilized by aliens visiting our world.[40]

Then there is another comment in the earlier-noted Military.com story: "Incidents around nuclear facilities are also noted for special attention." This is an indirect confirmation regarding events at nuclear installations cited earlier in this book. While many people interpret ET interest in our nuclear sites, whether of a military or peaceful nature, to be benevolent, as if they are merely reminding us of our folly, such interest may instead be out of a desire to track our ability to compete – and resist – and to remind us of our current incapacity to block their power of preventing our use of a nuclear deterrent against them, should the need arise. There is also the consideration that if extraterrestrials have a stake in something of value on our planet, then they would be protecting their perceived "proprietary

38. "An international team of researchers from Lancaster University, Royal Holloway London, Landau Institute, and Aalto University in Helsinki observed time crystals by using Helium-3 which is a rare isotope of helium with one missing neutron. The experiment was carried out in Aalto University." https://www.lancaster.ac.uk/news/time-crystals-impossible-but-obey-quantum-physics
39. https://arlingtoninstitute.org/volume-24-number-24-12-15-21/
40. https://www.sandboxx.us/blog/navy-team-floats-idea-for-a-spacetime-modification-weapon-more-powerful-than-nukes/

interests" in not having "their" resources damaged, contaminated or destroyed in a human-caused catastrophe such as a severe nuclear accident or atomic war. In other words, they may not be as much concerned with human wellbeing as with their own easy access to our resources from which they benefit. To me however, alien interest in nuclear advances – not just in weaponry but in power generation and other research – should send a hint toward our scientists and engineers regarding the source of extraterrestrials' superior manipulation of electromagnetic forces, hence the previous news item about the U.S. Navy patents.

It is evident now – and has been so apparent since the first analyses in the 1940s and 1950s – that ETs have mastered the techniques of detection and manipulation of electromagnetic forces on even a very subtle level, such as the slight energies generated by human nervous systems and brains – enabling them to affect human perceptions, emotions, even thought processes. They also appear to have mastered the subtleties of generating and controlling gravity and anti-gravity waves and fields. It is the extraterrestrial mastery of the detection, creation and manipulation of electromagnetic fields and forces that gives them a clear military superiority over the most advanced technology having been fully developed by Earthlings as of today – possibly. Ironically, or perhaps not, it seems that more primitive weapons can be effective, if certain conditions exist.

Regarding the sensing and manipulation of electromagnetic forces, fields, rays, waves: all humans, barring disability, have the capacity to sense electromagnetic energies via eyesight. We can, of course, manipulate light sources to affect our perceptions of electromagnetic radiations in the visible electromagnetic light spectrum. Moreover, humans evidently have the capacity to sense the electromagnetic field of our planet Earth. [41] Other creatures on our planet have special sensory capabilities: spiders are able to detect electrical fields in the atmosphere. The platypus possesses extremely sensitive electric sensors in its bill that can pick up charges of as little as 0.05μV. Sharks have superior receptors with electro-sensing thresholds down to 0.005μV/cm – a measure of ultra-violet light.[42] As for the utilization of electromagnetic force: electric eels use their nervous systems to accumulate electrical energy with enough power to stun and kill prey and other predators. Lightning bugs can create and transmit light through

41. "Many humans are able to unconsciously detect changes in Earth-strength magnetic fields, according to scientists at Caltech and the University of Tokyo." https://www.caltech.edu/about/news/evidence-human-geomagnetic-sense

42. http://faculty.washington.edu/chudler/amaze.html

bio-chemical means, as can many deep-sea creatures. The Massachusetts Institute of Technology has just announced the development of a miniature fuel cell that uses the sugars in a human body to generate electricity.[43] With applicable technology and/or biological development, it is conceivable that other wavelengths on the electromagnetic spectrum, such as thoughts, could also be detected and projected.[44]

It is postulated that with alien spacecraft in their utilization of gravitic/anti-gravitic waves, forces and fields to propel their space vehicles, such manipulations will also be simultaneously configured to generate countervailing waves, forces and fields within and immediately around their spacecraft to keep them and their occupants from being crushed or ripped apart by the forces of inertia and momentum as the objects conduct extreme maneuvers such as sudden changes in direction, abruptly halting to hover, then shooting away at hypersonic speeds. As mentioned previously, alien spacecraft would also likely be enclosed within a protective envelope of electromagnetic forces to "shield" the spacecraft from drifting and darting debris in deep space. However, it is evident that at times these energy shields are shut off, possibly because the force fields interfere with the aliens' detection of human-generated or natural electromagnetic waves, or to save power, or possibly just due to negligence or error on the part of ET pilots. Should that be the case, then extraterrestrial spacecraft could conceivably be brought down by a sudden influx of electromagnetic energy, such as by a lightning bolt or powerful enough radio or radar beacons, as indicated earlier. Also as we have seen, extraterrestrial craft have the ability to not only sense but to remotely shut down our more advanced systems of defense and offense, such as missiles – whether ICBMs or air-to-air – and radars, radios, other sensors and equipment, including electric-power generators. (UFOs were reported in areas where power blackouts have occurred.)

However, as shown in the incident above Peru, old-fashioned kinetic weapons such as guns firing bullets not reliant on an electromagnetic interface, just a manual or simple electrical trigger, can, at least in theory, hit an alien spacecraft if it has its shielding shut off. In the Peruvian event, it is possible the aliens reactivated their force field just as the aircraft's

43. https://news.mit.edu/2022/glucose-fuel-cell-electricity-0512
44. FDA Approves Neuralink Human Brain Implant Trials. Within the news item, dated 26 May, 2023: ". . . brain implants could cure a range of conditions including obesity, autism, depression and schizophrenia as well as enabling web browsing and telepathy . . ." https://www.newsmax.com/finance/streettalk/neuralink-brain-implant-humans/2023/05/26/id/1121273/n

bullets were about to strike their craft, absorbing the bullets and minimizing damage. Likewise, if we accept as true the story of pistol shots fired by Lieutenant Morgan into the unidentified flying object above Great Britain during the First World War, and also the alleged shoot-down by the Red Baron of a strange craft over Belgium, then, in theory, these incidents could happen despite a very advanced countervailing alien technology – provided that it is temporarily inactivated. The same would apply to the MP allegedly shooting an alien on the ground at Fort Dix. The extraterrestrials' inability to deal with bullets may explain why they are reported to seem to panic and hurriedly evacuate back into their spacecraft and take off when humans, particularly armed humans such as law-enforcement officers or military personnel, show up nearby.

It is also possible that an energy beam with enough force, such as proposed or current ground-based X-ray[45] lasers or particle beams could knock down alien spacecraft, even if their force fields are activated.[46] The United States Navy is reported to soon be installing beam weapons on some of its ships.[47] At least a few of these vessels are robotic, or "drone" craft without human crews. So, our technology is indeed becoming advanced to a degree that we are now, perhaps only distantly, approaching the level of engineering sophistication where we can challenge alien spacecraft entering our airspace through the use of beam weapons. The extraterrestrials, no doubt monitoring all of our communications media, including the internet, are aware of this fact.

Also in this regard: I am pleased to learn that, as of 24 March 2023, the U.S. military is making a move toward defending the United States from missile

45. For an in-depth look at the quest to develop X-Ray laser – described earlier as "hot" X-Rays, see: "The History of the X-ray Laser," by Jeff Hecht. https://www.optica-opn.org/home/articles/volume_19/issue_5/features/the_history_of_the_X-Ray_laser/
Also: "X-Ray Laser." https://www.globalsecurity.org/space/systems/xrl.htm
These articles conclude that the United States and its allies [some basic theoretical work was completed by Geoffrey Pert at the University of Hull in Britain] was unsuccessful. I believe the system was perfected but kept from public knowledge, and therefore that of potential enemies. See: "Directed Energy Missile Defense in Space (Part 5 of 15)" https://www.princeton.edu/~ota/disk3/1984/8410/841005.PDF
46. *The Shape of Wars to Come* David Baker. Stein and Day. Briarcliff Manor, NY. 1981. pp.192-193.
Also: *Beam Defense: An Alternative to Nuclear Destruction.* By the Scientific Staff of the Fusion Energy Foundation. Aero Publishers. Fallbrook, CA. 1983.
47. https://nationalinterest.org/blog/buzz/us-navy-ships-will-soon-have-new-laser-weapon-199412

attack through the use of directed-energy weapons,[48] and also to observe that these systems could, at least theoretically at this point, be used for the planetary defense of Earth against spacecraft, of whatever origin. The vulnerability here would be the power supply, which must be fortified to prevent failures.

In any halfway decent intelligence "estimate of the situation," one must attempt to understand the motivations of all parties – friendly, neutral, potentially or openly hostile. I suspect that the UFOs following, leading, dogging, "toying with" the ships and planes of the United States Navy,[49] among others, may be part of an ongoing program by aliens to probe our defenses – to see if and how we will respond, and the effectiveness of our response. Obviously, if we destroy one or more of their spacecraft with our beam weapons, the "game" of "cat-and-mouse," or whatever we are "playing at" or engaged in will reach a new level of conflict, and possible repercussions should the armed forces of our planet engage successfully against alien space vehicles prematurely. It is best to wait; to bide our time until we can be as certain as possible that we are able to operate at technological and military parity – or, better still, superiority – against possible, even if deemed improbable, extraterrestrial adversaries.

Extraterrestrial technological superiority presents us with a substantial challenge, but one that must be met even if we set aside the possibilities of alien-abduction, hybrid production, and mind-control to dominate our species – just the fact that an alien presence is here for unexplained reasons, and is not only surveying but possibly exploiting the resources of our planet, even if we are not one of those resources, is sufficient justification. These circumstances alone are enough cause for the human race to assert its sovereignty and to stand up against any such invasive activities.

Invasive? Yes, because we face three levels of possible ET involvement: incursion, as would be the case if we and our planet are under extraterrestrial surveillance and investigation, even if just of a scientific nature, but especially if this is an extraterrestrial intelligence-gathering effort as a precursor to military activity. Then there is intrusion – as mentioned in the

---

48. "MDA [Missile Defense Agency] director considering new directed energy, electronic warfare capabilities for future missile defense.

    Vice Adm. Jon Hill mentioned directed energy technologies like high-power continuous wave lasers, a pulsed laser or high-powered microwaves as options the MDA could explore." By Mikayla Easley. 24 March 2023.

    https://defensescoop.com/2023/03/24/mda-director-considering-new-directed-energy-electronic-warfare-capabilities-for-future-missile-defense/

49. https://www.dailymail.co.uk/news/article-10324965/A-warship-FIRED-drone-swarm-terrorized-Navy-destroyers-California-weeks-2019.html

"Foo-Fighters" section, when we saw that Allied surveillance and attack night fighters flew "intrusion" missions to penetrate enemy air space and analyze and neutralize their defenses. If UFOs and aliens are here to exploit our natural and/or human resources, that would be a major intrusion. Then we have the possibility of invasion for, if some of the abductees and associated researchers and counselors are correct, then our planet is the target of a gradual and relentless, intergenerational, interplanetary invasion through the manipulation of human psychology and biology.

Supposing that even a bare minimum of an alien threat exists, of which at least some world governments are aware, that fact alone would be sufficient for suppressing the truth out of concern about a worldwide public panic. As Nick Pope has remarked on television, "Perhaps the truth is too frightening to be revealed." (Pope has appeared on numerous television shows; I heard the remark and although I cannot recall the specific program, he deserves credit for it.)

It occurs to me that the erratic flight patterns, engagement with Earth's aircraft in midair "dogfights," light displays seemingly flashed to attract attention, other unpredictable aerial antics may be employed not only to mystify and annoy, they may be decoy tactics utilized to distract ground controllers and planes from some other extraterrestrial activity, just as rodeo clowns engage in extreme behaviors to focus the attention of a bull or wild horse – a "bucking bronco" – from the rider the animal had just ejected from its back, allowing the cowboy to flee to safety.

If we eliminate the more sinister possibilities, and if the antics of ETs piloting UFOs are more the products of pranksters than gangsters – still, their indiscriminate intrusions into our airspace, feigned suicide dives on our aircraft and other mischievous misbehaviors such as crafting crop circles (even if they do not engage in animal mutilations, human abductions and hybridizations, and mind-manipulation) are enough for Earthlings to attempt to put a stop to the reckless acts of ETs. But how to do this?

Throughout history, groups of people, social classes, minority populations, smaller countries, weaker alliances and lesser empires have made concessions and been conciliatory toward greater powers while behind the scenes they built-up their economic, social, political, scientific and especially military potential until they could confront and defeat their stronger competitors or oppressors, or at least neutralize them.[50] This must

50. "Assessing China's Strategy to 'Hide Capabilities and Bide Time.'" https://divergentoptions.org/2022/02/21/assessing-chinas-strategy-to-hide-capabilities-and-bide-time/

be the strategy of planet Earth, as represented by the United States and its military, and possibly at least some of its allies, such as the United Kingdom and some Commonwealth nations. This is now even acknowledged in legislation in attempting to investigate, analyze then duplicate alien technology to enable the human race to stand up to extraterrestrial exploitation on an even footing. Of course, other nations would likely also join in this effort. (An impartial view of human history suggests the possibility that some nations or factions may decide to ally themselves with ETs in a partial conquest of Earth that leaves their collaborators in control of their own subject territories.)

After a successful, united effort to catch up technologically with our ET competitors we could enter into negotiations and make agreements with beings from beyond our planet on a basis of mutual strength, equality and respect. In order to achieve this goal, secrecy – in abundance – has been necessary so far, and may continue to be so to a limited degree for a long time to come. This is so because when you tell your friends you also inform your opponents; and we, demonstrably, are in opposition to the aims of extraterrestrials – assuming that they exist and are performing as described by the many witnesses cited in this book and elsewhere. In these regards, I truly believe that while extraterrestrials encroaching into our skies, and occasionally on the ground, are demonstrably in the superior position vis-à-vis the human race, again, we are not that far behind, and, in view of what we – our scientists, engineers and technicians – have speculated about, engineered, and are even now fabricating, our species is capable of being successful in the catch-up game, and we are doing so – fast.

What Can *You* Do?

Don't panic! President Franklin D. Roosevelt was correct: "The only thing we have to fear is fear itself." We must collectively roll-up our sleeves and join in a united, worldwide effort to diligently protect our species and planetary interests. We shall do so through maintaining a confident attitude as we work together to improve not only our technology but also ourselves; to elevate our human race to its highest potential – going beyond the evidently tightly regimented and closed-to-individual-opportunity, collectively stagnant societies and cultures of ETs.

Do not immediately assume the worst, or ridicule or belittle people who report UFO sightings, abductions, or other odd encounters with strange beings, and/or other bizarre-seeming events such as psychic phenomena.

These people (abductees and/or other experiencers) are traumatized victims, not hoaxers, fools, crazies – or "cranks and weirdos." Be supportive – of our fellow humans, and of our collective efforts of planetary and species defense.

A friend of nineteen years, and former USAF Technical Sergeant, upon learning of my writing of this book, informed me that in 1949, when he was just 11 and working with his brothers in the then extant farm fields of Irvington, near today's Fremont, California, they observed a silver-colored saucer being pursued by a USAF jet toward Moffett (Air) Field. He said the UFO suddenly gained speed and left the plane far behind. I am sure he would never have told me of the incident – and I believe him, 100 per cent – if I had not mentioned this project, probably out of concern for disbelief, ridicule, etc.

With regard to the latter: our governments and military and intelligence organizations are, or were, being foolish in ridiculing and harassing people reporting close encounters with UFOs and ETs, as some witnesses and experiencers assert. Instead, these people must be regarded as human-intelligence (known in intelligence-gathering circles as "HUMINT," as opposed to, for example, electronic intelligence – "ELINT") assets to be humanely treated and compassionately exploited through voluntary contact and benevolent interrogations. Wise counseling and advice must be extended beforehand to abduction and close-encounter victims. In this way we can learn as much as possible about the aliens so we may have enough useful intelligence to help us deal effectively with extraterrestrials.

I urge everyone to use their influence – and do not be discouraged, we all have influence – on government officials to engage in such a program. In view of the recent Defense Intelligence Reference Document (DIRD) released by the Defense Intelligence Agency and published by *The Political Insider*, such an effort has evidently been under way by government in conjunction with the civilian UFO group MUFON.[51] The ancient Chinese sage and insightful instructor in military affairs Sun Tzu has advised that a wise military leader should know one's enemy as well as or better than one knows one's self to almost guarantee a victory. This must be our goal, and UFO witnesses and experiencers of close encounters with ETs are our most valuable human asset in knowing our potential enemies better than we know ourselves.

51. https://thepoliticalinsider.com/the-truth-may-very-well-be-out-there/?utm_source=home-headline-stories

If confronted by extraterrestrials, it seems that humans are able to resist and even overcome alien attempts at mind control through ET "remote hypnosis." As noted, negative attitudes such as doubt, cynicism, sarcasm, anger, hostility and hatred put off, subdue and seem to neutralize psychic phenomena such as ESP, which extraterrestrials allegedly rely upon to in turn mentally subdue and control intended abductees prior to kidnapping them. Some abductees report that when they have "snapped out of it" and became hostile and attempted, or even just contemplated, violence or escape, the ETs – especially the "Greys" – become very alarmed and immediately leave the area. It seems as if negative emotions projected at them adversely affect the psychic sensitivities of extraterrestrials. Therefore, it is apparent that projecting such emotions at aliens – whether "Greys" or others – could conceivably put them off their game enough that they could quickly depart the area and abandon all intentions of attempting a kidnapping or other actions damaging to human mental and/or physical wellbeing. Perhaps projecting an image in one's mind of ETs bursting into flame, melting, exploding or otherwise perishing could send them on their way. In any case, such a course of action is worth trying, especially if while doing so one is grabbing a firearm, releasing the safety, chambering a round, and – for me at least – taking aim, and promptly opening fire. (Not forgetting that I am often alone, at the edge of the wilderness, in an area with some history of UFO activity at times.)

Forcible resistance is not as impractical as it may seem at first because for unknown reasons, Earth's alien visitors are generally reported to be extremely reluctant to engage in open physical combat. This could be the result of a treaty or agreement among different alien species; a "grand directive" or law against harming more primitive or "endangered species" such as humans may be regarded. Or, ETs may wish to avoid confrontation and armed struggle while they pursue a more subtle, long-term program of conquest, as through the creation of alien-hybrid overlords to subvert and rule over us. So, on an individual or small-unit level, resistance may be possible, and even successful, even as, again, we should avoid a major clash to keep the peace long enough for us to achieve extraterrestrial levels of technological and military development.

My Conclusions

I recognize that many readers of this exploration of a history of military encounters with UFOs will have decided that I am either just another reckless infidel in the temple, or merely an establishment defender of the faith. I believe I am neither … or perhaps both… I have investigated what others have reported and relayed it to my readers. Some will declare "Conspiracy theory!" Real conspiracies do exist – sometimes for sinister purposes and at other times with a beneficial intent (such as keeping a surprise birthday party secret). I believe that a conspiracy to shield the public from the terrifying implications of the presence of extraterrestrials in our world for not necessarily benevolent purposes has had some justifications before now. Yet I also believe that such secrecy has already served its purpose and that it is now time to level the truth with everyone and to forthrightly face the extraterrestrial challenge together as a united front. I suspect this was the intent of President Reagan's 21 September 1987 address to the 42nd Session of the United Nations General Assembly in New York when he said, in part:

> Can we and all nations not live in peace? In our obsession with antagonisms of the moment, we often forget how much unites all the members of humanity. Perhaps we need some outside, universal threat to make us recognize this common bond. I occasionally think how quickly our differences worldwide would vanish if we were facing an alien threat from outside this world.[52]

It may very well be that such a menace does actually threaten humanity today, and it also may be that President Reagan and his advisors were aware of such a situation in 1987, and were just beginning to hint at the truth.

We must continue to do all we can to improve our technological situation vis-à-vis an extraterrestrial presence that may be inimical, or at least indifferent, to the wellbeing of humanity, whether the aliens have already arrived here or not – and I do now believe they have.

I hope my conclusions, which I have reached very reluctantly, are incorrect, and that the apparent visitors to our planet have benign intent. However, we know that the best defense is not only a good offense but also to possess the precursor to a good defense: to have the technical ability to wage an effective defense or offense is the first order of business. We can only acquire that advanced capability if we are willing to spend the

52. https://www.reaganlibrary.gov/archives/speech/address-42d-session-united-nations-general-assembly-new-york-new-york

time, energy, and resources to discover the technologies to provide a good species and planetary defense. Sun Tzu also advised that the best military commander achieves victory not by waging war to obtain one's ends but rather to assure victory without even becoming involved in physical combat at all. However, in a worst-case scenario, where future military encounters by the people of Earth with UFOs/ETs could be of a violent nature, then our species would have a fair chance of emerging as the victor and not the vanquished if we master the advanced technologies necessary to neutralize the advantages of any potential adversary.

Even if we set aside all of the evidence – eyewitness testimony; recent government concessions; even mild speculation, such as that by Stephen Hawking; other, more ominous warnings by professional investigators – the fact is that we humans have, literally, been broadcasting through radio waves our existence to the entire universe for about a century. If we suppose that UFOs as alien spacecraft and extraterrestrials themselves have not been here yet, it is still an imperative that we advance our technological level as far as possible in order to have the capacity to defend our planet and species from incursion and invasion by entities and forces as yet unknown. This is because, as one who grew up in the mean streets of a tough town, I know for a fact that weakness invites aggression.

Finally, as has been shown to us so many times throughout our human history – at Thermopylae; with regard to Israel in 1948, 1967 and 1973; the heroic resistance of the people of the Soviet Union and other countries such as France and Yugoslavia in combating Nazi aggression from 1940–41 until 1945; the resistance of Chinese, Vietnamese, and Filipinos against Imperial Japan from 1937 until 1945; and the truly remarkable achievements of the courageous struggle of Ukrainians in 2022, 2023, and 2024 – to quote President Dwight D. Eisenhower: "It's not the size of the dog in the fight, it's the size of the fight in the dog."

May There be Peace on Earth and Good Will Toward All.

The End… or is it?

Bibliography

Andrews, Colin; with Spignesi, Stephen J. *Crop Circles: Signs of Contact*. New Page Books. Franklin Lakes, NJ. 2003.

Baker, David. *The Shape of Wars to Come*. Stein and Day. Briarcliff Manor, NY. 1981.

Bauer, Conrad. *Military UFO Encounters*. Maplewood Publishing. No city listed. 2019.

Berliner, Don; and Whitley Streiber. *Unidentified Flying Objects Briefing Document - The Best Available Evidence*. Dell. New York. 2000.

Bruce, J.M. *British Aeroplanes 1914–18*. Putnam. London. 1957.

Clarke, David; and Roberts, Andy. *Out of the Shadows: UFOs the Establishment and the Official Cover-Up*. Piatkus. London. 2002.

Cole, Christopher and E.F. Cheesman. *The Air Defence of Britain 1914-1918*. Putnam. London. 1984.

Corso, Lieutenant Colonel Philp J.; with Birnes, William J. *The Day After Roswell*. Pocket Books. New York. 1997.

Cramp, Leonard. *UFOs and Anti-Gravity: Piece for a Jig-Saw*. Adventures Unlimited Press. No city listed. 1997.

Fawcett, Lawrence; and Greenwood, Barry J. *Clear Intent: The Government Coverup of the UFO Experience*. Prentiss-Hall. Englewood Cliffs, NJ. 1984.

Filer, Major George III, USAF (Ret.), as told to Guerra, John L. *Strange Craft*. Bayshore Publishing. Tampa, Fl. 2018.

Friedman, Stanton T.; and Berliner, Don. *Crash At Corona: The U.S. Military Retrieval and Cover-Up of a UFO.* Paragon House. New York. 1992.

Good, Timothy. *Above Top Secret*. William Morrow, New York, 1988.

Good, Timothy. *Alien Contact: Top-Secret UFO Files Revealed.* William Morrow. New York. 1991.

Good, Timothy. *Need to Know: UFOs, the Military and Intelligence*. Pan Books. London. 2007.

Good, Timothy. *The UFO Report*. Avon. New York. 1989.

Greenwood, Barry J.; Fawcett, Lawrence. *Clear Intent: The Government Coverup of the UFO Experience.* Prentiss-Hall. Englewood Cliffs, NJ. 1984.

Hobana, Ion; and Weverbergh, Julien. *UFOs Behind the Iron Curtain.* Bantam. New York. 1975.

Hopkins, Budd; and Rainey, Carol. *Missing Time: A Documented Study of Alien Abductions*. August Night Press. No city given. 1981.

Hopkins, Budd; and Rainey, Carol. *Sight Unseen.* Pocket Books. New York. 2003.

Hopkins, Budd. *Witnessed.* Pocket Books. New York. 1997.

Jacobs, David M., Ph.D. *Secret Life: Firsthand Documented Accounts of UFO Abductions*. Fireside. New York. 1993.

Jacobs, David M., Ph.D. *Walking Among Us: The Alien Plan to Control Humanity*. Disinformation Books. San Francisco, CA. 2015.

Jones, H.A. *The War in the Air, Volume 3*, The Clarendon Press, Oxford, 1931.

Joseph, Frank. *Military Encounters With Extraterrestrials*. Bear & Co. Rochester, VT. 2018.

Jung, Carl Gustav. *Flying Saucers: A Modern Myth of Things Seen in the Skies*. Princeton University Press. No city listed. 1991.

Kean, Leslie. *UFOs: Generals, Pilots, and Government Officials Go on the Record.* Three Rivers Press, New York, 2010.

Keyhoe, Major Donald E. "Aliens from Space." Doubleday. Garden City, NY. 1973.

Ledger, Don; and Styles, Chris. *Dark Object*. Dell. New York. 2001.

Leifland, Leif (1995). *…Secret Matters Not So Far Disclosed.* Vårstormar 1944.

Stockholm: PROBUS Förlag. ISBN 91-87184-37-0.

Lier, Dr. Roger. *UFOs Do Not Exist: The Greatest Lie That Enveloped the World*. The Book Tree. San Diego, CA. 2014.

Mack, John E., M.D. *Abduction: Human Encounters with Aliens*. MacMillan. New York. 1994.

Pope, Nick; Burroughs, John; Penniston, Jim. *Encounter in Rendlesham Forest: The Inside Story of the World's Best-Documented UFO Incident*. Thomas Dunne Books. New York. 2014.

Pope, Nick. *Open Skies, Closed Minds: For The First Time A Government UFO Expert Speaks* Out. Simon and Schuster. London. 1996.

Pope, Nick. *The Uninvited: An Exposé of the Alien Abduction Phenomenon*. The Overlook Press. Woodstock, New York. 1997.

Randle, Lieutenant Colonel Kevin D. *A History of UFO Crashes*. Avon. New York. 1995.

Randle, Lieutenant Colonel Kevin D. *Case MJ-12*. Harper-Torch. New York. 2002.

Randle, Lieutenant Colonel Kevin D.; Estes, Russ; Cone, William P., Ph.D. *The Alien Abduction Enigma*. Forge. New York. 1999.

Randle, Lieutenant Colonel Kevin D.; and Donald R. Schmitt. *The Truth About The UFO Crash At Roswell*. Avon. New York. 1994.

Randle, Lieutenant Colonel Kevin D.; and Schmitt, Donald R. *UFO Crash at Roswell*. Avon. New York. 1991.

Ruppelt, Captain Edward J. *The Report On Unidentified Flying Objects*. E-artnow. No city listed. 2020.

Salas, Robert. *Unidentified: The UFO Phenomenon*. New Page Books. Pompton Plains, NJ. 2015.

Salas, Robert; and Klotz, James. *Faded Giant*. Booksurge. No city given. 2005.

Schindele, David D. *It Never Happened, Volume 1: U.S. Air Force UFO Cover-up*. EdgarRock Publishing. No city listed, 2017.

Scientific Staff of the Fusion Energy Foundation. *Beam Defense: An Alternative to Nuclear Destruction*. Aero Publishers. Fallbrook, CA. 1983.

Smith, Clayton; Hall, Richard. *The UFO Evidence: (unidentified Flying Objects.)* National Investigations Committee on Aerial Phenomena. Washington, D.C. 1964.

Smith, Paul Blake. *MO41, The Bombshell Before Roswell*. W & B Publishers. Kernersville, NC. Revised, 2020 edition.

Stonehill, Paul. *The Soviet UFO Files*. Bramley Books. Godalming, Surrey, UK. 1998.

Vallée, Jacques. *Confrontations*. Ballantine Books. New York. 1990.

Vallée, Jacques; and Aubeck, Chris. *Wonders in the Sky*. Penguin. New York. 2010.

Woodman, Harry. *Early Aircraft Armament*. Smithsonian Institute Press. Washington, D.C. 1989.